GOD'S LIGHT

GOD'S LIGHT

THE PROPHETS OF THE WORLD'S GREAT RELIGIONS

Edited by JOHN MILLER *and* AARON KENEDI

Introduction by PHILIP ZALESKI

MARLOWE & COMPANY
NEW YORK

Published by Marlowe & Company
An Imprint of Avalon Publishing Group Incorporated
245 West 17th Street • 11th Floor
New York, NY 10011

Editor's note: Changes for consistency have been made to the essays
in this book.

Cover and interior design: Miller Media
Cover photograph: Getty Images
Permissions research: Shawneric Hachey
Proofreading and copyediting: Mimi Kusch

God's light : the prophets of the world's great religions—a companion to
God's breath /
    edited by John Miller and Aaron Kenedi.
        p. cm
    ISBN 1-56924-444-8
    1. Religious biography.   I. Miller, John, 1959-II. Kenedi, Aaron.

BL72.G63 2003
200'.92'2—dc22
[B]

9 8 7 6 5 4 3 2 1

Printed in the United States of America
Distributed by Publishers Group West

God is the light of the heavens and of the earth. His light is like a niche in which a lamp — the lamp encased in glass — the glass, as it were, a glistening star. From a blessed tree it is lighted, the olive neither from the East nor of the West, whose oil would well nigh shine out, even though fire touched it not. It is light upon light. God guideth whom He will to His light, and God setteth forth parables to men.

Qur'an, 24:35

To the few who carry the weight
so that the many may rise up.

CONTENTS

GOD'S LIGHT

INTRODUCTION

A FEW YEARS AGO, wandering the streets of lower Manhattan on a sticky August day, I came upon Union Square Park, famous for its nineteenth-century workers' rallies and its twenty-first-century farmer's market. Needing a respite from the sun, I made a beeline for the shade of some stunted trees in the southwest corner. Halfway there, I stopped in my tracks. In front of me stood something so unexpected that I could hardly believe my eyes: a towering bronze statue of Mohandas Gandhi, in loin cloth and shawl, staff in hand, head craned forward and knees bent as if striding rapidly toward a crowd of British soldiers or a session on his spinning wheel.

What startled me wasn't finding the statue — parks breed statues as surely as pigeons — but finding, in a public park controlled by the government of the City of New York, as secular an institution as one can find, a statue of a man famed worldwide as a spiritual leader. Gandhi was a political activist and an honored statesman, and perhaps it was this secondary aspect of his character that paved the way for the erection of the statue. But primarily Gandhi was a seeker of truth, a man of prayer, and a preacher of peace, a serious student of the Bhagavad Gita, the New Testament, and the Qur'an, whose main concern was the life of the spirit. "What I want to achieve — what I have been striving and pining to achieve these thirty years — is self-realization, to see God face to face, to achieve Moksha," he wrote in summation of his struggles. "I live and move and have my being in pursuit of this goal." Thus the famous epithet bestowed upon him by the people of India, mahatma, meaning great souled. As if in conscious gratitude for Gandhi's religious role, a bright garland of flowers (vaijayanti), a ubiquitous offering in Hinduism, adorned the statue's long, ascetic neck.

Here, I thought, was a sign of hope. From Miami to Moscow, our urban areas teem with figures of warriors on horseback and politicians in striped suits. We are very skilled at honoring the rich and powerful. Why not instead honor the true heroes of the world? Portraying Gandhi is a step in the right direction. How grand it would be, as we stroll through our city streets, to see representations of the founders of the great religions, of saints, sages, martyrs and mystics, of the lamed vavnik, the thirty-nine holy people who uphold the world. One can still find something of this sort in lands where traditional ways have not yet died out; I have walked in these regions and rejoiced in their wayside chapels, crossroad statues, and corner altars. Whatever brings us back to God deserves our love, attention, and praise.

This is why *God's Light*, edited by John Miller and Aaron Kenedi, is cause for celebration. A bright garland of literary flowers, it offers fourteen essays on seven of the world's great religious figures: Buddha, Jesus, Krishna, Lao Tzu, Moses, Muhammad, and Rumi. There is no sign here of the pedant's dustbin or the reductionist's hacksaw. Instead, we are offered what we so desperately need: contemporary approaches to timeless teachings of the great traditions. The essays — by novelists, scholars, and, in one instance at least, a saint of the first order — affirm the individuality, indeed, the uniqueness of each of the great figures under discussion. Moses, as seen by Zora Neale Hurston and Elie Wiesel, is a mighty magician, a man of power. Lao Tzu, according to Alan Watts and Max Kaltenmark, is a puckish philosopher with a taste for paradox and wry insight. Krishna, reports Stephen Mitchell and Vanamali, is the perfection of distilled illumination, grace, and love. So too for Muhammad, Rumi, Buddha, and Jesus. Together they present a fascinating typology of the religious luminary — God, God-man, enlightened one, prophet, seer, poet, dancer — reminding us of the density and depth of the world's religious traditions and of their profound differences.

Nonetheless, each of these people calls to every one of us; each has something to teach us, whatever our creed. A Christian who names Jesus as Lord and Moses as prophet and saint can learn much from the philosophical investigations of Buddha. A Hindu to whom Krishna is the wisest and most endearing of avatars can benefit greatly from the precepts for holy living found in the hadith of Muhammad. How could this not be the case? For each of these holy men claims — and anyone who studies them in depth would be hard put to deny — a portion of divine revelation in their teaching. When we listen to them, we hear, in varying degrees (how much or how little we must determine for ourselves), the very voice of God. The same opening to divine wisdom is available to those readers with no religion of their own, those who have been raised in secular households, or those who, for one reason or another, have abandoned the tradition that sustained their mothers and fathers. This book may lead them to reexamine their reasons for walking away from the call of their ancestors, or it may help them to discover a teaching that revitalizes their hopes and prayers.

It may be that something even greater will come of a collection such as this. No one can predict the will of God, and while it seems clear that revelation, in the sense of the establishment of authentic new religions, is a closed book, God still whispers in the souls of individual men and women, and new manifestations of the spirit, new forms of holy life, continue to appear. In particular interest in this regard are the essays here about Jalaluddin Rumi, for the great Persian poet stands apart from the other figures in this book in being neither a divine incarnation nor the recipient of a great revelation. Rumi was one of us. His accomplishment was to express the mystical dimensions of Islam in poetry and dance. What Rumi did, you and I (in our own small ways) can do as well, making our work (be it writing books or cooking dinner) a means of transmitting beauty, goodness, and truth, a vehicle for God's love. Here one remembers another of the contributors to *God's Light*, Mother Teresa, who discovered a new form of Catholic Christian life by tending to the needs of the poorest of the poor in the forsaken slums of Calcutta. Mother Teresa proves that for those who heed the will of God nothing is impossible, and that the history of religious genius has not reached its end.

I said above that the essays in *God's Light* respect the differences between the great religious founders. But in reading through the volume, one discovers too a common note, one that sounds with clarity, depth, and insistence in the teachings of every master: the need to change one's life. This command goes out in equal measure to sinner and to saint. It takes many forms: rebirth in the Spirit, surrender to the will of God, the discovery of one's true being. Without this inner revolution, nothing is possible. We can see this principle at work in the life of Gandhi; his transformation from diffident intellectual to mahatma came about through an incessant commitment to self-study and self-perfection. "God can never be realized by one who is not pure of heart," he wrote. "Self-purification must therefore mean purification in all the walks of life." In Gandhi's case, this meant a steady diet of prayer, scriptural study, sexual abstinence, fasting, and other ascetic practices that stripped away impediments to holy living, along with a willingness to accept whatever came his way — even the clubs of British soldiers — as an occasion for spiritual improvement. One cannot read *God's Light* without forming the conviction that self-transformation in the light of eternal truth is available to us all, and that careful attention to the seven men profiled in this volume will point the way.

This isn't to suggest that *God's Light* is a kind of spiritual castor oil to be gulped down reluctantly in the hope of self-improvement. Not at all. Reading this book can be pure pleasure. What a marvelous range of voices, from the folk rhythms of Zora Neale Hurston to the gentle admonitions of Thich Nhat Hahn to the devout scholarship of Seyyed Hossein Nasr to the breathtaking purity of Mother Teresa. Finishing the volume, one feels that the remarkable late-twentieth-century blossoming of that curious genre known as spiritual writing continues apace in the twenty-first. It is a brave genre, daring to convey the broadest truths in the finest detail — that is to say, to combine art and insight in perfect balance. According to Thoreau, a book (and perhaps any piece of writing) "should contain pure discoveries, terra firma . . . and not the art of navigation by those who have never been out of sight of land." The essays that constitute this volume meet Thoreau's criterion. One longs for a sequel, for writings about Zoroaster, Confucius, St. Paul, the Baal Shem Tov, and many other religious giants who could fit comfortably in these pages. Until then, hats off. This is, I have no doubt, the sort of book that Gandhi would have loved.

— PHILIP ZALESKI
NORTHAMPTON, MA
AUGUST 16, 2003

BUDDHA

c. 483 B.C.

Buddha, the title of Prince Gautama Siddhartha, was the founder of Buddhism, born the son of the rajah of the Sakya tribe ruling in Kapilavastu, Nepal. At roughly thirty years of age he left the luxuries of the court, his beautiful wife, and all earthly ambitions for the life of an ascetic; after six years of austerity and mortification he saw in the contemplative life the perfect way to self-enlightenment. According to tradition, he achieved enlightenment when sitting beneath a banyan tree near Buddh Gaya, Bihar. For the next forty years he taught, gaining many disciples and followers. He died at the age of about eighty in Kusinagara, Oudh. His teaching is summarized in the Four Noble Truths, the last of which affirms the existence of a path leading to deliverance from the universal human experience of suffering. The goal is nirvana, which means "the blowing out" of the fires of all desires and the absorption of the self into the infinite.

PREFACE
by Jack Kornfield

IT IS SAID THAT SOON AFTER his enlightenment the Buddha passed a man on the road who was struck by the Buddha's extraordinary radiance and peaceful presence. The man stopped and asked, "My friend, what are you? Are you a celestial being or a god?"

"No," said the Buddha.

"Well, then, are you some kind of magician or wizard?"

Again the Buddha answered, "No."

"Are you a man?" "No."

"Well, my friend, then what are you?" The Buddha replied, "I am awake."

The word *buddha* means "one who is awake." It is the experience of awakening to the truth of life that is offered in the Buddhist tradition. For twenty-five hundred years the practices and teachings of Buddhism have offered a systematic way to see clearly and live wisely. They have offered a way to discover liberation within our own bodies and minds, in the midst of this very world.

History records that the Buddha was born as a prince in an ancient kingdom of northern India. Although as a youth he was protected by his father in beautiful palaces, as he grew older the Buddha encountered what we must all face: the inevitable sorrows of life. He saw the loss of all things we hold dear, and the aging, sickness, and death that come to every human being. Seeing this, he chose to renounce his royal title and leave his palace to become a seeker of truth, searching for the end of human sorrow, searching for freedom in the face of the ceaseless round of birth and death.

For some years the Buddha practiced as an austere yogi in the forests of India. In time he realized that his extreme asceticism had brought him no more freedom than his previous indulgence in worldly pleasure. Instead, he saw that human freedom must come from practicing a life of inner and outer balance, and he called this discovery the Middle Path.

Having seen this, the Buddha seated himself under a great banyan tree and vowed to find liberation in the face of the forces that bring suffering to humankind. He felt himself assailed by these forces — by fear, attachment, greed, hatred, delusion, temptation, and doubt. The Buddha sat in the midst of these forces with his heart open and his mind clear until he could see to the depths of human consciousness, until he discovered a place of peace at the center of them all. This was his enlightenment, the discovery of *nirvana*, the freeing of his heart from entanglement in all the conditions of the world. The realization of truth that he touched that night was so profound that his teachings about it have continued to inspire and enlighten people all over the world to this day. Over the centuries, one and a half billion people, one quarter of the human race, have followed the Buddha's way.

From the Buddha's enlightenment, two great powers were awakened in him: transcendent wisdom and universal compassion. Setting in motion the Wheel of the Dharma, the Buddha wandered first to the Deer Park in Benares and gave instructions to the yogis who had practiced with him in the forest. After this, for forty-five years he brought the teachings of wisdom and compassion to all who would listen. These teachings, which the Buddha called the Dharma, or Way, are an invitation to follow the path of enlightenment. They are an invitation to all who hear them to discover their own buddha-nature, the freedom and great heart of compassion that is possible for every human being.

To bring about the awakening of students of all temperaments, the Buddha taught a wonderful variety of spiritual practices. There are foundation practices for the development of loving-kindness, generosity, and moral integrity, the universal ground of spiritual life. Then there is a vast array of meditation practices to train the mind and open the heart. These practices include awareness of the breath and body, mindfulness of feelings and thoughts, practices of *mantra* and devotion, visualization and contemplative reflection, and practices leading to refined and profoundly expanded states of consciousness.

To carry on these teachings, the Buddha created an ordained *Sangha*, what is now one of the oldest surviving monastic orders on earth. These monks and nuns, who still number in the hundreds of thousands around the globe, follow the Buddha through a life of renunciation. But the teachings he left were not limited to renunciates. They can be understood and awakened in the heart of human beings in every circumstance, in every walk of life.

BUDDHA

by Thich Nhat Hanh

BUDDHA WAS NOT A GOD. He was a human being like you and me, and he suffered just as we do. If we go to the Buddha with our hearts open, he will look at us, his eyes filled with compassion, and say, "Because there is suffering in your heart, it is possible for you to enter my heart."

The layman Vimalakirti said, "Because the world is sick, I am sick. Because people suffer, I have to suffer." This statement was also made by the Buddha. Please don't think that because you are unhappy, because there is pain in your heart, that you cannot go to the Buddha. It is exactly because there is pain in your heart that communication is possible. Your suffering and my suffering are the basic condition for us to enter the Buddha's heart, and for the Buddha to enter our hearts.

For forty-five years, the Buddha said, over and over again, "I teach only suffering and the transformation of suffering." When we recognize and acknowledge our own suffering, the Buddha — which means the Buddha in us — will look at it, discover what has brought it about, and prescribe a course of action that can transform it into peace, joy, and liberation. Suffering is the means the Buddha used to liberate himself, and it is also the means by which we can become free. . . .

Siddhartha Gautama was twenty-nine years old when he left his family to search for a way to end his and others' suffering. He studied meditation with many teachers, and after six years of practice, he sat under the bodhi tree and vowed not to stand up until he was enlightened. He sat all night, and as the morning star arose, he had a profound breakthrough and became a Buddha, filled with understanding and love. The Buddha spent the next forty-nine days enjoying the peace of his realization. After that he walked slowly to the Deer Park in Sarnath to share his understanding with the five ascetics with whom he had practiced earlier.

When the five men saw him coming, they felt uneasy. Siddhartha had abandoned them, they thought. But he looked so radiant that they could not resist welcoming him. They washed his feet and offered him water to drink. The Buddha said, "Dear friends, I have seen deeply that nothing can be by itself alone, that everything has to inter-be with everything else. I have seen that all beings are endowed with the nature of awakening." He offered to say more, but the monks didn't know whether to believe him or not. So the Buddha asked, "Have I ever lied to you?" They knew that he hadn't, and they agreed to receive his teachings.

The Buddha then taught the Four Noble Truths of the existence of suffering, the making of suffering, the possibility of restoring well-being, and the Noble Eightfold Path that leads to well-being. Hearing this, an immaculate vision of the Four Noble Truths arose in Kondañña, one of the five ascetics. The Buddha observed this and exclaimed, "Kondañña understands! Kondañña understands!" and from that day on, Kondañña was called "The One Who Understands."

The Buddha then declared, "Dear friends, with humans, gods, brahmans, monastics, and maras as witnesses, I tell you that if I have not experienced directly all that I have told you, I would not proclaim that I am an enlightened person, free from suffering. Because I myself have identified suffering, understood suffering, identified the causes of suffering, removed the causes of suffering, confirmed the existence of well-being, obtained well-being, identified the path to well-being, gone to the end of the path, and realized total liberation, I now proclaim to you that I am a free person." At that moment the Earth shook, and the voices of the gods, humans, and other living beings throughout the cosmos said that on the planet Earth, an enlightened person had been born and had put into motion the wheel of the Dharma, the Way of Understanding and Love. This teaching is recorded in the *Discourse on Turning the Wheel of the Dharma (Dhamma Cakka Pavattana Sutta)*. Since then, two thousand, six hundred years have passed, and the wheel of the Dharma continues to turn. It is up to us, the present generation, to keep the wheel turning for the happiness of the many.

Three points characterize this sutra. The first is the teaching of the Middle Way. The Buddha wanted his five friends to be free from the idea that austerity is the only correct practice. He had learned firsthand that if you destroy your health, you have no energy left to realize the path. The other extreme to be avoided, he said, is indulgence in sense pleasures — being possessed by sexual desire, running after fame, eating immoderately, sleeping too much, or chasing after possessions.

The second point is the teaching of the Four Noble Truths. This teaching was of great value during the lifetime of the Buddha, is of great value in our own time, and will be of great value for millennia to come. The third point is engagement in the world. The teachings of the Buddha were not to escape from life, but to help us relate to ourselves and the world as thoroughly as possible. The Noble Eightfold Path includes Right Speech and Right Livelihood. These teachings are for people in the world who have to communicate with each other and earn a living.

The *Discourse on Turning the Wheel of the Dharma* is filled with joy and hope. It teaches us to recognize suffering as suffering and to transform our suffering into mindfulness, compassion, peace, and liberation. . . .

After realizing complete, perfect awakening (*samyak sambodhi*), the Buddha had to find words to share his insight. He already had the water, but he had to discover jars like the Four Noble Truths and the Noble Eightfold

Path to hold it. The Four Noble Truths are the cream of the Buddha's teaching. The Buddha continued to proclaim these truths right up until his Great Passing Away (*mahaparinirvana*).

The Chinese translate Four Noble Truths as "Four Wonderful Truths" or "Four Holy Truths." Our suffering is holy if we embrace it and look deeply into it. If we don't, it isn't holy at all. We just drown in the ocean of our suffering. For "truth," the Chinese use the characters for "word" and "king." No one can argue with the words of a king. These Four Truths are not something to argue about. They are something to practice and realize.

The First Noble Truth is suffering (*dukkha*). The root meaning of the Chinese character for suffering is "bitter." Happiness is sweet; suffering is bitter. We all suffer to some extent. We have some malaise in our body and our mind. We have to recognize and acknowledge the presence of this suffering and touch it. To do so, we may need the help of a teacher and a Sangha, friends in the practice.

The Second Noble Truth is the origin, roots, nature, creation, or arising (*samudaya*) of suffering. After we touch our suffering, we need to look deeply into it to see how it came to be. We need to recognize and identify the spiritual and material foods we have ingested that are causing us to suffer.

The Third Noble Truth is the cessation (*nirodha*) of creating suffering by refraining from doing the things that make us suffer. This is good news! The Buddha did not deny the existence of suffering, but he also did not deny the existence of joy and happiness. If you think that

Buddhism says, "Everything is suffering and we cannot do anything about it," that is the opposite of the Buddha's message. The Buddha taught us how to recognize and acknowledge the presence of suffering, but he also taught the cessation of suffering. If there were no possibility of cessation, what is the use of practicing? The Third Truth is that healing is possible.

The Fourth Noble Truth is the path (*marga*) that leads to refraining from doing the things that cause us to suffer. This is the path we need the most. The Buddha called it the Noble Eightfold Path. The Chinese translate it as the "Path of Eight Right Practices": Right View, Right Thinking, Right Speech, Right Action, Right Livelihood, Right Diligence, Right Mindfulness, and Right Concentration. . . .

If we are not careful in the way we practice, we may have the tendency to make the words of our teacher into a doctrine or an ideology. Since the Buddha said that the First Noble Truth is suffering, many good students of the Buddha have used their skills to prove that everything on Earth is suffering. The theory of the Three Kinds of Suffering was such an attempt. It is not a teaching of the Buddha.

The first kind of suffering is "the suffering of suffering" (*dukkha dukkhata*), the suffering associated with unpleasant feelings, like the pain of a toothache, losing your temper, or feeling too cold on a winter's day. The second is "the suffering of composite things" (*samskara dukkhata*). Whatever comes together eventually has to come apart; therefore, all composite things are described as suffering. Even things that have not yet decayed, such as mountains, rivers, and the sun, are seen to be suffering, because they will decay and cause suffering eventually. When you believe that everything composed is suffering, how can you find joy? The third is "the suffering associated with change" (*viparinama dukkhata*). Our liver may be in good health today, but when we grow old, it will cause us to suffer. There is no point in celebrating joy, because sooner or later it will turn into suffering. Suffering is a black cloud that envelops everything. Joy is an illusion. Only suffering is real.

For more than two thousand years, students of Buddhism have been declaring that the Buddha taught that all objects of perception — all physical (table, sun, moon) and physiological phenomena and all wholesome, unwholesome, and neutral states of mind — are suffering. One hundred years after the Buddha passed away, practitioners were already repeating the formula, "This is suffering. Life is suffering. *Everything* is suffering." They thought that to obtain insight into the First Noble Truth, they had to repeat this formula. Some commentators said that without this constant repetition, the Four Noble Truths could not be realized.

Today, many people invoke the names of the Buddha or do similar practices mechanically, believing that this will bring them insight and emancipation. They are caught in forms, words, and notions, and are not using their intelligence to receive and practice the Dharma. It can be dangerous to practice without using your own intelligence, without a teacher and friends who can show you ways to practice correctly. Repeating a phrase like "Life is suffering" might help you notice when you are about to become attached to something, but it cannot help you understand the true nature of suffering or reveal the path shown to us by the Buddha.

This dialogue is repeated in many sutras:

> "Monks, are conditioned things permanent or impermanent?"
>
> "They are impermanent, World-Honored One."
>
> "If things are impermanent, are they suffering or well-being?"
>
> "They are suffering, World-Honored One."
>
> "If things are suffering, can we say that they are self or belong to self?"
>
> "No, World-Honored One."

When we read this, we may think that the Buddha is offering a theory — "All things are suffering" — that we have to prove in our daily life. But in other parts of the same sutras, the Buddha says that he only wants us to recognize suffering when it is present and to recognize joy when suffering is absent. By the time the Buddha's discourses were written down, seeing all things as suffering must have been widely practiced, as the above quotation occurs more frequently than the teaching to identify suffering and the path to end suffering.

The argument, "Impermanent, therefore suffering, therefore nonself" is illogical. Of course, if we believe that something is permanent or has a self, we may suffer when we discover that it is impermanent and without a separate self. But, in many texts, suffering is regarded as

one of the Three Dharma Seals, along with impermanence and nonself. It is said that all teachings of the
Buddha bear the Three Dharma Seals. To put suffering on
the same level as impermanence and nonself is an error.
Impermanence and nonself are "universal." They are a
"mark" of all things. Suffering is not. It is not difficult to
see that a table is impermanent and does not have a self
separate of all nontable elements, like wood, rain, sun,
furniture maker, and so on. But is it suffering? A table will
only make us suffer if we attribute permanence or sepa-
rateness to it. When we are attached to a certain table, it
is not the table that causes us to suffer. It is our attachment. We can agree that anger is impermanent, without a
separate self, and filled with suffering, but it is strange to
talk about a table or a flower as being filled with suffering. The Buddha taught impermanence and nonself to
help us not be caught in signs.

The theory of the Three Kinds of Suffering is an
attempt to justify the universalization of suffering. What
joy is left in life? We find it in nirvana. In several sutras
the Buddha taught that nirvana, the joy of completely
extinguishing our ideas and concepts, rather than suffering, is one of the Three Dharma Seals. This is stated four
times in the *Samyukta Agama* of the Northern transmis-
sion. Quoting from yet another sutra, Nagarjuna listed
nirvana as one of the Three Dharma Seals. To me, it is
much easier to envision a state where there are no obstacles created by concepts than to see all things as suffering. I hope scholars and practitioners will begin to accept
the teaching that all things are marked by impermanence,

nonself, and nirvana, and not make too great an effort to prove that everything is suffering.

Another common misunderstanding of the Buddha's teaching is that all of our suffering is caused by craving. In the *Discourse on Turning the Wheel of the Dharma*, the Buddha did say that craving is the cause of suffering, but he said this because craving is the first on the list of afflictions (*kleshas*). If we use our intelligence, we can see that craving can be a cause of pain, but other afflictions such as anger, ignorance, suspicion, arrogance, and wrong views can also cause pain and suffering. Ignorance, which gives rise to wrong perceptions, is responsible for much of our pain. To make the sutras shorter and therefore easier to memorize, the first item on a list was often used to represent the whole list. The word *eyes*, for example, is used in many sutras to represent all six sense organs and *form* is often used to represent all Five Aggregates (*skandhas*). If we practice identifying the causes of our suffering, we will see that sometimes it is due to craving and sometimes it is due to other factors. To say, "Life is suffering" is too general. To say that craving is the cause of all our suffering is too simplistic. We need to say, "The basis for this suffering is such and such an affliction," and then call it by its true name. If we have a stomachache, we need to call it a stomachache. If it is a headache, we need to call it a headache. How else will we find the cause of our suffering and the way to heal ourselves?

It is true that the Buddha taught the truth of suffering, but he also taught the truth of "dwelling happily in things as they are" (*drishta dharma sukha viharin*). To succeed in the practice, we must stop trying to prove that everything is suffering. In fact, we must stop trying to prove anything. If we touch the truth of suffering with our mindfulness, we will be able to recognize and identify our specific suffering, its specific causes, and the way to remove those causes and end our suffering. . . .

In the *Discourse of the Four Establishments of Mindfulness* (*Satipatthana Sutta*), the Buddha offers four objects for our mindfulness practice: our body, our feelings, our mind, and the objects of our mind. Monks and nuns in many Buddhist countries memorize this discourse, and it is the text that is read to them as they leave this life. It is helpful to read the *Discourse on the Four Establishments of Mindfulness* at least once a week, along with the *Discourse on the Full Awareness of Breathing* and the *Discourse on Knowing the Better Way to Live Alone*. You might like to keep these three books by your bedside and take them with you when you travel.

The Four Establishments of Mindfulness are the foundation of our dwelling place. Without them, our house is abandoned; no one is sweeping, dusting, or tidying up. Our body becomes unkempt, our feelings full of suffering, and our mind a heap of afflictions. When we are truly home, our body, mind, and feelings will be a place of refuge for ourselves and others.

The first establishment is "mindfulness of the body *in the body*." Many people hate their bodies. They feel their body is an obstacle, and they want to mistreat it. When Sister Jina, a nun at Plum Village, teaches yoga, she always begins by saying, "Let us be aware of our bodies. Breathing in, I know I am standing here in my body. Breathing out, I smile to my body." Practicing this way, we renew our acquaintance with our body and make peace with it. In the *Kayagatasati Sutta*, the Buddha offers methods to help us know what is happening in our body. We observe nondualistically, fully in our body even as we observe it. We begin by noting all of our body's positions and movements. When we sit, we know we are sitting. When we stand, walk, or lie down we know we are standing, walking, or lying down. When we practice this way, mindfulness is there. This practice is called "mere recognition."

The second way the Buddha taught us to practice mindfulness of the body in the body is to recognize all of our body's parts, from the top of our head to the soles of our feet. If we have blonde hair, we recognize and smile to that. If we have gray hair, we recognize and smile to that. We observe whether our forehead is relaxed and whether it has wrinkles. With our mindfulness, we touch our nose, mouth, arms, heart, lungs, blood, and so on. The Buddha described the practice of recognizing thirty-two parts of our body as being like a farmer who goes up to his loft; brings down a large bag of beans, grains, and seeds; puts the bag on the ground; opens it; and, as the contents fall onto the floor, recognizes rice as rice, beans as beans, sesame as sesame, and so on. In this way, we recognize our eyes as our eyes and our lungs as our lungs. We can practice this during sitting meditation or while lying down. Scanning our body with our mindfulness in this way might take half an hour. As we observe each part of our body, we smile to it. The love and care of this meditation can do the work of healing.

The third method the Buddha offered for practicing mindfulness of the body in the body is to see the elements that it is made of: earth, water, fire, and air. "Breathing in, I see the earth element in me. Breathing out, I smile to the earth element in me." "Earth element" refers to things that are solid. When we see the earth element inside and outside of us, we realize that there is really no boundary between us and the rest of the universe. Next, we recognize the water element inside and outside of us. "Breathing in, I am aware of the element of water in my body." We meditate on the fact that our body is more than 70 percent water. After that, we recognize the fire element, which means heat, inside and outside of us. For life to be possible, there must be heat. Practicing this, we see over and over that the elements inside and outside our body belong to the same reality, and we are no longer confined by our body. We are everywhere.

The fourth element of our body is air. The best way to experience the air element is the practice of mindful breathing. "Breathing in, I know I am breathing in. Breathing out, I know I am breathing out." After saying these sentences, we can abbreviate them by saying "In" as we breath in, and "Out" as we breath out. We don't try to control our breathing. Whether our in-breath is long or short, deep or shallow, we just breathe naturally and shine the light of mindfulness on it. When we do this, we notice that, in fact, our breathing does become slower and deeper naturally. "Breathing in, my in-breath has become deep. Breathing out, my out-breath has become slow." Now we can practice, "Deep/slow." We don't have to make an effort. It just becomes deeper and slower by itself, and we recognize that.

Later on, you will notice that you have become calmer and more at ease. "Breathing in, I feel calm. Breathing out, I feel at ease. I am not struggling anymore. Calm/ease." And then, "Breathing in, I smile. Breathing out, I release all my worries and anxieties. Smile/release." We are able to smile to ourselves and release all our worries. There are more than three hundred muscles in our face, and when we know how to breath in and smile, these muscles can relax. This is "mouth yoga." We smile and we are able to release all of our feelings and emotions. The last practice is, "Breathing in, I dwell deeply in the present moment, Breathing out, I know this is a wonderful moment. Present moment/wonderful moment." Nothing is more precious than being in the present moment, fully alive and fully aware. . . .

All conditioned things are impermanent.
They are phenomena, subject to birth and death.
When birth and death no longer are,
the complete silencing is joy.

This verse *(gatha)* was spoken by the Buddha shortly before his death. The first two lines express relative truth, while the third and fourth lines express absolute truth. "All conditioned things" includes physical, physiological, and logical phenomena. "Complete silencing" means nirvana, the extinction of all concepts. When the Buddha says, "The complete silencing is joy," he means that thinking, conceptualizing, and speaking have come to an end. This is the Third Noble Truth in absolute terms.

The Buddha recommends that we recite the "Five Remembrances" every day:

1. I am of the nature to grow old. There is no way to escape growing old.
2. I am of the nature to have ill-health. There is no way to escape having ill-health.
3. I am of the nature to die. There is no way to escape death.
4. All that is dear to me and everyone I love are of the nature to change. There is no way to escape being separated from them.
5. My actions are my only true belongings. I cannot escape the consequences of my actions. My actions are the ground on which I stand.

The Five Remembrances help us make friends with our fears of growing old, getting sick, being abandoned, and dying. They are also a bell of mindfulness that can help us appreciate deeply the wonders of life that are available here and now. But in the *Heart Sutra*, Avalokiteshvara teaches that there is no birth and no death. Why would the Buddha tell us that we are of the nature to die if there is no birth and no death? Because in the Five Remembrances, the Buddha is using the tool of relative truth. He is well aware that in terms of absolute truth, there is no birth and no death.

When we look at the ocean, we see that each wave has a beginning and an end. A wave can be compared with other waves, and we can call it more or less beautiful, higher or lower, longer lasting or less long lasting. But if we look more a deeply, we see that a wave is made of water. While living the life of a wave, it also lives the life of water. It would be sad if the wave did not know that it is water. It would think, Some day, I will have to die. This period of time is my life span, and when I arrive at the shore, I will return to nonbeing. These notions will cause the wave fear and anguish. We have to help it remove the notions of self, person, living being, and life span if we want the wave to be free and happy. . . .

We began with the sentence, "Buddha was not a god. He was a human being. . . . "What does this mean? What is a human being? If the trees and the rivers were not there, could human beings be alive? If animals and all other species were not there, how could we be? A human being is made entirely of nonhuman elements. We must free ourselves of our ideas of Buddha and of human beings. Our ideas may be the obstacles that prevent us from seeing the Buddha.

"Dear Buddha, are you a living being?" We want the Buddha to confirm the notion we have of him. But he looks at us, smiles, and says, "A human being is not a human being. That is why we can say that he is a human being." These are the dialectics of the *Diamond Sutra*. "A is not A. That is why it is truly A." A flower is not a flower. It is made only of non-flower elements — sunshine, clouds, time, space, earth, minerals, gardeners, and so on.

A true flower contains the whole universe. If we return any one of these nonflower elements to its source, there will be no flower. That is why it is an authentic rose." We have to remove our concept of rose if we want to touch the real rose.

Nirvana means extinction — first of all, the extinction of all concepts and notions. Our concepts about things prevent us from really touching them. We have to destroy our notions if we want to touch the real rose. When we ask, "Dear Buddha, are you a human being?" it means we have a concept about what a human being is. So the Buddha just smiles at us. It is his way of encouraging us to transcend our concepts and touch the real being that he is. A real being is quite different from a concept.

If you have been to Paris, you have a concept of Paris. But your concept is quite different from Paris itself. Even if you've lived in Paris for ten years, your idea of Paris still does not coincide with the reality. You may have lived with someone for ten years and think that you know her perfectly, but you are living only with your concept. You have a concept of yourself, but have you touched your true self? Look deeply to try to overcome the gap between your concept of reality and reality itself. Meditation helps us remove concepts. . . .

One day, the Buddha went with Ananda to a monastery in Koshala. All the monks had gone out on alms round except one monk who had dysentery. He was lying exhausted, his robes and bedding covered in filth. When the Buddha saw this, he asked, "Where have the other monks gone? Why is no one looking after you?" The unwell monk replied, "Lord, all my brothers have gone out on alms round. At first, they looked after me, but when I was getting no better, I told them I would look after myself." The Buddha and Ananda bathed the monk, cleaned his room, washed his robes, and gave him a fresh robe to wear. When the monks returned, the Buddha said, "Friends, if we do not look after each other, who will look after us? When you look after each other, you are looking after the Tathagata."

There are true jewels and jewels that are not authentic. If someone gives spiritual teachings that contradict the Three Seals of impermanence, nonself, and nirvana, that is not authentic Dharma. When a community has mindfulness, peace, joy, and liberation, it is a true Sangha. A Sangha that does not practice mindfulness and is not free, peaceful, or joyful cannot be called a true Sangha. The Buddha also can be true or false. In the *Diamond Sutra*, the Buddha says, "If you look for me in forms and sounds, you will never see the Tathagata."

Looking into any of the Three Jewels, you see the other two. Buddha, Dharma, and Sangha inter-are. If you look after the Sangha, you are looking after the Buddha. When your Sangha is happy and advancing in the practice, the holiness of the Sangha increases, and the presence of the true Buddha and true Dharma become clearer. When you walk in mindfulness, you are taking good care of the Dharma. When you make peace with another member of your Sangha, you are looking after the Buddha. Going into the meditation hall, offering incense, and tidying the altar are not the only ways to look after the Buddha. Taking someone's hand or comforting someone who suffers is also to look after the Buddha. When you touch the true Sangha, you touch the Buddha and the Dharma. The Dharma cannot exist without a Buddha and a Sangha. How could the Dharma exist if there were no practitioners? A Buddha is a Buddha when the Dharma is in him or her. Each jewel contains the other two. When you take refuge in one jewel, you take refuge in all three. This can be realized in every moment of our life. . . .

Inclusiveness is the capacity to receive, embrace, and transform. Kshanti is often translated as patience or forbearance, but I believe "inclusiveness" conveys the Buddha's teaching. When we practice inclusiveness, we don't have to suffer or forbear, even when we have to embrace suffering and injustice. The other person says or does something that makes us angry. He inflicts on us some kind of injustice. But if our heart is large enough, we don't suffer.

The Buddha offered this wonderful image. If you take a handful of salt and pour it into a small bowl of water, the water in the bowl will be too salty to drink. But if you pour the same amount of salt into a large river, people will still be able to drink the river's water. (Remember, this teaching was offered 2,600 years ago, when it was still possible to drink from rivers!) Because of its immensity, the river has the capacity to receive and transform. The river doesn't suffer at all because of a handful of salt. If your heart is small, one unjust word or act will make you suffer. But if your heart is large, if you have understanding and compassion, that word or deed will not have the power to make you suffer. You will be able to receive, embrace, and transform it in an instant. What counts here is your capacity. To transform your suffering, your heart has to be as big as the ocean. Someone else might suffer. But if a bodhisattva receives the same unkind words, she won't suffer at all. It depends on your way of receiving, embracing, and transforming. If you keep your pain for too long, it is because you have not yet learned the practice of inclusiveness.

When Rahula, the Buddha's son, was eighteen, the Buddha delivered to him a wonderful Dharma talk on how to practice inclusiveness. Sariputra, Rahula's tutor, was there and he listened and absorbed that teaching, also. Then, twelve years later, Sariputra had the chance to repeat this teaching to the full assembly of monks and nuns. It was the day after the completion of the three-month rainy-season retreat, and every monk was getting ready to leave the compound and go off in the ten directions to offer the teachings to others. At that time, one monk reported to the Buddha, "My Lord, this morning as Venerable Sariputra was leaving, I asked him where he was heading, and instead of answering my question, he pushed me to the ground and did not even say, 'I'm sorry.'"

The Buddha asked Ananda, "Has Sariputra gone far yet?" and Ananda said, "No, Lord, he left just an hour ago." So the Buddha asked a novice to find Sariputra and invite him to come back. When the novice brought Sariputra back, Ananda summoned all the monks who were still there to gather. Then, the Buddha stepped into the hall and asked Shariputra formally, "Shariputra, is it true that this morning when you were going out of the monastery, a brother of yours wanted to ask you a question and you did not answer him? Is it true that instead you pushed him to the ground and didn't even say you were sorry?" Thereupon, Shariputra answered the Buddha, in front of all his fellow monks and nuns:

"Lord, I remember the discourse you gave twelve years ago to Bhikshu Rahula, when he was eighteen years old. You taught him to contemplate the nature of earth, water, fire, and air in order to nourish and develop the virtues of love, compassion, joy, and equanimity. Although your teaching was directed to Rahula, I also learned from it, and I have tried to observe and practice that teaching.

"Lord, I have tried to practice like the earth. The earth is wide and open and has the capacity to receive, embrace, and transform. Whether people toss pure and fragrant substances such as flowers, perfume, or fresh milk upon the earth, or toss unclean and foul-smelling substances like excrement, urine, blood, mucus, and spit upon the earth, the earth receives them all equally, without grasping or aversion. No matter what you throw into the earth, the earth has the power to receive, embrace, and transform it. I try my best to practice like earth, to receive without resisting, complaining, or suffering.

"Lord, I practice mindfulness and loving-kindness. A monk who does not practice mindfulness of the body in the body, of the actions of the body in the actions of the body, could knock down a fellow monk and leave him lying there without apologizing. But it is not my way to be rude to a fellow monk, to push him to the ground and walk on without apologizing.

"Lord, I have learned the lesson you offered to Rahula to practice like the water. Whether someone pours a fragrant substance or an unclean substance into the water, the water receives them all equally without grasping or aversion. Water is immense and flowing and has the capacity to receive, contain, transform, and purify all these things, I have tried my best to practice like water. A monk who does not practice mindfulness, who does not practice becoming like water, might push a fellow monk to the ground and go on his way without saying 'I'm sorry.' I am not such a monk.

"My Lord, I have practiced to be more like fire. Fire burns everything, the pure as well as the impure, the beautiful as well as the distasteful, without grasping or aversion. If you throw flowers or silk into it, it burns. If you throw old cloth and other foul-smelling things into it, the fire will accept and burn everything. It does not discriminate. Why? Because fire can receive, consume, and burn everything offered to it. I have tried to practice like fire. I am able to burn the things that are negative in order to transform them. A monk who does not practice mindfulness of looking, listening, and contemplating might push a fellow monk to the ground and go on without apologizing. Lord, I am not such a monk.

"Lord, I have tried to practice to be more like air. The air carries all smells, good and bad, without grasping or aversion. The air has the capacity to transform, purify, and release. Lord Buddha, I have contemplated the body in the body, the movement of the body in the movement of the body, the positions of the body in the positions of the body, the feelings in the feelings, and the mind in the mind. A monk who does not practice mindfulness might push a fellow monk to the ground and go on without apologizing. I am not such a monk.

"My Lord, I am like an untouchable child with nothing to wear, with no title or any medal to put on my tattered cloth. I have tried to practice humility, because I know that humility has the power to transform. I have tried to learn every day. A monk who does not practice mindfulness can push a fellow monk to the ground and go on without apologizing. My Lord, I am not such a monk."

Shariputra continued to deliver his "Lion's Roar," but the other monk could stand it no longer, and he bared his right shoulder, knelt down, and begged for forgiveness. "Lord, I have transgressed the *Vinaya* (rules of monastic discipline). Out of anger and jealousy, I told a lie to discredit my elder brother in the Dharma. I beg the community to allow me to practice Beginning Anew." In front of the Buddha and the whole Sangha, he prostrated three times to Shariputra. When Shariputra saw his brother prostrating, he bowed and said, "I have not been skillful enough, and that is why I have created misunderstanding. I am co-responsible for this, and I beg my brother monk to forgive me." Then he prostrated three times to the other-monk, and they reconciled. Ananda asked Shariputra to stay for a cup of tea before starting off on his journey again. . . .

The heart of the Buddha is in each of us. When we are mindful, the Buddha is there. I know a four-year-old boy who, whenever he is upset, stops what he is doing, breathes mindfully, and tells his mommy and daddy, "I am touching the Buddha within." We need to take care of the healthy seeds that are in us by watering them every day through the practice of mindful breathing, mindful walking, mindfully doing everything. We need to touch the Buddha within us. We need to enter our own heart, which means to enter the heart of the Buddha. To enter the heart of the Buddha means to be present for ourselves, our suffering, our joys, and for many others. To enter the heart of the Buddha means to touch the world of no-birth and no-death, the world where water and wave are one.

When we begin the practice, we bring our suffering and our habit energies with us, not just those of twenty or thirty years, but the habit energies of all our ancestors. Through the practice of mindful living, we learn new habits. Walking, we know that we are walking. Standing, we know that we are standing. Sitting, we know that we are sitting. Practicing this way, we slowly undo our old habits and develop the new habit of dwelling deeply and happily in the present moment. With mindfulness in us, we can smile a smile that proves our transformation.

The heart of the Buddha has been touched by our being wonderfully together. Please practice as an individual, a family, a city, a nation, and a worldwide community. Please take good care of the happiness of everyone around you. Enjoy your breathing, your smiling, your shining the light of mindfulness on each thing you do.

Please practice transformation at the base through deep looking and deep touching. The teachings of the Buddha on transformation and healing are very deep. They are not theoretical. They can be practiced every day. Please practice them and realize them. I am confident that you can do it.

JESUS

c. 6 B.C.

Jesus of Nazareth was apparently born in Bethlehem around 6–5 B.C. (before the death of Herod the Great in 4 B.C.) but began his ministry in Nazareth. After being baptized by John the Baptist in the Jordan River, he gathered a group of twelve close followers, or apostles.

The duration of his public ministry is uncertain, but it is from John's Gospel that one gets the impression of a three-year period of teaching. He was executed by crucifixion under the order of Pontius Pilate, the Roman procurator, owing to the unrest Jesus's activities were causing. The date of death is usually considered to be 30 or 33. Accounts of his resurrection from the dead are preserved in the Gospels, Pauline writings, and Acts of the Apostles; Acts also refers to his subsequent ascension into heaven.

PREFACE

by Mother Teresa

WHAT IS MY SPIRITUAL LIFE? A love union with Jesus in which the divine and the human give themselves completely to one another. All that Jesus asks of me is to give myself to Him in all my poverty and nothingness.

Jesus said, "Learn of me." In our meditations we should always say, "Jesus, make me a saint according to your own heart, meek and humble." We must respond in the spirit in which Jesus meant us to respond. We know Him better through meditations, and the study of the gospel, but have we really understood Him in His humility?

One thing Jesus asks of me: that I lean on Him; that in Him and only in Him I put complete trust; that I surrender myself to Him unreservedly. Even when all goes wrong and I feel as if I am a ship without a compass, I must give myself completely to Him. I must not attempt to control God's action; I must not count the stages in the journey He would have me make. I must not desire a clear perception of my advance upon the road, must not know precisely where I am upon the way of holiness. I ask Him to make a saint of me, yet I must leave to Him the choice of the saintliness itself and still more the means that lead to it.

> *Hungry for love, He looks at you.*
> *Thirsty for kindness, He begs from you.*
> *Naked for loyalty, He hopes in you.*
> *Sick and imprisoned for friendship. He wants from you.*
> *Homeless for shelter in your heart, He asks of you.*
> *Will you be that one to Him?*

The simplicity of our life of contemplation makes us see the face of God in everything, everyone, and everywhere, all the time. His hand in all happenings makes us do all that we do — whether we think, study, work, speak, eat, or take our rest in Jesus, with Jesus, for Jesus and to Jesus, under the loving gaze of the Father, being totally available to Him in any form He may come to us.

I am deeply impressed by the fact that before explaining the Word of God, before presenting to the crowds the eight beatitudes, Jesus had compassion on them and gave them food. Only then did He begin to teach them.

Love Jesus generously. Love him trustfully, without looking back and without fear. Give yourself fully to Jesus, He will use you to accomplish great things on the condition that you believe much more in His love than in your weakness. Believe in Him, trust in Him with a blind and absolute confidence because He is Jesus. Believe that Jesus and Jesus alone is life, and sanctity is nothing but that same Jesus intimately living in you; then His hand will be free with you.

Who is Jesus to me?
Jesus is the Word made flesh.
Jesus is the Bread of Life.
Jesus is the Victim offered for our sins on the cross.
Jesus is the sacrifice offered at holy Mass for the sins of
*   the world and for mine.*
Jesus is the Word to be spoken.
Jesus is the truth to be told.
Jesus is the way to be walked.
Jesus is the light to be lit.
Jesus is the life to be lived.
Jesus is the love to be loved.
Jesus is the joy to be shared.
Jesus is the peace to be given.
Jesus is the hungry to be fed.
Jesus is the thirsty to be satiated.
Jesus is the naked to be clothed.
Jesus is the homeless to be taken in.
Jesus is the sick to be healed.
Jesus is the lonely to be loved.
Jesus is the unwanted to be wanted.
Jesus is the leper to wash His wounds.
Jesus is the beggar to give Him a smile.
Jesus is the drunkard to listen to Him.
Jesus is the mentally ill to protect Him.
Jesus is the little one to embrace Him.
Jesus is the blind to lead Him.

Jesus is the dumb to speak for Him.
Jesus is the crippled to walk with Him.
Jesus is the drug addict to befriend Him.
Jesus is the prostitute to remove from danger
      and befriend Her.
Jesus is the prisoner to be visited. Jesus is the old to
      be served.

To me: Jesus is my God.
Jesus is my spouse.
Jesus is my life.
Jesus is my only love.
Jesus is my all in all.
Jesus is my everything.

Jesus, I love with my whole heart, with my whole being. I have given Him all, even my sins, and He has espoused me to Himself in all tenderness and love.

JESUS

by Reynolds Price

IT BEGAN WITH A GIRL who was loved by God. The girl was named Mary and was aged fourteen. She had been promised in childhood to the builder Joseph but her mother Anna was wasting with sickness and Mary had Joseph's leave to stay home till her mother was walking again or dead. So the girl lived on in her mother's house which was one dry room that backed on a cave. Her father had been a priest of the Temple but died years back in the battering sun as he walked from Jerusalem down to Bethlehem, a town of six hundred souls, the home of King David dead a long thousand years.

On a spring afternoon in the year before King Herod died in filth and worms, Mary brought water in from the well and was kneeling beside her sleeping mother to wipe the feverish face and arms when a silent voice gripped the girl's strong hand. She'd heard the voice twice before but only in music, a keen distant chanting.

Now the chant was distant words so high that the girl looked down to see if fear had waked her mother.

Anna lay still on her clean pallet.

The first words again and again were a name *Sweet Mary.*

The girl went on soothing her mother. Mary had known her own beauty for two years but this was a prideful demon to shun.

The next high words were separate but clear. *You — God's choice — your son — his son.*

Baffled but calm as she'd never been, Mary faced the door to the world and said Yes with a single nod. When her hand came back to her mother's brow, her mother was dead.

Mary spent an hour washing the body and wrapping it in the linen they had saved for this last purpose. Then she stood and walked toward Joseph's shop.

Joseph lived in the back and slept on boards. But at dark that day he moved in beside young Mary at last — the law allowed it after betrothal — and they were married by midsummer though only in law. Near her there in her old home, Joseph slowly learned of the terror planted in her womb and growing daily. Through the long wait his pallet lay apart from Mary's by the reach of his arm, and there were days that summer and fall when Joseph pressed iron nails deep into his hands to let out part of the pain he felt but never told. This girl had been taken and used to the dregs before he touched her.

So early that winter — a freezing night when Mary called Joseph's name in the dark before the pain broke from her in groans — Joseph brought the lamp, saw she was wet but clean of blood, then ran uphill to the midwife's house.

As the midwife stepped out onto the path she gave him her own jar to fill at David's spring.

Long after they moved to Nazareth in Galilee where Joseph's brother Clopas owned land and a building business, when Joseph would stop to watch Mary's boy — with Mary's likeness in the lean dark face — he recalled the strangeness that came down on him as he trotted home that night with water. *My heart had seized up in my chest. A nighthawk hung in the air beyond me all but in reach. Through the open door of a house in lamplight, I saw three men and a dwarfish girl stalled in the cold — bread in their fingers aimed at their lips but still as bones. Yet when I looked the stars were wheeling. Then suddenly blood roared again in my ears, and I went toward home.*

At home the midwife had led Mary back to the cave that served as a stable and pen. The colt and the hens had warmed the space; and when Joseph bent to look in the door, the boy was already born and dugging his mother's breast.

Her eyes had found their lifelong sight, but she looked to Joseph and told him the boy would be named Jesus.

Joseph raised the boy, the first in a line of five sons and three daughters. He led the sons to the synagogue school where they each surpassed him by learning their letters and reading the law and prophets on sight. He found good husbands for the girls.

And the eldest boy, the one from Bethlehem, repaid the

training Joseph gave him. After he and his brothers left school for work in the family trade, Jesus would go to the rabbi at night and read the law and prophets till late. Before he was grown he knew them well; and many nights while his kinsmen slept, Jesus walked alone in the hills. He could look down on the plain of Jezreel where God and his armies had fought Israel's enemies and where the great battle of the last days would rage. He could look to the lights of Herod Antipas' capital Sepphoris three miles from Nazareth — a marble city with a palace, a theater, baths and a temple to the deified man Augustus Caesar. The boy learned the story of all he saw.

Every spring he went up with his family to eat the Passover feast in Jerusalem, honoring the night when God's mercy spared the slave hovels where Hebrews lived in Pharaoh's Egypt but killed the firstborn in their masters' homes. Old King Herod's new Temple in Jerusalem, built on the site of Solomon's Temple, was all but finished after decades of work. There among its ivory and gold, young Jesus talked with any priest or lawyer who would hear his questions. He was already asking if God was truly the Father of all and if so then who could watch the world of blood and hate and think God was loving?

Back in Nazareth Jesus showed keen skill at the smithing forge among his four brothers who were masons and carvers. And from the day when Joseph died, young Jesus bore the first son's duty to tend his mother who at forty was hunched with all she'd borne as God's choice — the lean girl Mary who was bent now and worn.

But when Jesus passed his thirtieth year, he turned his back on the home he'd known. His mother and all his brothers and sisters stayed in Nazareth, but in the spring Jesus walked south through Galilee and on down the banks of the Jordan through country held by Rome now and ruled at the will of Tiberius Caesar by the puppet sons of old Herod the Great. Their moves were watched by the merciless eye of Pontius Pilate, Caesar's prefect in Palestine. When Jesus reached a bend in the river near Jericho, he saw the man he'd come to find — a man whose fame had reached even Nazareth.

It was near sundown and the mob who daily came from Jerusalem — lawyers, priests, rich women, whores, wretches — had ridden southwest back up through hills toward the golden Temple or were cooking over their fires on the east bank. The famous man that Jesus had come for was John the Baptizer. John had cried out here since the winter solstice against all evil hearts around him.

John warned of God's taut patience and wrath, the imminent coming down of God's last plan in fire and terror. He would say "One stronger than I is coming whose sandal I'm not fit to loosen. The winnowing fan is in his hand. He'll utterly sweep his threshing floor and gather the good wheat into his barn. He'll burn the chaff in roaring fire. Take shelter now. Thresh your own grain."

John offered a ritual washing from error, for readiness. Near dusk as it was, John was still at the edge of the river this day, still waiting in his camel skins. To the eye he made a believable image of the prophet Elijah whose return was expected as the near forerunner of God's anointed. Many hoped that the longed-for man, God's son Messiah, would roll Rome into the Roman sea, mount Israel's throne — and open souls to God's whirlwind — God's hand in history redeeming time. What John was waiting to welcome had come. Jesus beyond him was surely the man. John sensed him on sight, beckoned the younger man toward him, then forded the river to the waist-deep midst.

Jesus stripped and waded to meet John.

John met Jesus' eyes with half the blaze of recognition; but when Jesus gave no nod or sign, then John's eyes faltered. So he seized Jesus by the hair and buried him backward in the stream.

When he drew Jesus up, John's eyes still questioned him.

But Jesus faced the dusky zenith. Whatever John or the cooking stragglers saw or heard, Jesus watched the sky torn open above, a white dove sifting down through the air and what he heard was that same voice his mother heard but kept in secret. It said *You are my only Son.*

A fire blazed in the actual water.

For more than a month Jesus walked alone in the desert past Jericho, the crags and wastes by the hot Dead Sea, Earth's deepest pit. . . .

As he walked the lake's broad shore and hills, he told whomever would pause to listen the news he'd learned alone in the desert — that the reign of God would break in on them any day, that they must turn from waste and hatred to ready themselves for a fierce coming judgment and then for the endless reign of love. His hearers were farmers and fishermen, their wives and children, the occasional rabbi and village crank, the whores, cheats, and scapegoats.

From among them he chose two pairs of brothers. The first were Simon son of Jonah and his brother Andrew, then John the son of Zebedee and his brother James — all four were fishermen. The sons of Zebedee were heirs to their father's thriving business which sold dried fish to prosperous households as far south as Jericho and Jerusalem, a two-day trek. Even the High Priest bought their fish at his back door downhill from the Temple.

The way Jesus called them was the first strange thing. One late spring evening he came along the strand near their town Capernaum and as he saw them beaching boats and mending nets he told them "Come. We'll fish for humans."

For reasons they never plumbed, the four men dropped their work and followed him. Where he led them first was to Simon and Andrew's house. He was weak with hunger.

But Simon's mother-in-law was down with a lingering fever and not till Jesus went to her pallet, crouched beside her whispering, then took her hand and raised her up did she have the strength to cook a supper for the five men newly bound together as teacher and pupils.

In that small town word leaked at once that the teacher Jesus had brought Simon's mother from the edge of death and by the time the men finished eating, a crowd had gathered at the narrow door.

Among them was a leper too grim to watch. The crowd stood back when the leper pressed through Simon's door to stand above where Jesus sat. He said to Jesus "You can heal me if you want to."

Jesus stayed in place but met the man's eyes, managed a smile, and said "I want to."

The leper was healed. By the time he'd run out into the street, his open sores were sealing and fading. . . .

Word of that night swept the whole lakeshore and the hills behind. And while Jesus meant to go on telling people of the imminent breaking in of God and the need for love and mercy meanwhile, he was met in every town and field by mobs of the sick who silenced his teaching. Even healthy people brought him their cripples in carts and barrows.

Balked as he was he felt real anguish and pity at the sight of the power of demons on Earth and he healed when he could, when he knew he was trusted. Even back home in Capernaum he could hardly rest.

One day he was inside teaching his pupils and a few of the lawyers who'd come from Jerusalem to check on rumors. The door was shut on the crowd outside, but a pair of desperate men from the hills climbed onto the house with their paralyzed brother and broke through the mud and straw roof with poles. Then they lowered their brother's pallet near the spot where Jesus sat and they begged him for healing. . . .

Soon John the Baptizer . . . asked for a simple answer from Jesus "Are you really the one to come or not?"

Jesus waited all night, then called the messengers to him at dawn and said "Tell John this. The blind see, the lame walk, lepers are clean, the deaf hear and speak, the dead are raised, and the poor learn the news of God's coming reign. Bless him who trusts me." It was all he said.

But when John's messengers nodded and left, Jesus turned to the pupils stunned beside him and said one more thing "Foxes have holes, the birds have nests but the Son of Man has nowhere to lay his head."

Peter and Andrew at least were offended. They'd given him room and board for weeks.

Others thought he was crazy. Some turned back home abandoning hope in what they thought he'd meant and offered — rest, power, and glory in God's coming reign.

But after a troubled while the Twelve held firm around him stumped as they were.

So Jesus called them apart in secret. He gave them power over foul demons and to heal the sick. He said that they were to go through all the towns and farms of Galilee, telling the hearers of God's coming reign. "Go two by two with no gold or silver, no extra shirt, just sandals and a stick and announce to Israel the good news that God is at hand. Bless the house that receives you. When a town won't receive you shake its dust from your feet. Amen I tell you it will be far better for Sodom and Gomorrah on Judgment Day than for that town.

"I'm sending you out like sheep among wolves. Be wise as snakes and guileless as doves and when they attack you here run there but never rest from telling God's news to the lost and wicked — they're welcome too just as they are in the midst of their lives. Both God and the angels welcome wrongdoers more gladly than the good. Amen I tell you, you won't have gone through the towns of Israel before the Son of Man comes in glory."

The pupils were amazed at his expectation, but they tried to obey him and they went off in pairs. . . .

Then the Twelve returned from their separate travels on a day like any other day. No one could see that the reign of God had come or was closer.

Jesus saw their bafflement and said "Let's go to the wilderness and rest." Any thoughts of his own were inward and secret.

They got in the boat, sailed east again on the lake, and found a secluded place where Jesus could pray a little apart even from them and they could rest with no sad mobs of the sick and idle.

After a while though someone found them and a crowd gathered in the wilderness with no food or shelter.

Many violent and outcast men and women were among them. There was nothing to do but face the mob so Jesus told them this story about the Father's thirst for their souls. He said "A man had two sons. The younger one said to his father 'Father, give me my share of all that will come to me.' So the father divided his belongings between them. A few days later the younger son packed all he had and traveled far off. There he wasted his share in wild living and when he had spent everything a hard famine struck that place. The son was desperate so he hired himself to a man who sent him out to pasture his swine.

"The son would gladly have eaten the roots the swine ate — no one gave him anything. But once he finally came to himself, he said 'My father's slaves have food to spare but I'm starving here. I'll go to my father and tell him "Father, I've erred against Heaven and you. I'm not worthy to be called your son. Treat me like one of your hired hands.' Then he went homeward toward his father.

But while the son was still at a distance his father saw him and had pity. He ran and kissed him. The son said 'Father, I've erred against Heaven and you. I'm not worthy to be called your son.' But the father said to his slaves Quick, bring the best coat and put it on him. Put a ring on his hand, shoes on his feet, and kill the fat calf. We'll eat and be glad for this son of mine was dead and is now alive. He was lost and we've found him.' They began to be glad.

"Now the elder son was out in the field and as he got near the house he heard music and dancing. He called one of the slaves and asked what this meant and the slave told him 'Your brother is home and your father has killed the fat calf because he's got him back safe and whole.' But the elder son was angry and refused to go in.

"His father came out and begged the elder son but he answered his father 'Look, all these years I've served you and never disobeyed your orders yet you never gave me even a kid so I might celebrate with my friends. But when this son of yours returned — the one that squandered your money on whores — you killed the fat calf for him.' So the father said to him 'Son, you're always with me and all that's mine is yours. It's fitting now to be grateful and glad for your younger brother was dead and is back alive. He was lost and is found.'"

When Jesus had taught them about God's hunger for their souls, evening was coming and he took pity on them. He said to Philip "How are we going to feed these people?"

Philip said "We aren't. Two hundred denars wouldn't buy bread for them."

But Andrew, Simon's brother, said "There's a boy here with five barley rolls and two fish."

So Jesus said "Make the people sit down" — there was deep green grass where they were.

The people sat down. With women and children there were some five thousand.

Jesus took the boy's rolls and fish. He thanked God for them, then passed them out to the seated crowd as much as they wanted.

When all were full the pupils picked up twelve baskets of uneaten scraps.

And when the men took the meal as a sign that God's anointed had truly come and his reign was at hand, they talked of seizing Jesus on the spot and making him king.

Jesus left quickly and the pupils followed. . . .

From there Jesus led the Twelve northeast to the flanks of Mount Hermon and the hamlets near Caesarea Philippi. More and more he was walking ahead of them or praying apart. But once on a lonely stretch of road he stopped, turned back, and asked the pupils "Who do people think I am?" He had never told them outright whatever he thought.

They could see that now he needed to know. So they told him "Some say you're Elijah, some John the Baptizer, some say you're a prophet."

Jesus pressed them. "But you — who do you say I am?"

There was silence till Simon spoke out. "You're Messiah." The Jews had long awaited Messiah, a man whose Hebrew title means *Anointed*. Again some thought he was meant to free them and repair their pride in God's chosen people. Some thought he would come as a warrior chief. Some thought he'd be an eternal priest.

But as soon as Simon spoke Jesus warned the pupils to say nothing of this. Then as they walked he began to tell them that now the Son of Man must suffer many things, be refused by the lawyers and priests, and be killed. "Then I will rise on the third day" he said. He spoke quite plainly.

Simon took him aside and began to warn him of such wild words — he thought Messiah was meant to reign in painless eternity.

But Jesus wouldn't take the rebuke. It defied his growing sense of his fate. He turned on Simon saying "Get behind me, Satan. You're thinking of human things, not God's." But after a while he said to Simon "Simon son of Jonah, now I'll call you Peter" (*Peter* means *Rock*). And to the other pupils he said "This is Peter and on his shoulders I'll lay my whole plan. The gates of Hell itself won't shake it." Then he went on talking about his fate — pain and death and rising again.

The pupils and even Peter were baffled. They'd waited for places in God's coming reign but now they said nothing.

Then after six days Jesus took Peter, James, and John

apart from the others and led them on to the heights of Mount Hermon. He barely spoke through the arduous climb. Then near the peak and alone in their presence, he was changed in form. His clothes turned a very shining white like nothing a human can make on Earth. His face was gleaming, and Elijah and Moses were talking with him, one at each side.

Peter was cold with fright so he said "Rabbi, it's fine to be here! Let's pitch three tents — one for you, one for Moses, and one for Elijah." He didn't know what he was saying. They were terrified.

A cloud came down and covered them; a voice from the cloud said "This is my Son, the one I love. Hear him."

Peter's arms and legs were frozen; and he said to himself *I've given too much to this one man, and now he shows me this wild sight — me with a home and a hungry family I've left to chase what's either Messiah or the shrewdest demon I've yet known. Should I run for my life or fling myself off this high rock? My family might starve but no one would see my dead shamed face.*

Then suddenly Peter and the others looked round and saw themselves alone with Jesus.

As they came down the mountain, Jesus ordered them to tell no one what they'd seen till the Son of Man should die and rise alive from the dead.

The pupils were baffled but asked him nothing.

So Jesus set his face toward Jerusalem.

The loyal baffled Twelve came behind him — he had that power still.

Behind the Twelve came the loyal women who'd helped him according to the little they had.

On the way a young man ran up and knelt to Jesus saying "Kind teacher, what must I do to win eternal life?"

Jesus said "Why call me kind? No one is kind but God. You know the commandments — *'Do not kill, do not commit adultery, do not steal, do not give false witness, honor your father and mother.'*"

The man said "Teacher, I've done all that."

Gazing at him Jesus loved him and said "One thing's lacking then. Go sell all you own and give it to the poor. You'll have treasure in Heaven. Then follow me."

But the young man was shocked.

Jesus said "Look, your miserable brothers and sisters — all of them children of Abraham too — live in filthy rags and starve. Your house is stocked with all good things."

So the young man went away grieving. He had great possessions.

Looking round at the pupils, Jesus said "It's easier for a camel to go through the eye of a needle than for a rich man to enter God's reign. . . ."

It was the feast of Dedication and Jerusalem was mobbed with pilgrims to the Temple. Jesus and the pupils stayed east of the city on the Mount of Olives but daily he walked in the porches of the Temple and announced his news to all, Jew or Greek.

Some trusted him at once from the news they'd heard. Others hounded his steps in the hope of trapping him in some blasphemous or seditious claim — everyone in power feared his hold on the poor and outcast.

One group asked him by what right he did his work, who gave him his power?

Jesus said "Answer me one thing and I'll tell you by what right I do my work — John's baptism, was it from God or humankind?"

They reasoned among themselves "If we say 'From God' he'll say 'Then why didn't you obey him?' but if we say 'From men'" — they were slow to say that, knowing how the people had honored John. So they said "We don't know."

Jesus said "Then I won't tell you where I get my power."

One of the lawyers, knowing he'd answered them well, said "Sir, what commandment stands first of all?"

Jesus said "First is '*Hear, Israel, the Lord our God is one Lord and you shall love the Lord your God with all your heart, with all your soul and with all your strength.*' Second is this '*You shall love your neighbor like yourself.*' There's no commandment greater than these."

The lawyer said "True, teacher. There's no other beside God and to love one's neighbor like oneself is more than all burnt offerings and sacrifices."

Jesus told the man "You're not far from the reign of God. Remember God's word when he said '*Amen I will have mercy and not sacrifice.*'"

Then they brought him a woman caught in the very act of adultery. They stood her before him and said "Moses ordered us to stone such a woman. What do you say?"

Jesus stooped and wrote on the ground with his finger as if he hadn't heard them.

So they asked him again.

He stood and said "The one that's pure among you, let him throw the first stone." Again he stooped and wrote on the ground.

One by one, from the oldest to the youngest, the men walked off and left Jesus alone with the woman.

Jesus said to her "Woman, where are your accusers? Is no one condemning you?"

She said "No sir."

He said "Neither do I. Go and wrong no more. . . ."

Then in Bethany on the Mount of Olives in sight of the Temple a man named Lazarus fell sick. He was Jesus's friend and the brother of Jesus's friends Mary and Martha. The sisters sent word to Jesus beyond the Jordan and though he loved Lazarus and the sisters he waited two days before saying he'd go to Bethany.

At once the pupils tried to dissuade him. They said "Rabbi, you're in trouble there so near Jerusalem."

Only Thomas was eager. He said "I'm ready to die beside him."

Jesus set out, the others fell in, and when they'd passed the Dead Sea and Jericho and climbed the long rise to Bethany, Lazarus had been in the grave four days.

Meeting Jesus on the road Martha even said "Sir, if you'd come sooner he wouldn't have died."

When Mary met him she said the same.

But Jesus walked straight past them to the grave where his friend lay wrapped and cold. When he got there he could not conceal his grief. It made him shudder hard and weep.

Many had come from Jerusalem to mourn. They all watched Jesus.

And at last he said "Take the stone off the grave."

Martha said "But sir, he'll stink by now."

They rolled the stone off the dark grave shaft.

Then groaning again and in a loud voice Jesus cried "Lazarus, come out!"

The man who was dead four days came out still wrapped in grave linen.

Jesus kissed him and said "Untie him. Let him live."

All who'd stood by watching were startled. Many trusted in Jesus.

But others went back to Jerusalem and told the chief priests and the ruling council.

Among themselves the council said that if they let Jesus work among them then all the people would follow him and soon the Romans would come and crush them — Jesus, his rabble, the nation around them, the priests and the Temple.

Caiaphas the High Priest finally said "It's better that one man die for the people than that we and all the nation be slaughtered." And from that day the priests and the council searched for a way to catch him on safe ground apart from his mob and kill him quickly.

Before they could act Jesus withdrew again, this time to a town named Ephraim north of Jerusalem near the wilderness. He understood that his time was near and more and more he walked out alone and slept apart. Again and again he asked himself if he'd been wrong about God's love — could any father who presided over the demons of sickness and pain, want, hate, and loss be rightly called *loving* by his lone afflicted creatures?

But the Twelve were still with him waiting still.

Then the time for Passover came in early April. Pilgrims moved toward the Temple from all the nation and from foreign lands and the city swelled many times over.

By the first day of Passover week Jesus thought he had answered his awful question — how could it matter if the Father loved his creatures? The Father was the only God; if Jesus was his Son then the question was meaningless — God's will was sovereign for joy or pain. So he led the pupils back along the eastern approach to the crest of the Mount of Olives. Looking down on the city and the nearby hamlet of Bethphage he called two of the pupils and said "Go to that hamlet there and you'll find a tethered colt on which no one's ever sat. Untie it and bring it here. If anyone asks what you're doing say 'The teacher needs it and will send it right back.'"

Just as he said they found a colt tied to a door outside in the street and they brought it to Jesus, throwing their coats across its back.

Jesus sat on it, rode down the Mount to the depth of the valley, and began the steep climb to the Temple.

Many spread their coats in the road and others spread leafy branches from the fields. The ones in front and those behind cried out *"Hosanna! Blessed is he who comes in the Lord's name!"* Few of them recalled what the prophet Zechariah had said long ago,

Rejoice greatly, O daughter Jerusalem!
Look, your king comes to you.
Triumphant and glorious is he,
Humble and riding on an ass,
On a colt the foal of an ass.

Even the pupils didn't understand though some of the lawyers said to him "Teacher, calm your pupils."

Jesus answered "Amen I tell you if they were silent the stones themselves would cry out."

The priests were only biding their time. Herod was watching. The Romans were watching.

Jesus dismounted at the Temple doors, looked round the courts that were sparsely filled so late in the day, then went back out.

That night Jesus led his pupils again uphill to Bethany where they dined with Lazarus and his sisters Martha and Mary.

At the end of the meal, Mary came forward with a pound of expensive perfumed ointment. She wiped Jesus's feet with it and dried them with her hair. The splendid odor filled the whole house.

Judas who kept the common purse for Jesus and the pupils was plainly indignant and said "Why wasn't this ointment sold for three hundred denars and the money given to the poor?"

But Jesus said "You'll have the poor with you always but not me. Let Mary be. She'll keep the remainder to sweeten my corpse."

No one but Jesus smiled.

On the following morning he entered the Temple courts. He'd brought a stout cord which served as a whip and with it he drove out the merchants, their sacrificial livestock, and the money handlers who defiled the place by exchanging coins for the Temple tax. As they ran he cried out "Remember it's written *'My house shall be called a house of prayer for all nations.'* But you have made it a bandits' cave."

The priests were watching.

The rest of that day and the next three days as Jesus taught and argued in the Temple his enemies worked to lure him into their trap. They even tried to catch him in sedition. Some lawyers approached him and said "Teacher, we know you're honest and that no one counts heavily with you since you aren't partial to appearances but teach God's way. So tell us is it right to pay tribute to Caesar? Should we pay or not?"

Jesus said "Why tempt me? Show me a coin."

They showed him one.

And he said "Whose picture is this and whose inscription?"

They said "Caesar's."

So he told them "Give Caesar's things back to Caesar. Give God's things to God."

Later to the crowd he denounced the lawyers. "Beware these lawyers. They love to parade in long robes, be bowed to in the market, take the best seats in synagogue and at banquets. Yet they likewise eat up widows' houses under cover of prayer. They'll get the reward of their pride and their lies." Then turning on the lawyers at hand Jesus said "Great sorrow to you, false teachers. You're like whitewashed tombs that shine in the light but inside are full of dead bones and filth. You're a nest of vipers-who'll save you now? Those who trust me are saved by God's truth. Truth sets them free. . . ."

On the Wednesday Jesus sat with the pupils on the Mount of Olives and looked toward the Temple porches and courts. White marble and gold dazzled in sunlight. Giant hewn stones braced it stronger than any building on Earth. Yet Jesus told the pupils plainly "See those great buildings? There'll be no stone left standing on stone which shall not be toppled."

When the pupils were baffled his feeling deepened and he cried toward the city "O Jerusalem, Jerusalem, killing the prophets and stoning the messengers. How often I'd have gathered your children as a hen gathers her brood to her wings but you wouldn't come. And now the days are strictly numbered till the sun goes dark, the moon fades, and all the powers of Heaven quake with the coming trial. For then you'll see the Son of Man coming on clouds with power and glory, sending his angels to gather the chosen from pole to pole. He'll separate the souls as a shepherd parts his sheep from the goats — the sheep on his right hand, goats on his left.

"Then the Son will say to those at his right hand 'Come O blessed by my Father. Inherit the kingdom readied for you from the start of the world. For I was hungry and you fed me, thirsty and you gave me drink, I was a stranger and you welcomed me, naked and you clothed me, sick and you visited me, in prison and you came to me.'

"The righteous will say to him 'Lord, when did we see you hungry or thirsty or a stranger or naked and serve you or sick or in prison and visit you?' And the Son will answer them 'Amen I tell you when you did that to the least of my children you did it to me. . . .'"

And late that same night Judas Iscariot who was one of the Twelve went to the priests and offered to betray Jesus's nighttime whereabouts. No one ever knew why he made that choice.

But as the priests heard Judas's offer, they were glad and promised him money if he found an occasion to lead them to Jesus when he was alone apart from the mob.

On Thursday which was the first day of unleavened bread when they sacrificed the Passover lamb, the pupils said to Jesus "Where do you want us to go and arrange for you to eat the feast?"

He sent two of them saying "Go into the city. You'll be met by a man with a water jug. Follow him. Wherever he enters tell the owner 'The teacher says "Where is my guest room so I can eat the Passover with my pupils?"' He'll show you a big room upstairs spread and ready. Prepare for us there."

The pupils went out and found the room as he told them.

So as evening fell Jesus came with the Twelve. When they'd taken their places around the table Jesus took off his shirt, wrapped a towel around himself, poured water into a bowl, and began to wash the pupils' feet, drying them with the towel at his waist.

He got to Peter but Peter protested "Lord, you'll never wash my feet."

Jesus said to him "If I don't wash you, you'll have no part in me."

Peter said "Then not just my feet but my hands and head too."

Jesus washed them all, even Judas who was set on his course now.

As they were eating Jesus said "Amen I tell you one of you will betray me, one eating with me here."

The pupils were distressed and said to one another "Surely not me."

Jesus said "One of you who dips bread into the dish with me — better for that man if he'd not been born."

Then Judas left on his errand. He knew where Jesus would go after this to be apart.

As they finished eating Jesus took a last loaf and blessing it he broke and gave it to them saying "Take. This is my body." Then lifting a cup and giving thanks, he gave wine to them.

All drank it.

He said to them "This is my blood of the promise poured out for many. Amen I tell you never in any way will I drink of the fruit of the vine till that day when I drink it new in the reign of God." Then when all had drunk, he led them in a final solemn joyous dance — a rite that mirrored the course of the stars, the currents of time, during which they sang the truth he'd told them only now,

A light I am to you who see,
A glass I am to you who look,
A door I am to you who knock,
A road I am to you who walk.

When that was done Jesus said a last thing "You have seen your brother, you have seen your God."

And after singing the final hymn they walked down the side of Zion and up the dry bed of the Kidron brook to a garden at the foot of the Mount of Olives where they'd stayed that week. And Jesus said to them "All of you shall stumble tonight for it's written

I'll strike down the shepherd
And the sheep shall be scattered,

But after I'm raised I'll go ahead of you to Galilee."

They'd still never understood his word *raised.*

But Peter told him "Even if everybody stumbles not I."

Jesus said to Peter "Simon, Simon — look — Satan begged hard to have you to thresh like harvest wheat. I've prayed for you that your faith won't fail."

Peter said "Oh Lord, no way, no way."

Jesus said to him "Amen I tell you — you, today, tonight before the cock crows twice — you'll deny me three times."

But Peter just kept saying "If I must die with you no way would I deny you."

All the others said likewise.

They came to a plot of land called Gethsemane or *Oil*

Press. Jesus told the pupils "Sit here while I pray." Taking Peter, James, and John with him he went on farther under the olive trees and began to be deeply appalled and harrowed. He said to the three men "My soul is anguished to death. Stay here and watch. It was ripe in his mind now — the Father might here require the Son to throw his own life in the press of time to ease the coming down of the reign. The prospect scalded.

So going on a little, Jesus fell to the ground and prayed that if it were possible the hour of sacrifice might turn away. He said "*Abba*, Father, everything is possible to you. Take this cup from me — still not what I want but you." He came, found the three pupils sleeping, and said to Peter "Simon, are you sleeping? Couldn't you watch with me one hour? Watch and pray so you don't come to testing. Oh the spirit is ready but the flesh is weak."

They didn't know how to answer him.

Going back alone Jesus prayed the same words. But then the wrongs of all humanity were laid on his head, and at last he felt the weight of the ransom he'd vowed to pay.

This time Peter heard the prayer and saw great drops of sweat like blood on Jesus' face. He meant to stand and go toward Jesus but his legs were weak from the long day.

So Jesus came again and found them sleeping since they didn't know how to answer his need.

Once more Jesus pled alone with the Father. Then he came back a third time and said to the three men "Sleep now and rest. It's over. I paid. The hour came. But look, the Son of Man is betrayed into wrongdoers' hands. Get up. Let's go. See, the one who betrays me is nearing."

At once while Jesus was still speaking, Judas Iscariot appeared and with him a cohort of Roman soldiers and a squad with swords and sticks from the chief priests, lawyers, and elders. The traitor had given them a signal — "Whomever I kiss is he. Seize him and take him off securely." Coming up to Jesus then, Judas said "Rabbi!" and kissed him lovingly.

The men got their hands on Jesus and bound him. . . .

Now the priests and the council took testimony from many liars that Jesus had said "I'll tear down this Temple made by hand and after three days I'll build another that's not handmade." Even so the witnesses were not consistent.

Rising in the center of the chamber the High Priest said to Jesus "Won't you answer to what these men testify?"

But Jesus was silent standing there.

So the High Priest said "Then you are Messiah, the Son of the Blessed?"

Jesus said "I am and you shall see the Son of Man sitting at the right hand of power and coming with clouds of Heaven."

The High Priest tore his robe at that, meaning Jesus had finally sealed his doom.

All the council likewise condemned him to death. Some spat on him, covered his eyes, struck him and said "Now prophesy!"

Even the slaves treated him to blows.

And while Peter was down in the courtyard one of the

High Priest's maids saw him warming himself. She said to him "You're with the Nazarene Jesus."

But Peter denied it saying "I don't know him. What are you talking about?" Then he went out to the porch and a cock crowed.

Seeing him the maid said to those standing round "This man is one of them."

Again Peter denied it.

After a little those standing round said to Peter "Surely you're one of them. Anybody can hear you're a Galilean."

Peter began to curse and swear. "I don't even know this man you mention." Then a second time the cock crowed and Peter remembered Jesus saying "Before the cock crows twice you'll deny me three times." Dwelling on that he wept bitterly.

In the morning the priests, the lawyers, the elders, and all the council handed Jesus over to Pilate at Roman headquarters in the former palace of Herod the Great by the western gate. For fear of defiling themselves that day and being unfit to eat the Passover they stayed outside while the soldiers led Jesus.

Pilate asked him "You're the King of the Jews?" Jesus said "You say."

Pilate asked him "Then what have you done? Are you some zealot?"

Jesus said "My reign is not here and now. If it were my friends would fight for me."

Pilate said "So you're a king?"

Jesus said again "You know the truth."

Pilate said "What's the truth?"

Jesus said no more.

Then Pilate went out to the waiting accusers and said "You have your custom that I free one prisoner at every Passover. Do you want me to free the King of the Jews?"

They all cried "Barabbas! No, give us Barabbas." Barabbas was a jailed bandit.

Pilate said "Then what must I do with Jesus?"

They cried "Crucify him!"

So Pilate had the soldiers take Jesus and whip him. Then they dressed him in a royal purple robe, plaited a crown of thorns for his head, saluted him as King of the Jews, mocked and spat on him and returned him to Pilate.

Pilate led Jesus back outside. To the waiting accusers he said "Here's the man."

They only cried again "Crucify him!"

Pilate handed Jesus to a squad of soldiers who stripped him of his robe, laid the armpiece of his cross on his shoulders, and led him north through the city to die. When Jesus stumbled under the weight, they forced one Simon from Cyrene to bear it.

So they went north through the Gennath gate and came to the hill Golgotha, *Skull Place*, in a limestone quarry long since worked out. They gave Jesus wine that was drugged with myrrh, a token mercy. Then they stripped him naked, nailed his arms at the wrist to the armpiece, then hoisted that upright onto the stake and nailed his feet. At his head they posted the charge against him written in Latin, Hebrew and Greek. It said "Jesus of Nazareth King of the Jews."

Below him, as was their privilege, the soldiers divided his clothes. His coat was woven in a single piece so rather than tear it they cast lots for it. Then at Jesus's right and left they crucified two thieves.

It was about noon.

The passersby insulted Jesus by wagging their heads and saying "So! — the man who'd destroy the Temple and build it in three days. Save yourself. Step down from the cross."

The chief priests also watched and mocked him.

Even the thieves beside him cursed him.

None of his friends were near at hand. Only the women who had followed from Galilee stood at a distance watching in grief. Among them were Mary from Magdala, Mary the mother of the younger James and Joses, and Salome. They tried to console his mother who was with them.

The blank sky gave no sign whatever of angels on clouds proclaiming the reign.

At last a great darkness settled on the place and at three in the afternoon Jesus shouted in a loud voice *"Eloi Eloi lema sabachthani?"* It means "My God, my God why did you desert me?"

Some of the bystanders thought he was calling Elijah. One of them ran, filled a sponge with vinegar, put it on a stick and held it up to his mouth to drink, saying "Let's see now if Elijah saves him."

No one saved him.

So Jesus cried out loud again and breathed his last. . . .

At daylight Sunday morning the two Marys and Salome returned to the tomb with cloths and spices to wash and anoint Jesus' body. All the way they asked themselves "Who'll roll back the stone?" — the stone was huge. But when they reached the actual tomb the stone was rolled back. The entrance was open. Two of the women balked in fear.

Mary from Magdala walked forward though, telling herself at every step *The world is frozen now in death. At last the demons have fouled his body. Even my hand that would wash his corpse is helpless in chill air before me. All my life has passed by useless.* When she took the last step she saw a young man on the right of the tomb where the corpse had lain.

The man wore a white coat; and when he saw Mary near he said "Don't be afraid. Are you hunting Jesus the dead Nazarene? He was raised. He's gone. Go tell all his pupils and Peter that he's going ahead to Galilee. You'll see him there as he told you before."

Going out again the women fled. They were shuddering and wild with shock and for a cold hour they told no one nothing.

When the women finally broke their story the pupils doubted and feared a trap.

But Peter and John ran toward the tomb.

John got there first, stopped at the entrance, and bent to look in. He saw the linen lying empty.

Peter went straight in, saw the linen and also the face cloth apart from the linen folded neatly.

John went in then, examined the linen, and believed. Then he and Peter returned to where the pupils had hid for fear of their enemies.

But Mary from Magdala had followed them back to the tomb and now she stood alone weeping at the entrance.

A man behind her said "Woman, why weep?"

Mary turned but did not know him as Jesus. She thought he was a gardener. She said "Sir, if you've taken him show me where."

The man said "Mary —"

Then she knew. She cried out "Rabbi!" and knelt to clasp his knees.

Jesus said "Stop holding me" and raised her upright. Then he told her plainly what to tell the pupils — he was risen indeed.

After that he went to the High Priest's servant and gave him part of the linen shroud that had covered his own dead body in darkness.

When Mary got to the pupils with her news they were even more amazed. They stayed in hiding afraid and uncertain. But that night when they'd finished eating Jesus suddenly stood in their midst — the door had been locked. They were terrified and thought he was a ghost.

He said "No fear. I am — look." He showed them the holes in his wrists and feet and the wound in his side. Then he asked for something to eat. They brought him part of a broiled fish and a comb of honey and he ate in plain view. Then he told them again he was bound for Galilee.

After that Jesus showed himself unmistakably to James his brother. James had sworn that he would never eat or drink again till he had seen the risen Lord so Jesus came to him, took bread and wine, blessed them, and said "Eat, brother, and drink your fill for the Son of Man is risen from among them that sleep."

He also came to Judas the traitor, touched him firmly, and ringed his wrist though he said no words and left still silent.

Then Judas went out to the field he'd bought with his blood money and hanged himself.

Jesus likewise appeared unquestionably to upward of five hundred people who'd known him. It was later in Galilee that he left the remaining pupils.

Peter and Andrew, James and John sons of Zebedee, Thomas, a man named Nathanael, and two more pupils returned to Capernaum to wait for his coming as the Son in glory. One night Simon said "I'm going fishing."

The others said "We're coming with you."

They went out, got into the boat and all that night caught nothing.

But when it was dawn Jesus stood on the shore, not that the pupils knew it was Jesus.

Jesus called to them "Boys, nothing to eat?"

They called back "No."

He said "Cast to starboard. You'll find some."

They cast the net and then could barely drag it, there were so many fish.

John said to Peter "It's the Lord."

Peter hearing that tucked his coat up — under it he was naked — and threw himself into the lake.

But even in sight of Jesus again the other pupils came on in the boat hauling the lucky net of fish. They were only a hundred yards from shore. When they landed they saw a charcoal fire laid, a fish lying on it and bread.

Jesus said to them "Bring some of your fish."

Peter got up — he'd been panting in the shallows — and helped beach the net: They'd caught a hundred fifty-three fish, but the net wasn't torn.

Jesus said, "Come eat."

None of the pupils dared ask him "Who are you?" knowing it was Jesus raised from the dead

When they'd eaten in silence Jesus pointed to all the men and said to Peter "Simon son of Jonah, do you love me more than these?"

He said "Yes Lord, I love you."

Jesus said "Feed my lambs." Then a second time he said "Simon son of Jonah, do you love me?"

Peter said "Yes Lord, you know I love you."

Jesus said "Tend my young sheep." A third time he said "Simon son of Jonah, do you love, me?"

Not understanding that Jesus was letting him cancel each of his three denials, Peter was grieved that he'd asked him a third time. He said "Lord, you know everything. You know I love you."

Jesus said again "Tend my young sheep."

Peter nodded yes and took more bread. The other pupils watched in silence.

Then Jesus rose and walked away to the east in the new light of that last day.

It had been two years since they first met him and they'd never see him again on Earth. It would only be slowly that they came to see how, in the time they shared his life, his hard ordeal and calm return had ended things as they'd been from the start. He'd reconciled an outraged God to them and their kind, all human creatures till the end of time.

And whatever they lacked that final dawn, they gave the rest of their lives to his other task, the task he failed — to make all people know that God is at hand with his flaming love, comprehensible at last — and they never lost hope to see him come again on clouds in the Father's power to claim them. One of their cries in their own language was. *"Maranatha"* — "Lord, come now!" They thought he had promised that.

In other lives their cry has lasted near two thousand years.

MOSES

c. 1250 B.C.

A major character of Israelite history, Moses is portrayed in the Book of Exodus as the leader of the deliverance of Hebrew slaves from Egypt and the recipient of the Ten Commandments at Mt. Sinai. In Exodus, stories about his early life depict his escape from death as an infant by being hidden in the bulrushes, his upbringing in the Egyptian court, his flight to Midian, and his divine call to lead the Hebrews out of Egypt. Stories of this deliverance describe Moses predicting a series of miraculous plagues designed to persuade the Pharaoh to release the Hebrews, the Passover narrative, and the miraculous escape led by Moses through the "sea of reeds." Traditions then describe Moses's leadership of the Israelites during their forty years of wilderness wandering, and his death before the Hebrews entered Canaan, the Promised Land. He was traditionally considered the author of the five books of the Law, the Pentateuch of the Hebrew Bible, but this is doubted by modern scholars.

PREFACE

by Zora Neale Hurston

MOSES WAS AN OLD MAN WITH A BEARD. He was the great law-giver. He had some trouble with Pharaoh about some plagues and led the Children of Israel out of Egypt and on to the Promised Land. He died on Mount Nebo and the angels buried him there. That is the common concept of Moses in the Christian world.

But there are other concepts of Moses abroad in the world. Asia and all the Near East are sown with legends of this character. They are so numerous and so varied that some students have come to doubt if the Moses of the Christian concept is real. Then Africa has her mouth on Moses. All across the continent there are the legends of the greatness of Moses, but not because of his beard nor because he brought the laws down from Sinai. No, he is revered because he had the power to go up the mountain and to bring them down. Many men could climb mountains. Anyone could bring down laws that had been handed to them. But who can talk with God face to face? Who had the power to command God to go to a peak of a mountain and there demand of Him laws with which to govern a nation? What other man has ever seen with his eyes even the back part of God's glory? Who else has ever commanded the wind and the hail? The light and darkness? That calls for power, and that is what Africa sees in Moses to worship. For he is worshiped as a god.

In Haiti, the highest god in the Haitian pantheon is Damballa Ouedo Ouedo Tocan Freda Dahomey and he is identified as Moses, the serpent god. But this deity did not originate in Haiti. His home is in Dahomey and is worshiped there extensively. Moses had his rod of power, which was a living serpent. So that in every temple of Damballa there is a living snake, or the symbol.

And this worship of Moses as the greatest one of magic is not confined to Africa. Wherever the children of Africa have been scattered by slavery, there is the acceptance of Moses as the fountain of mystic powers. This is not confined to Negroes. In America there are countless people of other races depending upon mystic symbols and seals and syllables said to have been used by Moses to work his wonders. There are millions of copies of a certain book, *The Sixth and Seventh Books of Moses*, being read and consulted in secret because the readers believe in Moses. Some even maintain that the stories of the miracles of Jesus are but Mosaic legends told again. Nobody can tell how many tales and legends of — Moses are alive in the world nor how far they have travelled, so many — have collected around his name.

So all across Africa, America, the West Indies, there are tales of the powers of Moses and great worship of him and his powers. But it does not flow from the Ten Commandments. It is his rod of power, the terror he showed before all Israel and to Pharaoh, and THAT MIGHTY HAND. . . .

Moses sat up on the mountain passing nations through his mind. Way late in the day he climbed up to a place where he had been resting every afternoon for a long time. He was watching the development of a family of reptiles under a rock beneath a bushy growth. So he went on up putting words into the mouths of the various little creatures that he saw on the way. What these creatures had to say about people had plenty of seasoning.

Moses rounded a large boulder in sight of the spot where he was going and went on easily. There was the bush, and there was the rock under it. He was within a few feet of it when the bush burst into furious flame. Moses could not believe his eyes, but neither could he shut them on the sight. Because the bush was burning brightly but its leaves did not twist and crumple in the heat and they did not fall as ashes beneath charred limbs as they should have done. It just burned and Moses, awed though he was, could no more help coming closer to try and see the why of the burning bush than he could quit growing old. Both things were bound up in his birth. Moses drew near the bush.

"Moses," spoke a great voice which Moses did not know, "take off your shoes."

"How come, Lord? I know no voice like that can't be like mine."

"This ground you are walking on is holy ground. Take off those shoes."

"Yes, sir, Lord." Moses loosened his shoes and took them off without once taking his eyes off of the burning bush that did not wither. Moses stood barefooted and barehanded and trembled with awe.

"Moses!"

"Yes, sir!"

"Come closer, Moses. There is something that you must hear."

"I'm coming." Moses faltered nearer the flame and stood. For the first time in all his life he felt naked, meek, and void.

"Moses, look on the ground in front of you."

Moses looked down, and started back in terror.

"What is it you see, Moses?"

"It's a snake! It's a deadly poison snake," Moses said in fear, and started to run away down the mountain.

"Moses!"

"Yes, sir, Lord."

"Come back here." Moses came because the mysterious voice commanded, but he came in fear. "Moses," the voice ordered, "pick up that snake." Moses shriveled and shrank from the order. "Pick it up by the tail."

Moses gathered his strength and stooped. He seized the snake by the tail expecting to be bitten immediately. But except for a curious tremor of life that somehow communicated itself to the hand of Moses and from his hand to his arm and from his arm throughout his body, it might have been the wooden image of a snake. It was heavy for its length in wood, but it was stiff and motion-less like stone. Moses was amazed that the writhing ser-pent on the ground could have become so quickly the lifeless thing in his hands. It was a walking stick carved in imitation of a snake.

"Moses, put it down." Moses dropped the rod and it became a living snake again. Suddenly his fear left him. He picked up the snake in that certain way again and it became again a rod to his right hand. It was his, he knew by the feel of it. It was the rest of him. But the voice came again.

"Moses, I want you to go down into Egypt."

"Into Egypt? How come, Lord? Egypt is no place for me to go."

"I said Egypt, Moses. I heard my people, the Hebrews, when they cried, when they kept on groaning to me for help. I want you to go down and tell that Pharaoh I say to let my people go."

"He won't pay me no attention, Lord. I know he won't."

"Go ahead, like I told you, Moses. I am tired of hear-ing the groaning in my ear. I mean to overcome Pharaoh this time. Go on down there and I'll go with you."

"And those people, Lord, they won't believe in me. I don't talk their kind of talk in the first place and then again, I got a stammering tongue. I never could make a speech. Send somebody else, Lord."

"You go on; I'll go with you. Open your mouth and I'll speak for you."

"Well, Lord, if I go, tell me what to say; they won't believe in me," Moses said with hopeless resignation. "I don't even know your name. Who must I tell them sent me?"

"Tell them I AM WHAT I AM."

"Yes, sir, I'll go tell them, but I know it won't do any good."

"Somebody with a speaking mouth will be provided to talk for you. Go down into Egypt, Moses, and lead my people to the place I have provided for them. I AM WHAT I AM."

The Voice was hushed. The bush no longer burned. In fact, it looked just like it had yesterday and the day before and the day before that. The mountain was just as usual with the wind yelling "Whoo-youuu" against its rocky knots. There was nothing to speak to the senses of Moses and verify what he had heard and to hold him to what he had so unwillingly promised. That is, nothing but the rod he held in his hand. Therefore it was not a vision and neither was it a dream. This bush had blazed with fire before his eyes, but it had not burned as was natural. A serpent had become a rod to his hand and a rod had become a serpent and back again. Life could never be again what it once was. He had promised a god to go down into hated Egypt and command a man whom he hated and who hated him to permit a people whom Pharaoh hated to leave his servitude and go free. Moses dropped to a shady rock and sat with his face covered until the sun got low and red. Then he dragged himself home behind his mumbling sheep.

MOSES

by Elie Wiesel

A LEGEND:

When Moses went up to heaven to receive the Torah, he found God in the process of adding to it various symbols and ornaments. Conscious of his role as spokesman, Moses asked shyly:

—Why not give the Torah, such as it is? Isn't it rich enough in meaning, sufficiently obscure? Why complicate it further?

—I must, answered God. Many generations from now, there will live a man named Akiba, son of Joseph, who will seek and discover all kinds of interpretations in every word, in every syllable, in every letter of the Torah. So, you see, I must put them there, so that he may find them.

—Would you show me that man, asked Moses, impressed. I should like to know him.

Since there was nothing — or almost nothing — that he could refuse His loyal servant, God said to him:

—Turn around, go backward.

Moses did as he was told. He turned backward and found himself projected into the future. There he was, in a Talmudic academy, sitting in the very last row, among the beginners, listening to a master delivering a course on Moses' teachings and work. What Moses heard was beautiful, probably even profound, but . . . too much for him. He understood nothing, not one concept, not one word. And a new sadness overcame him; he felt useless, diminished. Suddenly, he heard a question a pupil was asking the rabbi:

—What proof do you have that your views on the subject are correct? That your opinion, and only yours, is correct?

And the master, Rabbi Akiba, replied:

—I have it from my Masters, who had it from theirs, who for their part claimed Moses as their teacher. What I am telling you is what Moses heard at Sinai.

Amused, and flattered too, Moses — the first Jewish author — was mollified. But something continued to trouble him. He again turned to God:

—I don't understand, said he. Since You have at Your disposal a sage such as he, a teacher such as he, why do You need me? Let him be Your messenger to transmit the Law of Israel to the people of Israel!

But God interrupted him:

—Moses, son of Amram, be quiet! This is how I envision things!

Satisfied or not, Moses submitted. He insisted no more.

Yet, after a while he could not repress his curiosity:

—Tell me. . . . What will happen to him, later?

And once again God made him turn around to show him the future. And Moses saw Rabbi Akiba at the hour of death. He saw his agony, his martyrdom at the hands of the Roman executioners. And in his astonishment and distress he cried out for the third time:

—I do not understand, Almighty! Is this justice? Is this the reward for studying Your Law? Do those who live by it deserve such a death?

And once again God cut him short:

—Be quiet, son of Amram! Such is My will! This is how I envision things!

And Moses kept a respectful silence, just as, centuries later, Rabbi Akiba remained silent on the day when he faced both death and eternity.

Another legend:

When Moses learned that his hour had come, he refused to accept it. He wanted to go on living — though he was old and tired of wandering and fighting and being constantly tormented by this unhappy and flighty people he was leading across the desert.

He put on sackcloth, covered himself with ashes and composed fifteen hundred prayers; then he drew a circle around himself and declared: I shall not move from here until the decree is revoked.

And once more his words shook the universe to its very foundation; heaven and earth, in panic, consulted one another. What was happening? Had God decided to put an end to His Creation?

Then there came to Moses' aid the five Books of the Law which bear his name; they pleaded with God to extend his life. But their intervention was unsuccessful.

Then the fire joined its efforts to theirs — in vain. And the sacred letters too were rejected. Even the Name of God was turned down by God; its intervention proved useless as well.

Then followed an amazing dialogue between God and Moses, in which the Creator tried to persuade His trusted servant to submit to His laws:

—You must die, Moses, otherwise the people will turn you into an idol.

—Don't you trust me? asked Moses. Have I not yet proved my worth? Have I not destroyed the Golden Calf?

God could have replied that He trusted Moses but not the others. Instead He chose to make His point by appealing to His prophet's common sense.

—Moses, he asked, who are you?

—The son of Amram, said Moses.

—Who was Amram?

—The son of Yitzhar, said Moses.

—Who was Yitzhar?

—The son of Kehat, said Moses.

—And Kehat, who was he?

—The son of Levi, said Moses.

—And Levi?

—The, son of Jacob, son of Isaac, son of Abraham . . . And thus he continued to the first man, Adam.

—Adam? said God. Where is Adam?

—Dead, answered Moses. Adam is dead.

—And Abraham? And Isaac? And Jacob?

—Dead, said Moses. They are all dead. And the others too. All dead.

—Yes, said God, your ancestors are dead. And you, you alone wish to live forever?

But Moses discovered in himself new gifts of rhetoric:

—Adam? he said. Adam stole. I did not. Abraham? Abraham had two sons, one of whom did not belong to Your people. This is equally true of Isaac. But not of me. Both my sons are children of Israel.

At this point God seems to have lost His patience:

—Moses, he said more abruptly, you killed an Egyptian. Who ordered you to kill him? Not I.

And once more Moses found an answer.

—Yes, I killed one single Egyptian. But You? You killed many. You killed all the first-borns. And You want to punish me?

Still, Moses knew that no matter how good his argument, it did not change the situation. The divine will reflects a divine and not a human logic. And so, in desperation, he turned to all of creation for help:

—Heaven and earth, pray for me!

—No, said they, we cannot.

Then he pleaded with the sun and the moon to pray for him.

—No, said they, we cannot.

Next came the stars, the planets, the mountains and rivers.

—No, they all said. We cannot even pray for ourselves.

Then Moses turned to the sea:

—You, please intercede in my favor!

And the sea, cruel and vindictive, reminded him of their first meeting, long ago, when he was leading a newly liberated people toward challenging adventures.

—Son of Amram, the sea sneered at Moses, what is the matter with you today? Now you need me? You who struck me with your stick and made me withdraw in order to let your people pass?

And Moses realized how alone and helpless he was. And ruefully he whispered — almost to himself:

—Once upon a time I was king and I gave orders; now I am on my knees and the whole world is indifferent.

Whereupon, in a surge of generosity, the illustrious Angel of the Face, the *Sar Hapanim Metatron*, gave him the friendly advice to stop opposing God's plan:

—I was present when the decision was taken and I heard, I heard them proclaim that the decree was sealed and could not, would not be suspended.

Moses should have heeded such knowledgeable and well-meaning advice; he should have left in a gracious, dignified manner. But he did not. He went on refusing to die, pleading, crying for another day, another hour, as would any common mortal — and not the prophet of prophets who had imposed his vision on mankind, the teacher of teachers who had felt God's fiery breath on his naked face!

So great was his despair that he declared himself ready to renounce his human condition in exchange for a few more days of life:

—Master of the Universe, he implored, let me live like an animal who feeds on grass, who drinks spring water and is content to watch the days come and go.

God refused. Man is not an animal; he must live as a human or not at all.

—Then, said Moses, permit me to stay here as a bird, friend of the wind, returning to his nest every night, grateful for the hours it has lived.

Again God said no. Man must live and die as a man, like all men.

Then God used a striking expression:

—Moses, you must die. You have already made too many words.

But Moses was still not resigned. He fought fiercely to the end, until abruptly, he appealed to death to come, as we shall see later.

The reader cannot help but be troubled by Moses' violent passion for life. How could Moses, so zealous, so loyal, oppose the divine will? Or even question it? Is it not a privilege to die for God and His Glory?

Why was he so anxious to continue living? After all, he was not exactly young, having reached the age of one hundred and twenty. Furthermore, had his life been so happy, so rewarding? He had constantly been tested and punished by God and man. No one had ever shown him any gratitude or even friendship. His people had made him suffer so much that he had begun to doubt himself and his mission. They had distorted his ideals, betrayed his trust; there had been few joys in his life. Why, then, did he cling to it so passionately instead of going quietly, serenely toward infinite peace?

And even if he did want to live so desperately, why did he show it? Why did he make such a display of his appetite for life? Was this behavior worthy of the founder and leader of a nation? Most great men, as we know, tend to conceal their feelings and suppress their anguish; they try hard to welcome death with contempt, or at least indifference. How, then, is one to explain that one of the most extraordinary figures in history behaved so oddly? Could he have "forgotten" Rabbi Akiba, appointed by God, who was to accept martyrdom silently and even joyfully?

Moses, the most solitary and most powerful hero in biblical history. The immensity of his task and the scope of his experience command our admiration, our reverence, our awe. Moses, the man who changed the course of history all by himself, his emergence became the decisive turning point. After him, nothing was the same again.

It is not surprising that he occupies a special place in Jewish tradition. His passion for social justice, his struggle for national liberation, his triumphs and disappointments, his poetic inspiration, his gifts as a strategist and his organizational genius, his complex relationship with God and His people, his requirements and promises, his condemnations and blessings, his bursts of anger, his silences, his efforts to reconcile the law with compassion, authority with integrity — no individual, ever, anywhere, accomplished so much for so many people in so many different domains. His influence is boundless, it reverberates beyond time. The Law bears his name, the Talmud is but its commentary and Kabbala communicates only its silence.

Moshe Rabbénu, our Master Moses, incomparable,

unequaled. The only man ever to have seen God face to face. Guide and supreme legislator. The Talmudic expression "Such is the law that Moses received at Sinai" inevitably leads to the closing of any debate. He is both source of every answer and root of every question. Every question that will ever be posed to a teacher by his pupil, Moses already heard at Sinai, says the Talmud.

Nevertheless, his portrait as sketched by tradition is carefully balanced; we are shown his shortcomings as well as his virtues. Unlike the founders of other religions or great leaders in other traditions, Moses is depicted as human, both great and fallible. While every other religion tends to transform its founder into a semi-god, Judaism does everything to humanize Moses.

Occasionally one even gets the impression that the Talmud would like to convince us that the greatest of our leaders was not really qualified to fulfill his duties; none of his failings are concealed, nor are his abrupt changes of mood. He did not get along well with other men or even with the angels. He married the daughter of a pagan priest, lived far away from his people and once even went so far as to deny his origins. Moreover, he was a poor speaker — how could he hope to galvanize his public?

And yet. Were it not for him, Israel would have remained a tribe of slaves. Living in the darkness of fear, dreading light.

His life began with tears, his own. Batya, the Pharaoh's daughter, noticed a basket floating down the Nile and discovered in it a Jewish infant — she knew it was Jewish because it cried not like an infant but like an adult, like a community of adults — his entire people was crying in him, said one of the commentators.

Legend tells us that Moses did not wish to cry. On the contrary, he tried to hold back his tears, to remain calm and silent though he was afraid. But the angel Gabriel struck him hard to make him cry so as to arouse Batya's pity. This may explain the tense relationships Moses was to have later with the angels.

When he was brought to the royal palace, Moses stopped crying. And soon began to dazzle the king and his court with his intelligence. He became the most spoiled of children. And also the most precocious: at three years of age he displayed the gifts of a healer. And of a prophet. And since he was an exceptionally handsome child, people showered him with love. Batya, his adoptive mother, was constantly cajoling him. He was given all the advantages of the best education available; he studied with teachers from afar, stunning them with his industry and understanding. In hardly any time at all, he mastered several languages and the exact sciences. Pharaoh himself could not keep from covering the boy with signs of affection and often took him on his lap to play with him — an intimacy not without danger. One day, when the child playfully took the crown from the royal head and placed it on his own, the Pharaoh's counselors were dismayed; they called it high treason and the priests declared it a bad omen. All agreed that the child should be put to death before it was too late. Fortunately, one advisor — an angel in disguise — suggested a less radical solution. Set two plates before the child, one piled high with gold and precious stones, the other with burning coals: should the child reach for the gold, it would bear out that he indeed harbored suspicious intentions and that he had to be killed, but if instead he reached for the hot coals, then it would simply mean that he was attracted by shiny objects. This was done, and Moses indeed stretched out his hand to touch the gold and precious stones, but the angel Gabriel pushed him so hard that his hand seized a hot coal and brought it to his mouth. Thus Moses was saved — but his tongue was burned, and from then on he stuttered.

Thereafter he became more prudent and therefore more secure. Perhaps some of the royal advisors continued to suspect him, but we are not told about it. In fact, we are told nothing about his adolescence. Did he have any contact with his slave brothers? Was he aware of his origins? There is no mention of it either in the Bible or the Talmud. We are told only that one day *Vayigdal Moshe vayetze el echav — He grew up and went out to see his brethren.* (The Gerer Rebbe interprets this as meaning: Moses' greatness was that he went out to join his people.) How old was he then? Twenty, according to one source; forty, according to another. What is important is that he appeared among his brothers as a prince, with all the rights and privileges due his rank. An abyss separated him from the world of suffering. Yet the slaves' hunger and suffering did touch him; so much so that he decided to intervene.

The Midrash tells us that on that day Moses saw strong men carrying light burdens and weak men straining under heavy loads; old men performing the tasks of young men and young men doing work suited for old men; men assigned to do women's chores and women carrying out men's work. So shocked was Moses by this sight that he decided to intercede on their behalf and arrange that from that time on, everyone was assigned work according to his or her ability.

But Moses did not stop there. Once awakened, his sense of kinship with his people moved him to take further steps, involving more and more risks to himself. He improved their living conditions. He obtained for them the right to observe Shabbat, he took part in their internal affairs. In effect, he proclaimed himself protector of their interests.

One day, when he saw an Egyptian overseer torturing a slave, he threw himself on the man and killed him. From then on he spent all his time far from the palace, learning the mores and customs of these men and women persecuted by the powerful machinery of the empire. He wanted to understand, to help; to understand in order to be able to help more efficiently. He tried to comprehend the cruelty of the oppressors and that of some of the overseers chosen from the ranks of the slaves. Why did the victims, instead of helping one another, adopt the methods of their enemies? One day he saw two Jews quarreling. When one began to strike the other, he intervened. Rasha, he admonished the culprit, *you wicked man, why are you striking your brother*? In truth, it hardly seems to have been his business — why should an Egyptian prince care if two Jewish slaves felt like having a fight? But he

already felt committed as a Jew and people were beginning to take notice. These two Jews knew. And so the man
he had addressed answered insolently: Spare us your ser-
mons; are you planning to kill us *too*? The man knew
Moses' secret: that he had killed to save a Jew — and that
he himself was Jewish. Otherwise he surely would not
have dared to speak so rudely to one of the Pharaoh's
favorite princes.

Denounced, betrayed, Moses had to flee. The Talmud
tells us that an angel who resembled him like a brother gave
himself up in his place, and that while he was facing the exe-
cutioner, the real Moses escaped outside the country.
Another source tells of another miracle: all the men at the
royal court were stricken blind, deaf, or mute; those who
had seen or heard him leave could not speak of it.
Another text has it that Moses was arrested by the
Pharaoh's guards and condemned to have his head cut off,
but that his neck miraculously resisted the ax.

What is certain is that this was a turning point for
Moses, one of the most important in his life. It was not
easy for a young man used to a princely life and the
friendship of the great of this world to become a helpless fugitive overnight. Nor was it easy to break with his
friends and habits and adapt himself to the life of a
refugee.

When he accepted his new allegiance, Moses became
a stranger in more ways than one: a stranger to the
Egyptian people, to the Jewish peoples and to himself.

After many adventures the fugitive arrived in the land of

Midian, where he settled, having found food and shelter and work as a shepherd. He married a native girl — the daughter of the priest Yitro. Two sons were born to them, Eliezer and Gershom, and they led a peaceful, idyllic existence, devoid of problems, dangers or conflicts. Did he sometimes remember his parents, his persecuted brethren? Apparently not. At least nothing in the texts or legends alludes to it. Their fate was no longer his concern. A vast desert separated him from them and he was content.

Whatever was happening there, in faraway Egypt, no longer interested him. He took care of his family, of his flock, and that was enough for him to fill his time and justify his life as a man. Strange, for forty years Moses lived in his new adopted land without ever worrying about his family's fate. It seems unlikely somehow. What had taken place inside him? How is one to explain this sudden indifference? He who had risked his fortune, his freedom, his future to save one single life — why didn't he at least try to ascertain whether his people, an entire people, was still suffering or had been allowed some respite? This behavior does not fit in with Moses' temperament or with the logic of the events: to have opted for Judaism, at the price of a real sacrifice, only to give it up, just like that? It doesn't make sense.

There is one plausible explanation: Moses was disappointed in his Jews, and on several levels. They had not resisted, nor had they agreed to rebel. *Hasevel shesavlu bemitzraim* — They had settled into their "tolerance of suffering": resignation. (*Lisbol*, infinitive of *shesavlu*, means both to suffer and to tolerate.) He may have resented their inability to overcome their internal differences and unite against the enemy; there was too much pettiness, too much envy, too much selfishness. And then, too, they had betrayed him, their benefactor; for that there had been betrayal, he did not doubt. But who had been the informer? Well, let us see. When Moses killed the Egyptian overseer, who else had been present? Only one man: the very Jew whom Moses had saved.

For Moses this must have been a crushing experience — with terrifying implications. Could he have come to the conclusion that the Jews were, after all, not worthy of the freedom he wanted for them? That they had fallen too low, had become too used to servitude to be redeemable? Could that have been the real reason why he had fled the country? Not because of Pharaoh, but because of the Jews? He probably could have soothed the king's anger. After all, the man he had killed was an obscure overseer and such a crime was not considered terribly serious in ancient Egypt. Surely Moses would have been forgiven. But his fear of Pharaoh was insignificant compared to his disillusionment with the Jews!

Let us follow this hypothesis further and we shall understand why, when he arrived in the land of Midian, he concealed his identity. They assumed he was Egyptian and he chose not to correct their mistake. He was a hidden Jew in search of assimilation, so much so that his second son was not circumcised. Moses, once more, was far removed from his people, though this time deliberately. Nothing is more painful than the sight of victims adopting the behavior and laws of their executioners. If the Jews behaved like the Egyptians, why should Moses be concerned with their fate? He preferred to forget them.

In this context, we can perhaps understand why, at first, he refused to serve as God's messenger. It took God seven days to convince him, says a Midrash. Moses refused, advancing all kinds of arguments: Why me? Why not an angel? Or my older brother Aaron? I am a poor speaker; also I am married and I have children; my father-in-law will object. And furthermore, what am I supposed to tell the Jews when they start asking me questions, so many questions? What shall I say? And what shall I tell the Pharaoh when *he* begins to ask me questions? Clearly Moses had no wish to return to his brothers, no wish to reopen a wound that had still not healed.

Yet in the end he gave in. God always wins. The last word is always His, as was the first.

Also, consider the setting: the flaming bush in the immensity of the desert; the all-pervasive solitude, the anxiety, the Voice both distant and close, insisting, probing, throbbing, burning. How could any human being, even Moses, resist that Voice indefinitely? And so Moses gathered his family, bid his in-laws farewells and set out on his return journey, albeit with noticeable lack of enthusiasm. That very night he stopped to sleep at an inn. Why not rest the night? And thus postpone the moment when he would meet once more those brothers he had expected never to see again? And what if by some chance he were to happen on his informer? At this point Moses would undoubtedly have preferred to die. That was why he did not resist the mysterious assault by an angel. His wife Tzipora saved him; her quick move to circumcise their son was meant to remind both God *and* Moses of the covenant: Moses could not die, must not die, not yet. Israel needed him — and so did God — and Israel could not, must not, die.

We can find what ensued in the Book of Exodus. Event followed event at a feverish pace. Leaving the calm of the desert. Moses plunged into the whirlpool of history. In Egypt he witnessed and lets us witness the disintegration of an empire. Everything is falling apart and at dizzying speed. The participants in the drama are carried away by passions and unknown currents. The text becomes breath less, driven by an irresistible force. An epic poem with a thousand fragments joined in light. Everything is described in an intense, precise manner: the mood of the people, the fear of the slaves, the empty arrogance of the rulers, the calls to insurrection, the reverberations among the powerful as well as among the oppressed. What to do, what not to do? The first doubts on both sides, the first disagreements. Accept the challenge or submit. Tergiversations in the wretched huts as well as in the palaces darkened by malediction. What to do? What to say? Whom to follow? How was one to discern the signal of redemption, the sense of history?

At first Moses and his brother Aaron were alone, without allies or companions. Moses saw that his skepticism was justified: the slaves wanted to remain slaves. The Midrash tells us that, on their arrival in Egypt, Moses and Aaron were welcomed by the Elders of the tribes of Israel, who declared themselves ready to follow them to the end. They set out for the royal palace, but gradually, as they came closer, the Elders changed their minds. With each step the group shrank. By the time they entered the Pharaoh's residence, the two brothers remained alone. If the Elders had lost their courage, if the leaders had succumbed to fear, what could one expect from the average Jew?

No, the slaves were not ready to leave — no more than the Pharaoh was ready to let them leave. Had the Pharaoh been particularly shrewd, he could have said: You want an exodus? With pleasure. I can do without all these Jewish slaves. So take them, and good riddance. But one question: Have you asked *them* — are you sure *they* want to leave? Fortunately, God kept the Pharaoh from playing that game, thus sparing Moses the humiliation of facing slaves reluctant to follow him. One text tells us that while Moses was negotiating the liberation of the Jews with the Pharaoh, Aaron was engaged in trying to convince the Jews to accept freedom. This earned him the honor of becoming the first high priest.

When the negotiations proved fruitless, other methods were tried; the curses, the plagues followed one another, yet without resembling one another. Here again, the text fairly bursts with descriptive power. It is as though one can hear the cries, the lamentations, the shouted orders, picked up and transmitted. The last night, the last chance. A number of non-Jewish slaves and Egyptians decided to join the movement: never again would they have such an opportunity to leave. One can almost hear the Egyptian parents mourning the death of their children, and Moses' lieutenants jostling and exhorting the people: Let's go, let's go, fast, faster. The race against time had started; it was late, later than was thought. The fleeing slaves had but one night to break the vise, to escape their prison. Tomorrow the oppressor would regroup his forces. Tomorrow he would regret his weakness. Tomorrow was at hand, tomorrow was here.

One could see people running, running breathlessly, without a glance backward; they were running toward the sea. And there they came to an abrupt halt: this was the end; death was there, waiting. The leaders of the group, urged on by Moses, pushed forward: Don't be afraid, go, into the water, into the water! Yet, according to one commentator, Moses suddenly ordered everyone to a halt: Wait a moment. Think, take a moment to reassess what it is you are doing. Enter the sea not as frightened fugitives but as free men! And everyone obeyed. They paused in their rush toward the sea. And Moses turned to God with a prayer. But God reminded him that this was not the right moment: Tell the people of Israel to hurry! And the people, united as never before, swept ahead and crossed the Red Sea, which drew back to let the Jews go through. And, we are told, so awesome and charged with faith was this sight that the most humble of servant girls saw in it more divine mysteries than the prophet Ezekiel perceived centuries later. And Moses began to sing. The stutterer, who could never utter a sentence longer than *Shlakh et ami* — Let my people go — composed the most majestic, the most lyrical poem in Scripture.

How did the stutterer turn into a minstrel? (Today we

are told that while stutterers have difficulties in speaking, they have no problems in singing; this is probably true only since Moses.) The Hasidic explanation: *Vayaaminu baadoshem uv Moshe avdo* — And they had faith in God and in his servant Moses. For the first time an entire people rallied around Moses; for the first time he became its true spokesman. That was why he was able to sing; through him an entire people was singing.

Was this the moment of grace? The whole world became song. Even the angels began to sing, but God interrupted them with the most universally human call to order in the Talmud: *Maase yadai tovim bayam veatem omrim shira?* — My creatures are drowning in the sea — and you are singing? What if they are enemies of Israel and liberty — they are still human beings! How can you think of singing while human beings are drowning? Of course, the angels could have replied: What about the Jews, why is it all right for them to sing? The angels, perhaps out of politeness, did not ask the question. Besides, there was a difference: the Jews had just escaped disaster — the angels had not. As a surviving people, a people of survivors, Israel had the right — and duty — to express its gratitude.

Then, seven weeks later, came the big moment, the unique event in the memory of mankind: God was about to speak, to reveal His Law, to make His Voice heard. For three days the people and its leaders lived in expectation and purification; one must be worthy to receive the Law, worthy of being seen by God. Yet, if one is to believe Talmudic legend, there were those who were not impressed. On the morning of the day when all Israel was to have gathered at the foot of the mountain, some men and women were still asleep in their tents. And so God first manifested Himself with thunder and lightning in order to shake, to awaken those who were foolish enough to sleep while time and the heart of mankind opened to receive the Call of Him who lends mystery to all things. Then, abruptly, there was silence. And in this silence a Voice was heard. God spoke. What did He speak of? His secret work, His eternally imperceptible intentions? No, He spoke of man's relationship to man, of one individual's duties toward others. At this unique moment God wished to deal with human relations rather than theology. No wonder His audience was recalcitrant; after all, why not steal in a society where everyone else does? Why not kill in a world steeped in violence? The Talmud states it explicitly: Israel refused the Torah until God threatened them: *Kafa alehem har kegigit* — He lifted a mountain and held it over the crowd. It was either the Torah or death. They had no choice, and so they accepted the Law against their will and God was satisfied at last.

But not Moses. Moses, in his candor, would have liked to see his people accept the Law freely. And to freely pledge allegiance to the God who had promised to watch over its fate. But he said nothing. Forty days later everything was forgotten, everything collapsed. Standing at the top of the mountain, the tablets of the Law in his arms, Moses perceived an unwonted noise from down below: his people were dancing, rejoicing, worshiping the Golden Calf.

So angry was Moses, says one Midrash, that he was ready to kill . . . his own brother, Aaron. His disappointment was boundless: forty days after the Revelation at Sinai — a Golden Calf! Despite the magnitude of the events, of the divine manifestations, the crossing of the Red Sea and the other miracles, something of this stiffnecked people had stayed behind in bondage in Egypt!

This may explain Moses' ambiguous relationship with his people — and God. He desperately wanted the adventure to be successful . . . and it was not easy. He found himself constantly wavering between ecstasy and despair; failures followed triumphs, he never knew what to expect from his people.

Moses' outbursts of anger, even his abdication are understandable. This people he had chosen never gave him anything but worries. There was no pleasing, no satisfying them. Forever complaining, grumbling, protesting, regretting the stability — however precarious, even miserable — of the past; the certainties-however debasing-of bondage. Moses' Jews showed no faith, no joy in being participants in the making of history.

No sooner had they left Egypt than they already asked to return: *Why did you make us leave?* They asked Moses: *Aren't there enough graves in Egypt? Why do you want to bury us all in the desert?*

Three days after the miraculous Red Sea crossing, all they wanted to know was: *Ma nishte?* — What is there to drink? Barely one month later they recalled Egypt with nostalgia: it was so good there; we ate all we wanted. . . .

Even when Moses obtained the manna for them, they

were not satisfied. At one point he became so exasper-
ated that he cried out: *Oh, God, what am I to do with this
ungrateful people? One more incident, and they will stone
me to death!* On another occasion he had to remind them
that he had taken nothing from them, that he had not
become rich at their expense, and that he owed them
nothing. One does not make such statements unless one
stands accused.

Listen to a Midrash: Among the children of Israel,
there were those who followed Moses with their eyes,
saying: Look at this neck and look at that belly and those
legs; whatever he eats, he has taken from the Jews; whatever he drinks, he has taken from the Jews; everything he
owns comes from the Jews.

The line *And they were jealous of Moses* is commented
upon by one text in a very explicit manner: every husband
suspected him of engaging in illicit relations with his
spouse. Everyone seems to have tried to pull him down to
their own level.

Poor Moses, who had dreamed of inspiring them, elevating them, transforming slaves into princes, fashioning
a community of free and sovereign men. Here was his
dream — broken, shattered. The Jews, unchanged, were
still absorbed in their sordid intrigues and in-fighting.
They had seen God at work and had learned nothing.
They had witnessed events of cosmic importance and had
remained unaffected. *Hayesh adoshem bekirbenu im ayin?*
They were already doubting God's presence in their
midst. They were already doubting their purpose, their
very memory.

Moses had expected something else from this chosen people: another kind of vision, another kind of loyalty. After their liberation they should have lived proudly, as free men, not like a pack. of fugitives. *Vayekhal Moshe* — And Moses prayed — is interpreted in the Midrash as: They made Moses sick. Too many people plaguing him with too many problems. We imagine him morose, unhappy. Only once do we see him joyous: on the day his brother Aaron acceded to the office of high priest. Otherwise he seemed far removed from happiness, and even more, from collective rejoicing. He was burdened with too many responsibilities, too much grief. He handled everything alone, without any help, without the benefit of comradeship and reliable allies. On the contrary, he felt that he was not liked; that the people mistrusted him, envied him. Here and there, young prophets plotted behind his back. Notables — from the Korakh clan — even prepared a coup to force him out of power. The scouts he had dispatched to the land of Canaan — famous people all — came back with disastrous reports that the Promised Land was inhabited by giants in whose eyes they had felt very small and frail. Two nephews — Aaron's sons — had penetrated into the sanctuary while in a state of drunkenness. His brother himself had had a hand in the making of the Golden Calf.

Things only got worse as time went on. One text tells us that there were those who mocked him and treated him as if he were mad. Moses, the leader, the guide. When he presented the commandments to his people, he was interrupted by sneers: Are you going to lecture us, you stutterer? And: They took their children and threw them into his arms, shouting: Well, Moses, how are you going to feed them? What craft will you teach them? And: If he left his tent earlier than usual, they would ask: Why so early? If he left later than usual, they would ask: Why so late? If he left unnoticed, they would say: He is avoiding us, he is afraid of meeting us. Also: he explained the Law to them, but they refused to learn. After forty years of leadership, he still had to prove himself; every evening he had to tell them where they were and how many days had passed since Sinai. Only then were they prepared to admit that he was in full command of his mental faculties.

Who knows? Perhaps, God's decision not to let him enter the promised land was meant as reward rather than as punishment.

A flighty, ungrateful people. Moses had good reason to despair, to castigate — and he did so often. Some commentators say: too often and too severely. And that was why he was punished. Yet if others spoke ill of Israel, he was quick to come to its defense, passionately, fiercely; there are times when Jews — and Jews alone — may criticize other Jews. Moses defended them not only against their enemies but, at times, even against God.

Says the Midrash: only by pleading for his people did Moses become an *Ish Elokhim*, a Man of God.

For, in fact, he filled two equally difficult roles: he was God's emissary to Israel and Israel's to God.

The moment the angels spoke out against Israel — and that happened frequently — Moses took its defense.

When God decided to give His Law to Israel and the angels opposed His plan, Moses scolded them: Who then will observe it? You? Only man can assume the Law and live by its precepts.

And when his people sank to their lowest depths by dancing around the Golden Calf, Moses still found it possible to defend them: Whose fault is it, God, theirs or Yours? You let them live in exile, among idol-worshipers so long that they have been poisoned; is it their fault that they are still addicted? Then came his ultimatum: Either You forgive them everything or You erase my name from Your Book!

And when God said to him: *Ki shikhet amkha* — Your people have sinned — Moses replied with a sudden display of humor: When they observe Your Law, they are Your children, but when they violate it, they are mine?

Another time he remarked: Master of the Universe, do not get too angry, it is useless. Were You to destroy heaven and earth, Your people would survive — for that is what You pledged, remember? So why get angry?

In spite of his disappointments, in spite of his ordeals and the lack of gratitude he encountered, Moses never lost his faith in his people. Somehow he found both the strength and the courage to remain on Israel's side and proclaim its honor and its right to live.

All that he had been subjected to, all he had experienced notwithstanding, he knew how to accept every gift with gratitude. Moses was gratitude personified. Of his ten names, he retained that of Moses — because that was the name given to him by Batya, the Pharaoh's daughter; Batya who had saved his life.

When the great plagues befell Egypt, it was Aaron and not Moses who struck the Nile with his stick, transforming it into a river of blood. Moses would not do it, for he did not wish to harm the river that had saved his life.

Later, when Israel had to go and fight the nation of Midian, it was led by Joshua, not Moses; Moses would not fight his former adoptive country whose people had once given him shelter.

And now, let us return to our initial question: Why was Moses so attached to life, to the point of opposing God's will? Was that his way of protesting heaven's use of death to diminish, stimulate, and ultimately crush man? Was it his final act on behalf of his people? His way of teaching Israel an urgent and timeless lesson: that life is sacred always and for everyone — and that no one has the right to give it up? Did the most inspired and fierce prophet of all wish by his example to tell us, through centuries and generations to come, that to live as a man, as a Jew, means to say yes to life, to fight — even against the Almighty — for every spark, for every breath of life?

Of course, it is also possible that Moses refusing to die is nothing but the image of a still vigorous old man afraid to die; the image of a human being, with human shortcomings and anxieties. As his last hour approached, he refused to act out the role of saint or hero; he wanted to live and admitted it. He had never lied, not to others and not to himself; he was not going to start now, on the threshold of death.

Yes, he wanted to live and was not ashamed of it; he wanted to live at any cost, except at someone else's expense. The Midrash tells us that at the end God told Moses: You insist on belonging to the world of the living, so be it, you shall live — but then Israel shall perish; it must be one or the other, you or Israel. And Moses cried out: Let Moses die, let a thousand men like him die, only let not one child of Israel be touched. For one may not go beyond a certain limit; to live is good, to want to live is human, but not at the expense of another's death.

Moses was a humanist in all things. Even his courage, his generosity were human virtues; all his qualities and all his flaws were human. He had no supernatural powers, no talent for the occult. Everything he did, he conceived in human terms, concerned not with his own "individual salvation" but with the well-being of the community. Once he reached heaven, he could have stayed there, but he chose to come back. He could have kept the truth he had just discovered to himself, but he chose to share it with the others. Though chosen by God, he refused to give up on man. Just as God brought Moses closer to man, Moses brought Him closer to man; he lived to share.

Another story underlines that vulnerability in him which is the reason each of us recognizes oneself in him. At the end of their seemingly interminable exchange, God consented to let Moses live, on condition that he accept having his disciple Joshua become his Master and that of the entire people. Moses agreed and immediately regretted it, exclaiming: Rather a thousand deaths than one moment of jealousy!

Moses was capable of jealousy; the prophet was human.

Let us now listen to how he died:

When Moses finally agreed to accept the inevitable, he begged God not to place him into the hands of the Angel of Death, who frightened him. And God promised. Three times did the Angel of Death move toward Moses, yet he was powerless to do anything but look at him from afar.

Moses spent his last hour blessing Israel's tribes. He began blessing them one by one, but time was running out and so he included them all in one benediction.

Then, escorted by the priest Eleazar and by his son Pinhas, and followed by his disciple Joshua, he began to climb Mount Nebo. Slowly he entered the cloud waiting for him. He took one step forward and turned around to look at the people following him with their gaze. He took another, step forward, and turned around to look at the men, the women, and the children who were staying behind. Tears welled up into his eyes, he no longer could see anyone. When he reached the top of the mountain, he halted. You have one more minute, God warned him so as not to deprive him of his right to death. And Moses lay down. And God said: Close your eyes. And Moses closed his eyes. And God said: Fold your arms across your chest. And Moses folded his arms across his chest. Then, silently, God kissed his lips. And the soul of Moses found shelter in God's breath and was swept away into eternity.

At the foot of the mountain, shrouded in fog, the children of Israel wept. And all of creation wept. And in his sorrow, Joshua forgot three hundred commandments and acquired seven hundred doubts. And the bereaved people, blinded by grief, wanted to tear Joshua to pieces for having succeeded Moses, the saddest and loneliest and the most powerful prophet of Israel and the world.

But up above, the exulting angels and seraphim gave him a rousing welcome. Their joy reverberated throughout the celestial spheres. Everywhere Moses was celebrated as having been the most faithful of God's servants. The events that had filled his life on earth were glorified. Heaven glorified him seven times. And the waters glorified him seven times. And the fire glorified him seven times. And all of human history continues to glorify his name.

Nobody knows his resting place. The people of the mountains situate it in the valley. The people of the valley situate it in the mountains. It has become neither temple nor museum. It is everywhere and elsewhere, always elsewhere.

Nobody was present at his death. And so, in a way, he lives on inside us, every one of us. For as long as one child of Israel, somewhere, proclaims his Law and his truth, Moses lives on through him, in him, as does the burning bush, which consumes man's heart without consuming his faith.

KRISHNA

D.O.B. UNKNOWN

One of the most widely revered and popular of all Indian divinities, Krishna is worshiped as the eighth incarnation (avatar, or avatara) of the Hindu god Vishnu and also as a supreme god in his own right. Krishna (literally "black," or "dark as a cloud") was born into the Yadava clan, the son of Vasudeva and Devaki, sister of Kamsa, the wicked king of Mathura (in modern Uttar Pradesh). Kamsa, hearing a prophecy that he should be destroyed, tried to slay her children; but Krishna was smuggled across the Yamuna River to Gokula (or Vraja, modern Gokul), where he was raised by the leader of the cowherds, Nanda, and his wife Yasoda.

The child Krishna performed many miracles and slew demons and became the focus of numerous bhakti (devotional) cults, which over the centuries have produced a wealth of religious poetry, music, and painting.

PREFACE

by Stephen Mitchell

B
HAGAVAD GITA means "The Song of the Blessed
One." No one knows when it was written; some
scholars date it as early as the fifth century B.C.,
others as late as the first century A.D. But there is general
scholarly consensus that in its original form it was an
independent poem, which was later inserted into its
present context, Book Six of India's national epic, the
Mahabharata.

The *Mahabharata* is a very long poem — eight times
the length of the Iliad and the Odyssey combined — that
tells the story of a war between the two clans of a royal
family in northern India. One clan is the Pandavas, who
are portrayed as paragons of virtue; they are led by
Arjuna, the hero of the *Gita*, and his four brothers.
Opposing them are the forces of the Kauravas, their evil
cousins, the hundred sons of the blind King Dhritarashtra.
At the conclusion of the epic, the capital city lies in ruins
and almost all the combatants have been killed.

The *Gita* takes place on the battlefield of Kuru at the beginning of the war. Arjuna has his charioteer, Krishna (who turns out to be God incarnate), drive him into the open space between the two armies, where he surveys the combatants. Overwhelmed with dread and pity at the imminent death of so many brave warriors — brothers, cousins, and kinsmen — he drops his weapons and refuses to fight. This is the cue for Krishna to begin his teaching about life and deathlessness, duty, nonattachment, the Self, love, spiritual practice, and the inconceivable depths of reality. The "wondrous dialogue" that fills the next seventeen chapters of the *Gita* is really a monologue, much of it wondrous indeed, which often keeps us dazzled and asking for more, as Arjuna does:

> *for I never can tire of hearing your life-giving, honey-sweet words.* (10.18)

The incorporation of the *Gita* into the Mahabharata has both its fortunate and its unfortunate aspects. It gives a thrilling dramatic immediacy to a poem that is from beginning to end didactic. Krishna and Arjuna speak about these ultimate matters not reclining at their ease, or abstracted from time and place, but between two armies about to engage in a devastating battle. We see the ranks of warriors waiting in the adrenaline rush before combat, keying up their courage, drawing their bows, glaring across the battle lines; we hear the din of the conch horns, the neighing of the horses, the thunder of the captains and the shouting. Then, suddenly, everything is still. The armies are halted in their tracks. Even the flies are caught in midair between two wingbeats. The vast moving picture of reality stops on a single frame, as in Borges' story "The Secret Miracle." The moment of the poem has expanded beyond time, and the only characters who continue, earnestly discoursing between the silent, frozen armies, are Arjuna and Krishna.

In one sense, this setting seems entirely appropriate. The subject of Krishna's teaching is, after all, a matter of the gravest urgency: the battle for authenticity, the life and death of the soul. And in all spiritual practice, the struggle against greed, hatred, and ignorance, against the ingrained selfishness that has covered over our natural luminosity, can for a long time be as ferocious as any external war. During this time even the slightest clarity or opening of the heart is a major triumph, and metaphors of victory and defeat, of conquering our enemies and overcoming fierce obstacles, seem only too accurate, as if they were straightforward description. . . .

As fine as its chapters about spiritual practice and the sage are, the *Gita's* finest chapters are about God. The passages in which the poet has Krishna speak of himself are written at white heat, with an energy and a clarity that far surpass similar attempts in the other sacred texts of the world. These passages are sublime, crystalline, electric, stunning in their passion, their nimbleness, their density, the hugeness of their imagination, their metaphysical grace, and their readiness to cut free from rational limits. Krishna says, for example, that he is all that is. But all that is, is in him, though he is not in it. But he is the best of all that is. But he is beyond is and is not. Thus the poet keeps switching modes of reference, as our minds whirl, from one set of "I am's" to the next.

The *Gita* is usually thought of as a great philosophical poem. It is that, of course. It is also an instruction manual for spiritual practice and a guide to peace of heart. But essentially it is, as its title implies, a love song to God. However powerful its thinking, its intention is not to be a treatise but a psalm. The *Gita* is a love song to reality, a hymn in praise of everything excellent and beautiful and brave. It is a love song to both the darkness and the light, to our own true Self in the depths of being, the core from which all the glories and horrors of the universe unfold.

The passages in which Krishna speaks about himself are so splendid that a few short examples will suffice. First, a passage of great delicacy, where the poet's love for the most fundamental elements in human life shines through his philosophical disdain for "this sad, vanishing world":

> *I am the taste in water,*
> *the light in the moon and sun;*
> *the sacred syllable Ôm*
> *in the Vedas, the sound in air.*
> *I am the fragrance in the earth,*
> *the manliness in men, the brilliance*
> *in fire, the life in the living,*
> *and the abstinence in ascetics.*

I am the primal seed
within all beings, Arjuna:
the wisdom of those who know,
the splendor of the high and mighty. (7.8–10)

Next, in the wonderful ninth chapter, a passage that starts by seeing Krishna as all parts of the sacrificial rite and expands until he is not only all parts of the cosmos but even vaster than the category of "being":

I am the ritual and the worship,
the medicine and the mantra,
the butter burnt in the fire,
and I am the flames that consume it.

I am the father of the universe
and its mother, essence and goal
of all knowledge, the refiner, the sacred
Ôm, *and the threefold Vedas.*

I am the beginning and the end,
origin and dissolution,
refuge, home, true lover,
womb and imperishable seed.

I am the heat of the sun,
I hold back the rain and release it;
I am death, and the deathless,
and all that is, or is not. (9.16–19)

And from chapter 8, this startling quatrain, which seems to move at the speed of light, breathless with adoration:

> Meditate on the Guide,
> the Giver of all, the Primordial
> Poet, smaller than an atom,
> unthinkable, brilliant as the sun. (8.9)

The long passages in which Krishna describes himself are extraordinarily moving. They keep brimming over with love and boldness. Krishna's first-person pronoun is a resplendent act of the human imagination: it is the poet himself speaking as God so that he can speak *about* God. His love here is so intense and intimate that the reader must step into the words to see that every "I" is really a "you."

One element of Krishna's attitude that will impress even the most casual reader is his tolerance and inclusiveness. Even those who don't know him are held in the truly magnificent embrace of the following quatrain:

> However men try to reach me,
> I return their love with my love;
> whatever path they may travel,
> it leads to me in the end. (4.11)

And, at least in the first two-thirds of the poem, Krishna's large-hearted attitude toward the wicked reminds us of Jesus' God, who "makes his sun rise on the wicked and on the good, and sends rain to the righteous and to the unrighteous":

Even the heartless criminal,
if he loves me with all his heart,
will certainly grow into sainthood
as he moves toward me on this path.

Quickly that man becomes pure,
his heart finds eternal peace.
Arjuna, no one who truly
loves me will ever be lost.

All those who love and trust me,
even the lowest of the low —
prostitutes, beggars, slaves —
will attain the ultimate goal. (9.30–32)

The climax of the *Gita* is its eleventh chapter, in which Krishna appears to Arjuna in his supreme form. It is a terrifying theophany, a glimpse into a level of reality that is more than the ordinary mind can bear. Arjuna sees

the whole universe
enfolded, with its countless billions
of life-forms, gathered together
in the body of the God of gods. (11.13)

Krishna dazzles his sight, blazing

in the measureless, massive, sun-flame splendor of
[his] radiant form. (11.17)

KRISHNA

by Vanamali

T HE STORY OF THE LORD'S manifestation in the world as Krishna, scion of the Yadava clan, is one which has thrilled the hearts of all those who have been fortunate enough to have heard it. It is the glorious tale of how the One who is *aja*, or unborn, and *arupa*, without form, was born in this world of dualities with a form that has delighted the hearts of people for over five thousand years. It is the story of that Infinite, Eternal One, Who was born as Krishna, the son of the Yadava chief Vasudeva and his wife Devaki, Who was the nephew of Kamsa, the King of the Bhojas; Krishna, a prince Who was born in a dungeon and brought up as a common cowherd boy by their chieftain Nanda and his wife Yashoda in the village of Gokula. It is the story of a man Who was also God and of God Who was born as a man. There is no tale comparable to it in all times.

The main facts of His life can be gathered from the

Shrimad Bhagavata and the *Mababharata* — the first half of the story from the former and the second from the latter. He was born in captivity in the prison of the tyrant king Kamsa of Mathura as the son of Vasudeva and thus was known as Vaasudeva. Immediately after birth, He was transferred from Mathura to the cowherd settlement of Gokula, where He grew up as the foster son of their chief Nanda and his wife Yashoda. As a child He was mischievous and willful, charming all with His precocious acts. At the age of twelve He went to Mathura, where He killed His uncle Kamsa, thus freeing the Yadavas from the rule of the tyrant. He grew up to be a hero, valiant and invincible, and gradually assumed leadership of the Yadava and Vrishni clans, even though He did not accept the title of "King." He defeated many of the tyrant kings and made the Yadavas into one of the most powerful forces of His time. He founded His new capital on the island of Dwaraka on the western seacoast of India, which was then known as Bharatavarsha, and played an important part in shaping the cultural and political life of His times. Though He did not take up arms, He played a decisive part in the great war of the *Mahabharata*.

Even during His lifetime, He became canonized among these of His own clan, as well as among many others. He was looked upon as the incarnation of Vishnu, the godhead of *Vaishnava* theology and the Preserver in the trinity made up of Brahma, Vishnu, and Shiva. Vishnu later came to be identified with the solar deity of the Vedas, who is invoked in the great *Gayatri* hymn. In the course of time, Vishnu became the most dominant among the *Vedic* deities and came to be accepted as the Supreme Being. By worshiping Krishna as an incarnation of Vishnu one can gain the status achieved by striving yogis through the difficult forms of various *yogic* practices.

The charm of His *avatar* is the perfection with which He played every role He was called upon to play. He was a staunch friend, a dutiful son, an exciting lover, and a model husband not to just one, but to all women who desired Him. There was none who called to Him with intensity to whom He did not go with all speed!

"However a man approaches Me, in that same manner do I go to him," was His creed. In whatever guise people looked upon Him — as son, lover, friend, or husband — He went to them in that very form in which they visualized Him and satisfied their desires in that way. At the same time, He sublimated their desires and thus fulfilled their earthly lives and led them to eternal bliss. There was no one who approached Him, whether saint or sinner, in hatred or fear or love who did not attain liberation. The difference between a Kamsa, who tried to kill Him, and a Kuchela, who worshiped Him, is slight indeed. One approached Him with hatred and the other with love, but both thought of Him constantly and were thus rewarded with *moksha*, or liberation. An object of mortal dread and antagonism can produce as much absorption in the mind as an object of love. If this object of dread happens to be God, concentration on Him, though motivated by antagonism, must purify the person, just as potent but unpleasant medicine still effects a cure. This is what the *Bhagavad Purana* declares.

Thus Lord Krishna is not only the *Sat-chid-ananda*,

the existence-knowledge-bliss, of the Absolute without any diminution or contamination of His perfection, He is also the *Uttama Purusha*, the perfect person, amid all imperfect situations. He is the eternal boy, the paragon of masculine beauty, Who always retains His spiritual nobility, absolutely unaffected and unperturbed in every situation, be it amid the poverty and hardships of the cowherd settlement, the rigors of a hermitage, the seductive charms of dancing beauties, the gory scenes of the battlefield, in the self-destructive holocaust of His own kith and kin, or in peaceful interludes with His friends. As He Himself teaches, Krishna lived in this world of dualities as the lotus leaf in water, absolutely untouched and unaffected by the environment, a witness of situations, never a victim.

The river of time collects much flotsam and jetsam on its way, and the story of the Lord's life has been embellished with a wealth of detail, perhaps true, perhaps imaginary. Fact and fiction, truth and fantasy are entwined. But the final test of truth is Time itself. It is the true touchstone. It deletes the dross and retains the gold. The story of a divine manifestation is always filled with mystery and defies all attempts at human analysis. But it has the quality of being *svayamprakasha*, or self-illuminating, and therefore the person who narrates it will find illumination coming from within, for Krishna is the charioteer seated in the heart of everyone, the supreme *guru*. In and through the seemingly redundant detail that has woven itself around the story through the centuries, it retains its breathtaking beauty, for it is dominated by the powerful influence of Krishna's enchanting personality, in which the wisdom of the seer is mingled with the charm and simplicity of a child and the glory of God gushes forth in an inexhaustible fountain of divine love and wisdom.

The story of such a life can only be written by His grace and can only be understood by His grace. May that grace flow into us, inspire and enlighten us, and lead us to eternal bliss!

Though I'm totally incapable of grasping
Even the fringes of Thine infinite majesty,
Yet due to Thy supreme grace alone
I have dared to compile these lines
Containing the story of
Thy playful incarnation.

For this I ask Thy forgiveness.

May Thy choice blessings of long life, good health,
  and supreme beatitude
Be showered on all those who listen
To this account of Lord Narayana,
Narrated by Narayana Himself
In the form of my beloved Lord —
  Vanamali.

Glory to Lord Krishna-Vanamali — the wearer of the garland of wildflowers. . . .

As a man He was a *mahayogi*, the greatest of all yogis,

totally unattached, having complete mastery over Himself and nature, capable of controlling the very elements, if need be. His miracles were only an outflow of His perfect unity with God and therefore with nature. The spiritual gospel which He taught is known as the *Bhagavata Dharma* and is chiefly expounded in the *Bhagavad Gita*, the *Uddhava Gita*, and the *Anu Gita*. The simplicity of His teaching was such that it could be followed by any man, woman, or child, unlike the *Vedic* teachings, which were meant only for the elite. The *Vedic* religion had become elaborated into a vast system of complicated sacrificial rituals, which could be deciphered and performed only by the brahmins and conducted only by the *kshatriyas*. Out of the *Vedic* religion had developed the glorious philosophy of the *Upanishads;* which required high intellectual ability, moral competence, and training under a qualified spiritual preceptor, or guru, before it could he comprehended. The advent of Lord Krishna came at a time "when the common man in Bharatavarsha was without a simple religion that would satisfy his emotional wants and elevate him spiritually without taxing him too much intellectually. The *Bhagavata Dharma* provided a devotional gospel in which action, emotion, and intellect played equal parts, and proclaimed Krishna as Ishvara (God), Who had incarnated Himself for the sake of humanity, Who could be communed with through love and service, and Who responded to the earnest prayers and deepest yearnings of the ordinary person. Thus, Lord Krishna was not only a precocious child, an invincible hero, and a *mahayogi*, but He was the very God Whose contact transforms even sinners into saints, ignorant men into sages, sense-bound beings into spiritual ecstatics, and even animals into devotees. Krishna is the human version of the metaphysical Satchidananda *Brahman* (existence-consciousness-bliss) of the *Upanishads* Who took on a human form to help the ordinary mortal who cannot rise to union with the formless *Brahman* (the Indivisible Absolute) through the path of meditation and *samadhi* (super-conscious state), as advocated in the *Upanishads*. All His human actions during the span of His earthly life are, meant not only to bless His contemporaries and establish righteousness on earth, but to provide a spiritually potent account of His earthly deeds for the contemplation of posterity. By meditating on them they could establish with Him a devotional relationship like that which His great devotees had with Krishna during His lifetime. He is the expression of the redeeming love of God for man which manifests itself in different ages and in different lands, bringing spiritual enlightenment and bliss into the otherwise dreary life of humanity.

The theory of the *avatar*, or the descent of God into the human form, is one of the established beliefs of *Vaishnava* theism and is very difficult for the modern mind to conceive. If we believe in the unborn, impersonal godhead of *Brahman*, how can we accept the fact that it can be born as a human personality? The *Vedantic* view postulates that everything is divine. Every particle in the universe is imbued with the divine spirit. Far from the "Unborn" being unable to assume a form, *Vedanta* declares that all forms are the endless reflections of that One, Unborn Spirit Who is without beginning and without end. The assumption of imperfection by the perfect is the whole phenomenon of this mysterious universe and can only be attributed to the divine *lila*, or play. "*Avatar*" means "descent," and this descent is a direct manifestation in humanity by the divine in order to aid the human soul in its ascent to divine status. It is a manifestation from above of that which we have to develop from below. It is to give the outer religion of humanity an inner meaning which will enable it to grow into divine status that the *avatar* comes. The ordinary person has to evolve and ascend into godhead, but the *avatar* is a direct descent into the human form. The one is a birth from ignorance into ignorance under the shroud of *maya*, or the cosmic veil of illusion, and the other is a birth from knowledge into knowledge, with all powers intact and a full awareness and consciousness of His supreme status. He is thus a dual phenomenon, for He appears human and is yet divine. This has to be, for the object of the *avatar* is to show that a human birth with all its limitations can still be made the means for a divine birth. If the *avatar* were to act in a superhuman way all the time, this purpose would be nullified. He might even assume human sorrow and suffering, like Christ or Shri Rama, in order to show that suffering itself may be the cause of redemption. The *Krishn-avatar* is unique because even in hours of sorrow and travail, He showed Himself a complete master of the situation, thus exemplifying how one established in unity with the divine can remain unaffected in the midst of pain and sorrow. Hence, this *avatar* in the form of Krishna is known as *purnavatar*, or the complete descent of the entire divinity into the form of humanity. The *Bhagavad Purana* declares, *"Krishnasthu Bhagavan Svayam,"* Krishna is the Supreme Lord in His completeness.

Wars are first fought in the minds of men before they are fought in actuality. The bitterness and jealousy that had been festering in the minds of the cousins for many years culminated in the mighty Mahabharata war, which was fought in eighteen days.

The ten days following the new moon, on which the human sacrifice was to have been made, were spent in *ayuddha puja*, or the ceremonial worship of the weapons, by both sides. Winter rains had swept the field. Kurukshetra was wet and slushy when the great war commenced on the eleventh day of the bright fortnight, when the planet Krittika was in ascendancy in the month of Margashirsha. It was the auspicious day known as *Vaikunth Ekadashi*. Some modern calculators place the war on Friday, November 22, 3067 B.C. The great message of Lord Krishna to his friend Arjuna, known as the *Shrimad Bhagavad Gita*, was given on the morning of the first day of the battle.

The mighty epic of the *Mahabharata* reached its climax during the eighteen days of battle. The Lord's role in this war is similar to the role He plays in our lives as the inner guide and counselor, ever ready and willing to lead the chariot of our lives through the turbulent battlefield of Kurukshetra into the haven of a *dharmakshetra*, or divine life, if we, like Arjuna, give over the reins of our chariot into His capable hands and have utter faith and trust in Him. Though the Kauravas had numerical superiority, the Pandavas won, since the Lord Himself was Partha's *sarati* (Arjuna's charioteer). Even this humble role He was willing to take up for the sake of His devotee and friend who had surrendered his all to Him. This is one of the most sublime and elevating episodes in His enthralling life, His *Uttama Lila*, or Supreme Game. At the commencement of the battle, He boosted up Arjuna's flagging spirits with the glorious teaching of the *Bhagavad Gita* and the revelation of His Cosmic Form. In the following days, it was only due to His advice and skillful maneuvering of the chariot that the Pandavas won against insuperable odds. So also, if we have God with us, there is no adversity we cannot overcome.

The night before the war, Yudhishthira could not sleep. He told Krishna, "My Lord, I cannot bear the idea of fighting with our grandfather and the *gurus*. I hate the very idea of this war. How, are we to kill these Elders whom we have been worshiping for all these years?"

Krishna said, "Yudhishthira, you have been born as a *kshatriya*. So do your duty as one. Look at your grandfather. He has willingly undertaken to command the Kaurava army. Kripa, Drona, Ashvatthama, all of them could have refused to fight as Vidura did, but all of them agreed to help Duryodhana. So why are you flinching from doing your part?"

Krishna continued, "What sin is there, O Brother, in killing those who have sworn to kill us? These Elders, though knowing everything about us, have opted to side with Duryodhana, so why are you so frightened to fight them? We have to fight. There is no going back. The river, having once left its mountain fastness, is bound to go rushing down to meet the sea. The river of battle had already started on its course. None can stop it except the ocean of death!"

Both armies were now assembled on the plain of Kurukshetra by the side of the river Hiranavathi. The Pandavas were on the western side near the holy lake and the Kauravas on the eastern. The arena of battle extended over fifty-eight square kilometers of territory. The code of warfare had already been decided upon but, as will be seen, one by one in the following days, every rule was thrown overboard. War corrupts and makes man susceptible to every type of *adharma*. In the end, even the Pandavas succumbed.

On the morning of the commencement of the battle, the sage Vyasa went to the blind King Dhritarashtra at Hastinapura. Dhritarashtra was very anxious to have some idea of the happenings on the battlefield and so the sage endowed the king's Prime Minister, Sanjaya, with clairvoyance to enable him to give a firsthand report of the battle to the king. The events of the battle, as reported in the *Mahabharata*, are therefore spoken by Sanjaya.

The song of the Lord, known as the *Bhagavad Gita*, which contains the crux of His teaching to mankind, is placed at the very outset of the great war and comes in the middle portion of the epic, thus denoting its supreme importance in the eyes of its author, Vyasa. In the opening chapter of the *Bhagavad Gita*, Sanjaya gives a swift portrait to the blind king of the various generals stationed on either side and of the activities preparatory to battle. Flags were flying, drums were booming, conchs and trumpets were blaring, men were eager and restive, as were the horses. The two armies had drawn up in battle formation. The stage was set for the final scene in the mighty drama of their lives, the grand climax the cousins had been expecting and preparing for during the major portion of their lives.

Ten *akshauhinis* of the Kauravas were arranged in a formidable phalanx. The eleventh was directly under Bhishma, who was right in front. His horses were white, his chariot was silver, and his armor gleamed like silver in the morning sun. His banner was a golden palm with five stars. His noble mien gave great confidence to the Kaurava troops. Duryodhana was in the middle. His banner of a serpent embroidered on a golden cloth was fluttering gaily in the breeze,

Suddenly, Sanjaya's narrative was arrested by the appearance of the main characters: Arjuna, tall and handsome, standing in the chariot holding the bow Gandiva and Krishna, seated in front holding the reins in His steady hands, controlling the four milk-white steeds, which were straining at the bit and eager to charge into battle. The Lord's face was beautiful to behold. His lotus eyes were filled with compassion as He gazed at the flower of *Aryan* manhood which had assembled on the battlefield. Bhishma, Drona, and Kripa mentally saluted the noble pair, for they knew that they were beholding the *avatars* of Nara and Narayana. Hanuman had taken his place on Arjuna's terrible ape banner, striking terror into the hearts of the soldiers by his fierce gesticulations.

Arjuna told Krishna to take the chariot to the center

of the field between the opposing armies so that he could observe both sides and get an overall picture of the situation before the battle commenced. Obedient to his role as a charioteer, Krishna, the Lord of all the worlds, obeyed the command of His friend Arjuna and drove the chariot to this no-man's land between the opposing armies. Arjuna, the mighty hero of the age, surveyed the opposing army and saw, not his enemies, but his cousins, friends, relations, teachers, nephews, and grandsire. A tremendous psychological revulsion welled up in him. The full impact of the terrible destruction that was to take place hit him like a blow in the solar plexus. His whole body trembled with the shock, his mind reeled, his mighty bow Gandiva fell from his nerveless grasp, and he collapsed in a heap at the back of the chariot. Bringing forth many ethical and moral considerations for avoiding such a conflict, this mighty bowman told the Lord that he would not fight. To him who was thus in such a pitiable condition, Lord Krishna, his friend, philosopher, and God, imparted this most marvelous spiritual instruction, the highest spiritual instruction that can be given to humanity, known as the *Shrimad Bhagavad Gita*, or *The Song of God*. The Lord chose to sing His song in the middle of a battlefield with the background of drums and conchs and not in the silence of the forest, the sanctity of a temple, or the peace of an ashram. What was His purpose in choosing such a location? Arjuna and He had been very close. They had often been alone together when the Lord could have advised him, but He had not chosen to do so. Why was this? Why did He pick this peculiar location?

The philosophy of the *Gita* is not for the weak or

cowardly person who is afraid to face life as it is. It is for the heroic one, who is ready to face the challenges of life in the effort to evolve into godliness. The *Bhagavad Gita* does not teach an ethical sentimentalism that loves to look on nature as good and beautiful and refuses to face her grim and frightening mask. Unless we have the courage to face existence as it is, we will never be able to arrive at a solution to its conflicting demands. Harmony has to be achieved in and through the disharmony we cannot deny. War and destruction seem to be the principle not only of our material lives, but our mental lives as well. Life is a battlefield of good and evil forces. We are placed in the center of this field, now swayed by the good, now drawn by the evil. As in the Mahabharata war, the latter appears to be far stronger than the former.

Like Arjuna, we stand in this no-man's land between the opposing forces. Every moment we are faced with decisions and controversies. Perplexed and torn between the warring forces within ourselves, we know not which way to turn. The famous pictorial representation of the *Bhagavad Gita*, in which Arjuna is seated in the chariot with Lord Krishna holding a firm rein over the four white prancing horses, is an allegory of our conflicted life. The chariot represents the body, with Arjuna as the *jivatma*, or the embodied soul, seated within. Lord Krishna is the *Paramatma*, or the cosmic Soul, who has ever been his boon companion, but whom he has not so far recognized as the Supreme. The four horses represent the four aspects of the mind, *manas, buddhi, ahamkara,* and *chitta* (mind, intellect, ego, and superconsciousness). This mental equipment drives us like uncontrollable horses, hither and thither, in its mad quest for enjoyment. Arjuna, the embodied soul, was faced with a violent crisis that seemed quite incompatible with his aspirations for a spiritual life, or even for a moral life. But he had the sense to realize that by himself he was helpless, and therefore he had given over the reins of his life into the capable and willing hands of his divine charioteer, who steered him through this dangerous battle with ease, protected him, and led him to a glorious victory.

In all their years of friendship, Arjuna had never thought of turning to Krishna for advice because he had always considered himself competent to solve his own problems. Now, at that crucial hour when he should have been at the peak of his mental and physical powers, he found himself a wreck, his mind torn and perplexed as to his duty, and his body weak and helpless. Only then did he think of turning to the Lord and, having surrendered his ego, he begged Him to come to his aid.

The Lord within us, who is ever our boon companion, waits patiently for us to play out our game of make-believe as the sole hero of our life's drama. He waits patiently until the day dawns when we stumble and realize that without the director, we are helpless and turn to Him for help. At this point, the Lord rushes to us like a loving mother, points out the clear-cut path of duty, assists us to avoid the forces of evil, and even carries us across the treacherous crosscurrents of life, if necessary The message of the *Gita* is thus addressed to the fighter, the person of action, for whom life is a battlefield, as it is to all of us. Kurukshetra (field of the Kurus) has to be conquered before reaching the haven of *dharmakshetra* (field of virtue). Life is not merely a battlefield, but also a field where righteousness prevails.

The teaching of the *Gita* is therefore not merely a spiritual philosophy or an ethical doctrine but a *yogashastra*, which gives us a clear idea of the practical application of these doctrines in daily life. The recipient of the message is Arjuna, the prototype of the struggling human soul who is ready to receive the great knowledge through close companionship and increasing nearness to the Divine Self within him, embodied as his charioteer. The teacher of the *Gita* is, therefore, not only the God who is transcendent, but also the God in us who unveils Himself through an increasing knowledge. He is also the God in us who instigates all actions and toward whom all human life proceeds and travels. He is at once the secret guide to our actions, the highest source of all knowledge, and our closest friend, companion, and relation.

That is why the *Gita*'s message is still as fresh as when it was first given five thousand years ago, for it is always renewable in the personal experience of every human being. The central idea is to reconcile and effect a unity between the inner, highest spiritual truth in ourselves and the cosmos on the one hand, and the outer actualities of our life and action on the other. Thus, it is a guide for each one of us in our day-to-day lives. Whatever the problem we might face, whether horrifying or sanctifying, it can be solved by the application of the *Gita*'s teachings. Its meaning is so deep that the more we read it, the more we learn from it, and the more we live according to its teaching, the more our level of consciousness rises. Its message is of eternity and so it has a timeless significance for all of us. It is not a message conveyed in a mere temporal language to suit a specific occasion. Rather, the occasion was taken to convey to the eternal individual the knowledge of its relationship with the Eternal Absolute. The union of the *jivatma* with the *Paramatma* is the final consummation of the *Bhagavad Gita*. The word *gita* means song and the *Bhagavad Gita* is the song of God and therefore the song of Life — of Existence and Omniscience leading to Bliss — *Sat, Chit*, and *Ananda*.

The first chapter is known as Arjuna *vishada yoga*, or the *yoga* of Arjuna's despondency, in which he refuses to fight with his relations. The Lord listens to his arguments quietly, and it is only in the second chapter that He begins His beautiful sermon. Krishna explains to Arjuna that each person has a certain duty in life, his *svadharma*, which depends on his station, birth, and position in society as well as on his nature. This duty should be followed regardless of personal prejudices and without attachment to the fruits. The work itself brings its own reward.

The second chapter gives the philosophy of *sankhya yoga*, or the *yoga* of wisdom, in which the Lord declares the immortality of the soul and the mortality of the body. We grieve, for we think we are the body and therefore mortal. This is the root cause of all sorrow. The moment one understands that one is the *Atman* alone and that the body is a mere appendage that the *Atman* takes and uses for its own purpose and then discards like a worn-out garment, then there is an end to all fears, especially the fear of death. Though knowing ourselves to be the immortal soul, yet we have a duty to carry out the work appointed to us in life. This should be done while maintaining a balance of mind in the face of all dualities such as pleasure and pain, gain and loss, treating alike victory and defeat. The grandsire Bhishma was a perfect example of the *sthitaprajna*, or the person of perfection, as portrayed in the second chapter.

In the third, fourth, and fifth chapters, He delineates the glorious path of *karma yoga*, or the *yoga* of action. All of us have been given the organs of action by which we can make our way in the world. The law of the cosmos is to be endlessly active. Therefore, we who are part of this universe cannot remain inactive for even one minute. Yet, there is a mistaken understanding that if a person remains inactive as far as the organs of action are concerned, this can be called inaction. This is a misrepresentation of the law of *karma*, says Krishna. The greatest action is done by the mind and even one who is inactive physically is never inactive mentally. Again, there is a mistaken notion that physical action alone binds us to the law of *karma*. The Lord asserts that it is not action that binds, for if that were true, no creature could ever become liberated since none can be totally actionless. What binds us is the mind, which imposes certain reasons for doing the action, primarily the burning desire for the fruits of the action. Thus it is that the Lord makes His famous statement in the second chapter: "Your right is to the work alone and not to the fruits thereof."

Karma binds only when it is done for purely selfish

reasons. The same action, when done selflessly with no attachment to the results and in a spirit of surrender to the divine, becomes converted to *karma yoga*, a purifying process which leads to liberation, or freedom from the cycle of birth and death. When *karma* is blended with the glorious *vikarma* of love, then it is transmuted into worship and can be offered to the divine, just as one would offer a flower or fruit during the course of worship.

Whatever the nature of the work that one is called upon to perform in the discharge of one's station and calling in life, it can be considered an act of worship that can take us to *mukti*, or liberation. To renounce the action physically and dwell on it mentally is denounced vehemently by the Lord as the action of a hypocrite. Thus, a *sannyasi* (monk) who has physically renounced his hearth and home and retired to the Himalayas but continues to dwell upon the objects of renunciation with longing is deluding himself.

A householder who continues to discharge his duties in a spirit of detachment and as an offering to the divine is the true renouncer. We have only one right and that is the right to do our duty in a spirit of *yajna*, or sacrifice. The whole of creation works with this spirit of *yajna*. Nothing is done for oneself alone. Human beings alone defy this law and thus suffer, for no one can flout the cosmic laws with impunity. All of creation is a well-knit whole. Each and every thing in the cosmos is irrevocably bound to everything else. Those who refuse to see this and act purely for selfish reasons live in vain. Suffering and rebirth alone will be the fruits of their actions.

The sixth chapter gives a simple and effective method of *dhyana*, or meditation, by which the mind can be trained to achieve union with God. From the seventh chapter onward, the Lord touches on *bhakti yoga*, or the *yoga* of devotion. The Supreme possesses a twofold nature of matter and spirit. Matter is His lower nature. A true devotee is one who learns to see the spirit alone shining through every atom of matter. After many lives of progressive spiritual attainment, one acquires this type of spiritual vision, which sees Vaasudeva (the Lord) alone in everything. Such a soul is rare indeed! "*Vaasudeva sarvamiti sa mahatma sa durlabhaha* (Rare indeed is the noble soul who can see everything as Vaasudeva, as divine)."

The eighth chapter deals with the little-known and thus greatly feared state called death. The Lord tells Arjuna that whatever thought grips the mind at the time of death is the one which will propel it and decide for it the nature of its future birth. Thus, if one wants to attain God after death, one has to think of Him steadfastly at the time of death. But this is not as simple as it sounds, for at the time of death the mind automatically flies to the thought of that object which has possessed it during its sojourn in the world. If money has been the object of our life's pursuit, to money the mind will fly at the time of death. Thus, the Lord tells Arjuna that if he wants to think of God at the moment of death, he will have to habituate the mind to think of Him constantly. "*Mam anusmara yudya cha* (Think of Me constantly and fight)." Thus, the *yoga* of the *Gita* involves a twenty-four hour affair with the Divine Beloved, culminating in a total fusion at the time of death, when the physical body drops away and there is perfect union with the Divine.

Chapter nine gives the mystic secret by which one may attain liberation even in this very life. A devotee should surrender not only all outer actions but all inner thoughts at the lotus feet of the Lord. Even the negative thoughts should be surrendered, for He will slowly bring about a transmutation of the dross into gold. The one who is thus in constant communion with Him has no need to worry about anything more, for the Lord gives a solemn promise that He Himself will take care of his or her material and spiritual welfare. The Lord will supply all the wants, however mundane, leaving the person free to continue spiritual pursuits and He will lead such a one to salvation just as He did the Pandavas. Helpless and downtrodden, buffeted by the faithless winds of fate, they achieved victory and recovered their lost heritage because the Lord, was ever with them, making them perform seemingly impossible tasks, almost carrying them through the gory river of battle, as will be seen. The promise He makes to Arjuna is in fact given to all of us. "*Kaunteya pratijanihi na me bhakta pranashyati* (O Arjuna, I pledge to you that My devotee will never perish)."

Chapter ten gives the *vibhuti yoga*, or the *yoga* of divine glories, so that the mind of the devotee may learn to see Him in all things, both glorious and mundane. To begin with, we must train ourselves to see Him in the majestic things like the sun, the ocean, and the Himalayas, but later we must learn to behold Him even in the smallest and most insignificant objects of the world. One must learn to worship Him in both the elephant and the ant, in both the beautiful as well as the ugly, in both the sinner and the saint.

In the eleventh chapter, Krishna shows Arjuna His fearful form as *Kala*, or all-consuming Time, the greatest killer, the destroyer of all beings. This vision was different from the one He showed at the Kuru court. It was at once supremely beautiful and terrifying, for it was a direct answer to Arjuna's request to see His Cosmic Form. The love He bore Arjuna was so great that He was prepared to grant His every wish. The glory that Arjuna saw was that of the entire cosmos resting within the form of the Lord. The vision enabled Arjuna to understand not only that everything emanates from Him but that He Himself is everything.

"Time eternal and all-consuming am I, the Ordainer with faces turned to every side. I am death, which seizes all, as well as the source of life, from which it all emanates. That which is the seed of all things am I. Supporting this universe with but a tiny portion of Myself do I stand."

Arjuna realized that all beings are one in God. But the most important teaching of the chapter, which Arjuna grasped, was that even the actions which he thought of as his own were really not his, but the Lord's, using him as an instrument.

Arjuna was both terrified and enraptured as he gazed on the Lord's Cosmic Form. The countless hosts of both the Kurus and the Pandavas were seen entering into Him. Each arm, each hand, each weapon was an arm, a hand

and a weapon of the Divine Charioteer. Like moths rushing to a flame did all these living beings rush toward Him to be consumed in the fierce and terrible energy that was emanating from Him. This fearsome spectacle overwhelmed him. He shrank back and begged Krishna to forgive him for having treated Him in a familiar manner. All these years, Arjuna had considered Krishna to be only an exceptional human being, but now he saw to his consternation that His friend was in reality the one Friend of the whole universe.

"O God of gods! O Refuge of the Universe! Be kind to me!" he cried, appalled at the enormity of his offense. "Whatever disrespect I might have shown to You in the past, pray forgive me for You are possessed of boundless compassion."

Hearing this plea, the Lord once more resumed His previous form, that delectable form which enraptured all those who saw it. The Cosmic Form was shown to Arjuna to make him realize that a human being can neither create nor destroy. All action is, in fact, universal action. So long as we do not realize this, we are bound by the results of our actions, but once we do realize it, then we are no longer bound, for we act as instruments of the Divine. Our duty is only to make ourselves fitting instruments to be used by Him in whatever capacity He may think fit. "*Nimitta matram bhava savyasachin*," says the Lord. (Do thou be an instrument alone, O Arjuna.)

The final verse of the chapter sums up the entire teaching of the *Gita*. "O Son of Pandu the one who performs action for my sake, who considers Me as the

Supreme goal of life, who is devoted to Me, who is devoid of attachment, and who is without animosity toward any living being, that one alone finds it easy to attain Me. . . ."

THE MAHABHARATA WAR

Now everything was ready and the two armies were set to commence the war. Yudhishthira, over whose head waved the royal insignia of a pure white umbrella, was seated in his chariot gazing at the opposite side with a set and stern face, prepared to submit to the will of the Lord and abide by his duty, however unpalatable it might be. Next came the gigantic Bhima, who had no qualms about the task at hand and whose mighty arms ached for having been held back so long from grappling with the wicked Dusshasana. His face was red and fiery with repressed anger. Then came Arjuna, standing tall and radiant in the jeweled chariot with the four milk-white steeds driven by Lord Krishna, who was shining and resplendent like a thousand suns risen together. His look, filled with compassion, was enough to grant liberation to all those who died gazing at His immaculate form. The reins of the prancing horses were held lightly, yet firmly, in His slender fingers and His unfailing smile swept over the entire host as if in benediction. Next came the twins, Nakula and Sahadeva, slim and handsome, their chariots drawn by two steeds with flowing manes and tails and fiery eyes. Then came Drishtadyumna, general of the Pandava army, Draupadi's brother, born to kill Drona. Over each warrior waved his own special pennon.

On the opposite side, in the center of the army, Duryodhana appeared, riding on an elephant, beneath the umbrella of state. At the head of his forces, under a banner bearing the device of a palm tree, stood Bhishma, the ancient knight clad in white armor in a chariot driven by white horses. Behind him were Drona, with red horses, and the heroic Karna, waiting to succeed to the command at the fall of Bhishma. Duryodhana, who always suspected that Drona's and Bhishma's allegiance lay elsewhere, approached his preceptor and warned him in veiled terms of the consequences of disregarding his duty. "Behold, O Teacher, the mighty army of the Pandavas arrayed for battle under the command of your wise disciple Drishta-dyumna, the son of Drupada!"

This was a deliberate jibe at Drona, who had been stupid enough, so Duryodhana thought, to teach the art of warfare to the son of his archenemy Drupada, who had sworn to kill him. Duryodhana, of course, could never understand the high code of chivalry, that motivated great souls like Drona, Bhishma, and Yudhishthira. He warned Drona in no uncertain terms that his duty was to protect Bhishma at all costs. The grandsire roared like a lion and blew his mighty conch, which was a sign for the battle to commence. At that signal, Yudhishthira, to the amazement of the onlookers, dismounted and walked unarmed up to Bhishma and Drona. The Kauravas sneered mockingly, for they thought that this was a last cowardly gesture on the part of the Pandava king. Fearlessly, he walked up to the Elders, bowed low, and spoke. "In our desire for the kingdom, we have dared to array ourselves against you, who are worthy of worship. Pray forgive us and bless us and grant us permission to fight against you."

Drona and Bhishma were full of love and admiration for this great pupil of theirs, who had never deviated from the path of *dharma*. Both of them blessed him and gave him permission to fight against them. After Yudhishthira returned, Bhishma warned Duryodhana that he would never kill any of the Pandavas, who were like his grandsons, but that he would destroy ten thousand of their soldiers daily.

Krishna now took Arjuna to get the blessings of the grandsire, who welcomed them and said, "Hail, O Madhava (Krishna). You know the past, present, and future. Everything is a divine sport to you. As long as I carry weapons, I can never be killed by anyone but you, O Krishna. Therefore, I desire that you might take up arms against me. Let me see if You will grant my wish!" Then, turning to Arjuna, his favorite grandson, the old knight laid his hands lovingly and tenderly on his head and blessed him. With eyes filled with tears, Arjuna saluted the grandsire and returned. Yudhishthira now shouted to the opposing ranks, "Is there any one among you who is desirous to come over to our side? If so, you are welcome." At this, Yuyutsu, a great chariot warrior and the illegitimate son of Dhritarashtra by a maidservant, walked over to the Pandava camp and was welcomed.

Just then a small bird, a lapwing, who had built her nest on the turf in the middle of the battlefield, drew the attention of the Lord by her cries of anxiety and distress for her young.

"Poor little, mother," He said tenderly, "let this be your protection."

So saying, He removed the nest to the side of the field and placed a great elephant bell, which lay on the ground, over the nest. Through the eighteen days of raging battle that followed, the lapwing and its nestlings were kept in safety by the mercy of the Lord, who never failed to give it some food daily and who was the only one who could spare a thought to the smallest of His creations, even at such a crucial time as this. Similar was the care He took over every person on the battlefield, even though their limited vision may not have been able to appreciate this fact fully. Some deserved death and others life, and to each was given his just deserts. But everything was done so unobtrusively that it appeared to be by chance. It was ever His way to look on the world as if it were a play. Sometimes He would remove an obstacle so that the will of the players would have unimpeded scope and sometimes place an obstacle for the same reason. In this way, He allowed events to work themselves out according to the law of *karma*, striving ever to aid the course of destiny, even though this led in the end to the self-destruction of all things. In this battle He guided the fortunes of both sides in an unobtrusive manner, but for the sake of the Pandavas, who had surrendered their all to Him, He often broke His normal code of conduct and actively took a lead, even though His role as a charioteer was apparently that of the uninvolved witness. He thus saved them many times from the consequences of their own folly. If there was any *adharmic* (unrighteous) act to be done, He always did it Himself, for the Lord is always above His own laws, whereas for a human being to transgress these laws would result in infamy and ruin. A devotee may act in a quixotic and sometimes foolhardy way, but the Lord will intervene and save him, even at the risk of getting a bad name. With His wide-angle vision encompassing all the three states of Time — past, present, and future — He is ever able to judge and decide what is best for His creation. By the sheer power of their love for Him and the total surrender of their egos, the Pandavas compelled the Lord to do all things for them, just as Bhishma compelled Him by the power of his love to take up arms against him, as will be seen.

Bhishma sparked off the battle by his clarion call to the ranks. "O *Kshatriyas*! Here is a golden opportunity for you to exhibit your heroism. We are now standing on the threshold of heaven. The portals are open to you. To die of old age and disease on a comfortable bed in his own house is a shame for a *kshatriya*! To die on a battlefield fighting for a righteous cause is his supreme fortune. Dying thus, bravely, with your bodies pierced all over with arrows, you will go directly to heaven." So saying, he gave another blast on his conch. The battle cry was echoed by the opposing ranks and the horses and chariots charged forward with bloodcurdling cries.

The first day's battle, however, was fought on a cautious note. Both armies had been arranged in phalanxes which were difficult to penetrate. Arjuna, after humbly paying his respects to the grandsire, proceeded to engage him in a fierce combat. A few of the Kaurava brothers, as well as Shakuni and Shalya, came to his assistance, while Bhima and Arjuna's son Abhimanyu joined Arjuna. Bhishma's banner was felled by Arjuna and his horses killed by Abhimanyu, who then proceeded to rout Shalya, Shakuni, and the Kaurava brothers and went on to intercept Bhishma, who had turned away from Arjuna and was creating havoc among the Pandava ranks.

It was a wonderful sight to see the oldest and the youngest of the Kuru warriors forestalling each other with expertise! Finally, this brilliant lad of sixteen, who was almost his father's equal in warfare, managed to wound not only Bhishma but also Shalya and Kritavarma, who had joined the attack: Drishtadyumna challenged Drona, but was routed. Uttara, the young Prince of Matsya, now challenged Bhishma, cut off his staff, killed his charioteer, and destroyed chariot after chariot. After his training with Arjuna, he had turned out to be a formidable fighter. Bhishma was in a dilemma what to do with the boy, when Shalya aimed a deadly javelin at his heart and killed Uttara instantly. This was the first *adharmic* act of the war. Sveta, his elder brother, was furious at seeing how his young brother had been killed and turned his fury on Bhishma. He possessed an invincible bow from Lord Shiva and Bhishma found himself helpless against his onslaught. Realizing that Sveta was invincible so long as he held the bow, Bhishma taunted him, "Were you taught only archery? Can't you fight with a sword?"

The chivalrous Sveta immediately accepted the challenge and took up his sword. Now Bhishma, too, tarnished his fair name by cutting off Sveta's right arm with an arrow. Sveta continued to fight with his sword in his left hand, but Bhishma severed his other arm as well, and Sveta slowly bled to death. In utter dismay, Yudhishthira tried his best to console King Virata for the loss of both his beloved sons on the very first day of battle. Thus the day ended on a disastrous note for the Pandavas, and Duryodhana was jubilant.

The second day was a stalemate. On the third day, Bhishma arranged his army in the eagle formation and the Pandavas formed a crescent. Arjuna, as usual, engaged Bhishma. Gatotkacha, who was the gigantic son of Bhima by his *rakshasi* wife, created havoc in the Kaurava ranks. The *rakshasas* were capable of using many magical illusions, but Krishna forbade him to do so unless the other party resorted to similar tactics.

The sixth day was marked by great slaughter on both sides. Drona proved irresistible. After killing thirteen of the Kaurava brothers, Bhima fought and defeated Duryodhana, who fell unconscious and had to be carried off the field by his brother-in-law, Jayadratha. That night, Duryodhana went to Bhishma, who consoled him and gave him a potion to relieve his pain. On the seventh day, Bhima's tally of the Kaurava brothers reached twenty-six and Duryodhana, for the first time, wept in front of Bhishma, who told him, "It is too late to grieve now. Warriors should go to battle expecting to die. . . ."

Abhimanyu cleaved his way deep into the formation.

Drona, Shalya, Karna, Jayadratha, and a host of Kaurava warriors tried to oppose this brilliant boy, but he defeated them all and threw their entire army into confusion. Both Duryodhana and Dusshasana were defeated and had to beat a hasty retreat. Duryodhana's son, Lakshman, accompanied by ten thousand soldiers, now attacked Abhimanyu, but was killed by his brilliant cousin. Duryodhana could not bear it when he heard the news.

"This lad must be killed at all costs," he said, "by fair means or foul!"

All of them realized that he could never be conquered in a fair fight, since he had defeated all their best warriors individually. So, throwing fair play to the winds, the Kauravas now closed in on Abhimanyu and attacked him from all sides as he stood in the center of the lotus. Karna crept up from behind and broke his bow and Drona killed his charioteer. Abhimanyu was now surrounded by Drona, Karna, Kripa, Ashvatthama, Kritavarma, Dusshasana, Duryodhana, and Jayadratha. Like a lion facing a pack of jackals, he faced his opponents, undaunted by them, fitting son and nephew to Arjuna and Krishna. With amazing brilliance, he kept his attackers at bay, hoping against hope that his uncle would soon come to his rescue. With lightning movements of his sword, he managed to prevent even a single arrow from scratching him. Suddenly, he sprang onto Drona's chariot and smashed it to pieces. Looking at him disdainfully, Abhimanyu said, "You're a Brahmin and the commander of the Kaurava forces and yet you allow this injustice — six *maharathikas* to attack a single warrior like me!" He turned to Karna and said, "I thought at least you were capable of some nobility. Aren't you ashamed to have attacked me from the rear?"

He had no time to talk, for, disregarding the codes of warfare, Drona cut off the lad's right arm, which was brandishing the sword. Undaunted, Abhimanyu took up the sword in his left hand and continued to terrorize his opponents. But Drona cruelly sent another arrow with unerring accuracy and broke his sword. Now he was defenseless, his bow and sword broken, his charioteer killed, and his right arm cut off. Maimed and bleeding, Abhimanyu took up a fallen chariot wheel in his left hand, whirled it around, and thus kept his attackers at bay. Again he said, "I'm giving you a chance to redeem your honor. Come and fight with me one by one and I can still kill you all." Saying this, he rushed at Drona, whirling the chariot wheel and looking like Lord Vishnu Himself. He was a most remarkable sight as he stood there torn and bleeding, yet with a smile on his lips and the wheel held aloft in his left hand. Even before he could fling it at Drona, the six great heroes of the Kaurava army closed in on him and smashed the wheel to a thousand fragments. Abhimanyu now took up a mace. Once again, he said scornfully, "Come to me one by one, O Heroes, and I will still defeat you."

Abhimanyu now turned on Dusshasana's son and the two closed in deadly combat. Weak from loss of blood, the boy fainted for a minute. Before he could rise up, at Duryodhana's instigation, Jayadratha crept up from behind and smashed the weak and bleeding boy's skull with his mace, while Dusshasana's son pounced on his fallen body

and hacked him to death. Six great car warrior
to commit this most dastardly crime on the h
Kurukshetra. Arjuna's noble son was lying dead i
and grime of the battlefield and these ghouish men
danced around the corpse in exultation. The common soldiers beheld him as he lay in the mud like a lotus bud
trampled by a herd of mad elephants, and they wept
unashamedly. Vyasa says that even the vultures that flew
around the battleground incessantly seemed to be lamenting and saying, "Not thus! Not thus! We do not want any
share of this noble body!" The massacre of Abhimanyu
was such a dastardly act that it is supposed to mark the
end of the *Dvapara* Age and to usher in the Iron Age of
Kali, in which we now live. . . .

THE END OF THE WAR

Yudhishthira's state of mind on hearing of Abhimanyu's
death can well be imagined. He blamed himself bitterly
for his folly in having sent the boy to his doom. In the
meantime, Arjuna, after having defeated the Samsaptakas,
was returning, filled with foreboding for he knew not
what. The Lord knew very well what had happened and
invoked the aid of Indra, Arjuna's father, in order to save
him. Indra took the form of an old man, made a huge fire,
and was just preparing to jump into it when Arjuna and
Krishna came along. When Arjuna intervened, the old
man said, "You would do the same if you were in my
position, for I have just lost my only son."

In order to comfort him, Arjuna replied, "Please refrain from this ignoble act. I swear to you by Lord Krishna and my Gandiva that were I to lose my son, I would never stoop to such an act!"

The old man seemed appeased by this pronouncement. Arjuna returned to the chariot and Krishna drove off, but the Lord took the extra precaution of hiding Arjuna's weapons. On reaching the camp, Arjuna saw the silence and the way everyone seemed to be avoiding his eyes and he asked the Lord, "Tell me, what calamity has befallen us?" He looked at the Lord's face and saw a glimmer of tears in those lotus eyes.

"My nephew has been killed," He said.

Unable to bear the shock, Arjuna fainted. There was a deathly silence in the camp. None of the brothers could speak a word. On recovering, Arjuna took up the mangled remains of his beloved son and lamented. "O mighty Hero! You were able to discharge your arrows even before your enemies could string their bows, so how could they have killed you? Have you really gone to the realm of the dead? Why did I leave you and go? What will I say to your poor mother? O Brothers! Knowing how much I loved him, how could you have sent him alone to his doom? Sahadeva, light a fire. I want to join my son!"

Sahadeva obeyed without protest, for he knew that Krishna would save Arjuna. Yudhishthira was too scared to interfere, for he felt wretchedly guilty. All he could do was to look imploringly at Krishna. Arjuna, however, refused even to look at the Lord, for he knew that He could have saved his son had He so wished. Krishna summoned Indra again and the old man whom Arjuna had prevented from suicide now appeared and reminded him of his oath not to take his life.

It might be asked why the Lord had not stopped Abhimanyu's murder. The special message of Lord Krishna to Arjuna in the *Gita* is the message of the divinity in the human soul. By the force of the power generated in the performance of *nishkama karma*, or performance of one's duty without desiring the fruits thereof, it is able to unfold itself from the veil of its own lower nature and reach the full flowering of its divine status. The outcome of such action is our liberation from the limited ego and our elevation to a higher nature that is divine, enabling us to act in the world in the truth of the spirit, for the sake of God in the world and not for the sake of our own limited egos. To call Arjuna to such action, to make him aware of the power that was in him and that acted through him, was the purpose of the embodied Godhead. To this end, the divine Himself had become his charioteer. To this end, the vision of the world *Purusha* and the divine command to action had been given to him.

The sermon of the second chapter had shown him that, though the body is slain, the soul can never die, for one is purely temporal and the other eternal. Treating alike pleasure and pain, joy and sorrow, victory and defeat, his duty was to fight in the battlefield of life as an instrument of the divine. For this, both Arjuna and the rest of the Pandavas had to pass through the fire of sorrow and suffering many times in the course of their lives. The *avatar* of the Lord was not to put an end to the dualities of life, but to provide a firm bedrock of knowledge, faith, and action which would help one to rise above it as a *sthitaprajna*, one established in the highest knowledge.

He reminded Arjuna now of this great message of the second chapter, but Arjuna was sunk in gloom and no dry philosophy, however exalted, could comfort him. Knowing his psychology, the Lord rallied him, "O Arjuna! Why are you mourning like any woman? Instead of shedding tears like this, should you not be asking for the name of his murderer and taking revenge?"

Arjuna was a man of action and this was just the way to deal with him. He jumped up and having learned of Jayadratha's perfidy, he swore, "I swear by my Lord Krishna and my Gandiva that if I do not kill Jayadratha, who was responsible for my son's death, by sunset tomorrow I shall immolate myself in the fire!" The brothers were temporarily relieved and looked gratefully at the Lord.

"Arjuna begged Krishna to break the news of her son's death to Subhadra, since he could not face her. Krishna went to His dear sister. She could not control her grief on hearing the dreadful news. After allowing her to weep unchecked for some time, He spoke to her. "Dear Sister, you are the daughter of the clan of the Vrishnis, you are the wife of the greatest archer in the world, and the mother of a hero. Wipe your tears, as befitting the mother of such a son. Abhimanyu was killed by unfair means. He died the death of a hero. He was mercilessly murdered by six of the greatest warriors on the Kaurava side, since they could not tackle him single-handed. Cast away this sorrow and remember that today your son is with the gods. Arjuna has sworn to kill Jayadratha, who manipulated your son's death. Stop this weeping and comfort Uttara, who is bearing Abhimanyu's son in her womb. Guard her carefully, for danger awaits the fetus."

So saying, He took her to Uttara and after comforting both of them and Draupadi, He returned to Arjuna. The latter was waiting to worship Him before retiring to bed, as was his daily custom. After the *puja*, he offered flowers, fruit, and honey to Him. The Lord blessed him and told him to go to bed, for the next day would be the most taxing he had had so far. He would have to plow through the ranks of the Kauravas before reaching Jayadratha. The year was in the second half, *dakshinayana*, when the sun was in the southern solstice and would set early.

That night, Arjuna had a curious dream. He thought that he was taken by the Lord to Kailas, the abode of Lord Shiva. On the way, Arjuna felt weak and hungry, but refused to eat until he had finished his formal worship of the Shiva *linga*. Krishna told him to worship Him instead and Arjuna obeyed, offering the flowers and the garland made for Shiva to Him. The Lord sat in the pose of Dakshinamurti, the meditating Shiva, and accepted Arjuna's offerings. When they reached Kailas, Arjuna was astonished to see the garland he had offered to Krishna adorning the blue neck of Shiva. The latter knew what was passing through his mind and told him, "Know, O Arjuna, Krishna and I are one and the same! We are none other than the impersonal, formless Brahman."

Krishna now spoke, "We have come here so that

Arjuna can receive your blessings for killing Jayadratha, who has received some boons from you."

Jayadratha had practiced severe austerities to Lord Shiva to procure boons from him for the annihilation of the Pandavas. Though Shiva had given him the boons, he had also warned him that his evil machinations would have no effect against the Pandavas, who were protected by Krishna. Lord Shiva then demonstrated to Arjuna how the Pashupata weapon he had given him could be used to full effect, since that was the only weapon which could save him against what Jayadratha had.

In the meantime, Yudhishthira, in his obsession to adhere to *dharma* at all costs, ordered Gatotkacha, Bhima's son, to inform the enemy of Arjuna's oath. He was rudely received by Duryodhana, who was far from being grateful for the message and proceeded to abuse the messenger. When Jayadratha heard of his death sentence, he was all set to flee to his own country, but Duryodhana assured him that he would be given every protection. The next morning, he was sent to a hiding place twelve miles away from the Pandava camp.

On the morning of the fourteenth day, Arjuna was again challenged by the remnants of the Samsaptakas. He routed them in no time and pushed forward, but Drona intercepted him.

Arjuna spoke. "Though you played an active part in my son's death, yet you are my preceptor and I will not kill you, but let me pass for I must get to Jayadratha soon."

Drona was already bitterly regretting the part he had played and allowed him to pass unmolested. Arjuna fought his way through the ranks of the Kaurava army, which had been detailed to stop him at all costs from reaching Jayadratha before sunset. Next, he was accosted by Srutayudha, who had a mace that could kill anyone instantly, but if it hit an unarmed person it would ricochet back on him and destroy him. After a fierce interchange with arrows, Srutayudha flung his mace with deadly accuracy at Arjuna's chest, and once more the Lord saved him by changing the direction of the chariot so that the mace fell squarely on His own chest. As expected, it bounced back and killed its owner. Slowly, Arjuna was beginning to realize that he owed his life, every moment, not to his own skill but to the Lord's grace alone.

But the horses were tiring and the Lord, with His usual consideration for all His creatures, told Arjuna that they had to be rested before proceeding further. Arjuna agreed to fight on foot while the horses rested. Then Krishna said, "But Arjuna, they need to quench their thirst and there is no water in sight." Arjuna smilingly took up his bow and, invoking Varuna, god of waters, he shot an arrow into the ground.

Water gushed out and formed a pool. The Lord released the tired animals from the chariot and led them to the water. Gently He pulled out the arrows from their flanks and caressed them with a bewitching smile on His face. Without showing any sign of hurry, He spoke gently to them and made them relax with His loving touch. In the meantime, the Kaurava troops were harassing Arjuna, who kept them at bay with ease, as his son Abhimanyu had done the previous day. Calmly, the Lord harnessed the refreshed horses back to the chariot and the two of them cleaved their way through the Kaurava army, weaving in and out of the phalanxes. Subduing the army on either side, they sped forward like a forest conflagration.

As sunset was nearing, Arjuna fought with the fury of a man determined to avenge the death of his beloved son, but still they had not discovered their quarry. The red disc of the sun began to slip fast into the western horizon and once more the Lord intervened to save the life of his beloved devotee. Holding aloft His divine weapon, the *Sudarshana*, He masked the sun so that the Kauravas thought that it had set and Jayadratha crept from his hideout. Arjuna felt desperate and Krishna now expressed a wish to hear the twang of the Gandiva for the last time. Arjuna was past caring for anything and did as he was told. As the twang of the Gandiva reverberated in the air, striking terror into Jayadratha's heart, the Lord removed the *Sudarshana* and to the amazement of all, the setting sun appeared on the western horizon in a positive blaze of glory. Krishna galvanized Arjuna into action by shouting to him, "Look, Arjuna! There is the sun! It has not set and there stands the killer of your son, creeping out of his lair in the dark like a jackal!"

Arjuna was already preparing himself to jump into the fire, but the Lord's words made him spring into action. Using the Pashupata with deadly effect, he neatly severed Jayadratha's head from his body, but Krishna knew that the danger was not yet over. Jayadratha's father had obtained another boon — that whoever felled his son's head to the ground would perish. The father was sitting near the banks of the lake Syamantakapanchaka close to Kurukshetra and, quick as a thought, Krishna told Arjuna to keep shooting arrows so that Jayadratha's head would be relayed to his father's lap. The gruesome object dropped with a thud into the old man's lap as he was meditating at the lakeside. Instinctively, he threw it to the ground and his own head broke into fragments according to his wish.

Once again, Arjuna's life had been spared by the Lord, and all the brothers fell at His feet. As usual, He disclaimed all credit, "A noble man's anger is the most potent weapon," He said. "The gods will not sit idly and watch the good suffer, even though they may give boons to the wicked."

The negative vibrations aroused by the death of Abhimanyu were so great that the rules of *dharmic* warfare were waived aside and fighting continued into the night with the aid of torches. Gatotkacha now resorted to the use of his magic arts, for the opposite side was also using these tactics. He caused havoc in the Kaurava army, for being half *rakshasa*, his strength increased with the falling of night. Arjuna was itching to come to grips with Karna, but Krishna kept detaining him, for the time had not yet come. Karna was busy trying to restrain Gatotkacha, who brushed aside his weapons as if they were toys. A vast portion of the Kaurava army had been annihilated and Duryodhana begged Karna to kill Gatotkacha at all costs. Karna was in a dilemma, for only two of his weapons, the *Shakti* and the *Nagastra*, were capable of killing Gatotkacha and he had been reserving both for Arjuna, since he was allowed to use them only once. Reluctantly, at Duryodhana's repeated pleas, he discharged Indra's weapon, the *Shakti*, up into the sky, from which vantage point Gatotkacha was fighting. It pierced through the veil of illusion woven by the *rakshasa* hero and brought him down lifeless. But even in death, Bhima's son proved to be formidable, for he expanded his mighty form and crushed many Kaurava soldiers as he fell. The Pandavas were plunged in grief, but Krishna consoled them by saying that Arjuna's life had been partly saved, since the Shakti could no longer be used against him. This was the reason the Lord had not allowed Arjuna to come to grips with Karma before now.

The fifteenth day dawned and once more Duryodhana accused Drona of partiality for the Pandavas. Drona had been destroying the enemy troops without compassion, throwing overboard all codes of warfare that had been agreed upon. This unjust accusation, as well as his own indiscriminate slaughter of innocents, which was quite against his *svadharma* as a Brahmin, made him feel thoroughly disgusted with life. Yet he fought on and at last killed his childhood enemy Drupada. But this victory brought no joy to him. All the scenes of his boyhood spent with his friend flooded his mind and he felt a bitter disgust at the strange role that fate had forced upon him. Drishtadyumna rushed to avenge his father's death, but Drona routed him easily. Now Arjuna proceeded to engage the aged preceptor, but he proved to be invincible, for on that day he was fighting with utter disregard for his own life and none could approach him. The Lord knew what was passing through Drona's mind, how he was disgusted with life and ready to leave this world. He also knew that Drona could never be killed unless he laid down his weapons. This he would never do unless they could manage to convince Him of the death of his son Ashvatthama. He told Bhima to go and kill an elephant called "Ashvatthama" and prepared Yudhishthira as to what he should say if Drona questioned him. The former refused to tell a lie and had to be cajoled into saying the literal truth. Bhima returned and roared loudly so that Drona could hear, "I have killed Ashvatthama!"

Drona, however, did not trust Bhima and turned to Yudhishthira for confirmation. With great reluctance, Yudhishthira mumbled, "Yes, Bhima has killed Ashvatthama, the elephant."

However, the sound of the Lord's conch drowned the last two words, so that Drona had to infer that his son was dead. He was already disgusted with life and he started to behold celestial beings in the sky beckoning him to leave his mortal body. Then did the great Dronacharya lay down his arms and sit in meditation in his chariot. Drishtadyumna, who had been born to kill him, rushed forward and cut off his head, despite the exclamations of the others.

A temporary truce was now declared to lament over their fallen preceptor. When Ashvatthama heard of his father's death, he was so infuriated that he discharged the deadly *Narayanastra* against the Pandavas. This had been given to him by his father when he was a boy, since he had been jealous of his father's partiality for Arjuna and had begged him to give him some weapon not possessed by his disciple. It was a devastating weapon and Drona had warned him that it should be used only in the case of dire necessity and that it could not be used twice. The astra now came in the form of thousands of small missiles, threatening to engulf and destroy the entire Pandava clan. Krishna ordered everyone to throw down their weapons and prostrate in submission before the oncoming missile. Bhima alone stood up defiantly and it zoomed toward him. Krishna pushed him down in the nick of time and stood before him, and once again the astra proved to be helpless against the Lord. Ashvatthama was furious with everything and everyone including his father, who he thought had cheated him. Just then the sage Vyasa appeared and told him, "Your father did not cheat, you, O Ashvatthama! He gave you the *Narayanastra*, which is potent with the power of the Lord Narayana, and you have been foolish enough to use it against those who are being protected by Krishna, who is none other than the Lord Narayana."

Ashvatthama realized his mistake. He and Kripa now begged Duryodhana to stop the senseless slaughter, but the latter was now sure of a miraculous victory, for Karna had been installed as general of the Kaurava forces. Duryodhana ordered the Yadava army, the *Narayana sena*, to fight with Arjuna. Many of Krishna's own sons were in the army and Arjuna was most reluctant to fight with them, but Krishna, the perfect *karma yogi*, encouraged Arjuna to perform his duty unflinchingly. He was forced to fight and kill many of the Lord's sons, while He charioted him without a tremor.

Next, Karna tried to grapple with Arjuna, but had to turn away defeated. He went to Duryodhana and told him that he could kill Arjuna only if he had a charioteer of Krishna's caliber and asked him to request Shalya to take up this role. Shalya was not too happy to drive the chariot of someone Lowborn, but consented when Duryodhana pointed out the Lord's example. Since Shalya was noted for his acid tongue, Duryodhana warned Karna to exercise great control over his temper and not to retaliate whatever Shalya might say.

On the way to battle the next day, Shalya was determined to provoke and humiliate Karna and they had a wordy battle that very nearly broke up the union. Strangely enough, a similar scene was being enacted in Arjuna's chariot, with Krishna provoking him with such statements as, "Karna is invincible in a fair fight. You will need all your wits to defeat him."

But while Krishna's provocative words only served to strengthen Arjuna's determination to slay Karna at all costs, Shalya's served to inflame Karna so that he forgot the promise made to DuryoGhana and retaliated word for word.

Both Nakula and Yudhishthira were defeated by Karna. He refused to kill them since he had promised his mother to kill no brother but Arjuna. He, in turn, was hurt so badly by Bhima that he fainted, but Bhima desisted from killing him, for he was reserved for Arjuna. Now Sahadeva accosted him, but Karna let him go and pushed forward, until at last the two great protagonists came face to face. A fierce battle ensued in which Karna appeared to be getting the upper hand. When Krishna asked Arjuna what the matter was and why he was fighting in such a half-hearted manner, he replied, "I do not see Karna in front of me, but only my brother Yudhishthira. I don't know what the matter is, but I cannot fight with him now. Please take me away from here!"

So Krishna broke through the network of arrows made by Karna and took Arjuna to Yudhishthira's tent, where the latter was lying in severe pain from wounds inflicted by Karna. Even he reprimanded Arjuna mildly for shirking his duty and Arjuna, for once, became furious with his brother.

On the seventeenth day of battle, Karna prepared his weapons carefully and bade a loving farewell to Duryodhana, for he knew that the day of reckoning had come. In the meantime, Bhima came face to face with Dusshasana. The vivid scene of the disrobing of Draupadi flashed across his mind, so that he threw away the mace which was in his hand and caught hold of Dusshasana's hair. Using his fists and feet, he broke his right arm and wrenched if from its socket — the arm that had dragged Draupadi by her beauteous hair through the streets of Hastinapura into the open assembly of the Kurus — the arm that had done its best to tear her clothes away. With a diabolic cry, Bhima threw Dusshasana down, jumped on his chest, tore open his ribs with his bare hands, scooped out his heart, and proceeded to make good his oath of drinking his blood. Krishna stopped him in time and told him to spit it out, for he had already fulfilled his oath. Though he was still in a violent mood, Bhima complied, while the rest watched horrified. Karna was thoroughly demoralized by this macabre scene, for he also remembered that shameful incident of Draupadi's disrobing, his own comments, and the dreadful oaths taken on that day by the helpless Pandavas. Turning around, he beheld his only surviving son being killed by Arjuna after a brief duel.

Brushing away his tears, he girded himself for the final battle. Both of them realized that it would be a fight to the finish. As they fought on, using more and more potent weapons and tactics, they were each mentally applauding the other for his skill! The rest had stopped fighting and stood watching the duel between these two who had sworn to kill each other. The charioteers were maneuvering with great skill and care.

Finally Karna, realizing that all his best efforts were in vain, decided that the *Nagastra* (the snake missile) was the only weapon that could finish off Arjuna. Fixing it on his bow, he took careful aim at Arjuna's throat. The arrow, in the shape of a hissing cobra with mouth and fangs wide open, darted toward its mark like lightning. For the first time in his life, Arjuna, the great hero, lost his nerve and begged Krishna to save him. The Lord, who had saved him many times all through without being asked, now smiled comfortingly and effortlessly pressed the chariot down twelve inches into the mud. The *Nagastra*, which had been aimed at Arjuna's throat, just missed his head and carried away his helmet.

Karna now decided to resort to the *Brahmastra*, the most powerful missile, the *mantra* for which he had learned from his preceptor, Parasurama. To his dismay, he found that he could not remember a single word of the *mantra*, due to his *guru*'s curse. To make matters worse, his own chariot had also sunk into the mud and would not move. Shalya refused to get down to dislodge the wheel. Karna rebuked him for deserting him. At this, Shalya angrily flung down his whip, threw the reins into his face and left him to his fate. Karna was forced to jump out of the chariot and try to lift the wheel out of the quagmire, calling to Arjuna to stop the fight for a while. The latter was willing to do so, but Krishna, in His role as Karmaphaladatta (he who gives the fruits of actions), thundered at him, "Where, O Karna, was your talk of fair play when you and the Kauravas surrounded the boy Abhimanyu and slaughtered him?"

Karna remembered his own part in that dreadful episode and knew that the Lord spoke but the truth. With a sigh, he remounted and continued to fight from his stationary chariot but though Arjuna wounded him severely, he was unable to kill him. Krishna explained to Arjuna that Karna could not be killed until his entire stock of merit was exhausted. Taking on the form of a mendicant, the Lord Approached Karna for alms, but he had nothing to give Him, so the Lord said, "I have come to seek your *punya*, or spiritual merit. I shall be content with that." Karna knew it was another test for him, so he smiled and unhesitatingly replied, "Gladly will I give You all the merit I have accumulated, am accumulating, and might accumulate in the future, if it will satisfy You."

Thus by surrendering even his spiritual merit to the

Lord, who is the giver of all merit, Karna achieved immortality. But the Lord was not done with him as yet. He had come to test him to the utmost and He now said, "A gift to a Brahmin should be solemnized with an oblation of water."

Karna said, "I'm unable to find some water even to quench my thirst, but this I can do if it will satisfy you." So saying, he drew out an arrow embedded in his body and solemnized the gift with a spurt of blood. As he collapsed from loss of blood, the beggar gently supported him against the chariot wheel.

Feeling drops of water falling on him, Karna wearily opened his eyes and was thrilled to behold the glorious vision of the Lord upholding him with one arm and gazing at him with lotus eyes overflowing with love, from which a few drops of compassion had splashed on him.

"Your name and fame will live forever, O Karna!" the Lord said. "You have amply atoned for all your sins. Now ask for any boon and I shall grant it to you."

Karna whispered, "What terrible sins have I committed against my brothers and my sister-in-law! My only comfort is that I feel that I have paid my debt of gratitude in full to Duryodhana, and I have never failed to give to anyone whatever has been asked of me. If I have to take another birth, grant me the boon that once again I will never be able to deny anything to anyone."

The Lord smiled gently and said, "Your sins are insignificant when compared to the merit accrued by your charity and magnanimity. Your present physical suffering is due to those sins but fear not, Karna. By your final act of surrendering even your merit to Me, I Myself shall take on the burden of your sins and will relieve you from your physical pain." So saying, He gently released Himself and went back to Arjuna and told him to shoot the fatal arrow. Arjuna was reluctant to shoot at a fallen enemy, but took it as the command of God and discharged the Ancharika missile. Thus fell the mighty hero Karna. Though his sins were many, yet his heart was so large that one remembers him only for his love and not for his crimes. A heavenly voice now proclaimed that Karna was not a lowborn, but the son of Kunti and the brother of the Pandavas. Hearing this, Kunti came to the battlefield, where lay the fallen hero in the mud and grime and gore of Kurukshetra. Taking her dead son in her lap, she lamented long and loud over him, as she had promised she would do, and announced to all that he was her firstborn. The Pandavas, however, were not there to hear this.

Duryodhana rushed to the scene. If there was anyone in the world that he was genuinely fond of, it was Karna. When he realized that Karna had already known his parentage and had fought against his brothers only out of gratitude to him, he was inconsolable. Arjuna now realized why he had found a striking resemblance between Karna and his eldest brother and felt terrible at having killed him. Karna's wife Kanchanamala also came to the scene and threw herself on his body and mourned for him. All of them eventually turned on Krishna, for they felt that He had known everything and had not disclosed it at the proper time. They forgot the fact that God has no partiality for persons and that He only saw to it that each one got his just deserts.

The Lord said, "Karna himself requested Me not to reveal his secret until he had died. He sacrificed himself out of gratitude to Duryodhana. I am fully prepared to bear the responsibility for his death, just as I am prepared to assure you that he will never be born again. On two previous occasions I had given you hints about his identity, but you were not prepared to understand. None of you cared to enquire when Draupadi confessed to having a sixth person in her mind, nor when Arjuna retreated, thinking he saw Yudhishthira in him."

Thus ended the seventeenth day of battle. The eighteenth day dawned murky and gloomy, as if the weather gods themselves bemoaned the birth of such a day. The end was a foregone conclusion, but Duryodhana still hoped for a miracle. After consulting Ashvatthama, he chose Shalya as the new commander. As only a few heroes remained, they decided to avoid individual combats. Shalya now fought with an inspiration born of despair. Krishna suggested that Yudhishthira was the right person to fight with him. Yudhishthira amazed everyone by his dexterity with the javelin. After a long and well-matched battle, Yudhishthira hurled his javelin after invoking the Lord's name and it found its mark on Shalya's chest. The Lord explained that it was only the power of Yudhishthira's accumulated *dharma* that had vanquished Shalya. The Kaurava army was in shambles by now and thoroughly demoralized. Duryodhana tried to rally them and sent his remaining brothers to fight with

Bhima, who promptly finished off all of them. Shakuni's son, Uluka, was now singled out by Nakula, who fulfilled his oath by killing him under the very eyes of his father. Now it was Sahadeva's turn to make good his oath to kill the arch villain of the *Mahabharata* — Shakuni, Prince of Gandhara. He cut off his arms and left him to die in mortal agony.

The Pandavas now set out to exterminate the remnants of the opposing army. At the end of the morning, there were only four Kaurava chiefs left, Duryodhana, Ashvatthama, Kripa, and Kritavarma, general of the Yadava forces. Seeing the bloody field of his own making, spattered with the blood and heads of his own brothers and loved ones, the Kuru prince wept like a child. Forlorn and defeated, he decided to beat a hasty retreat and went to the Dvaipayana lake to cool himself. The other three followed him. Some hunters happened to hear their conversation by the lake and reported the matter to the Pandavas, who had been searching for their cousin. They hurried to the lake where Duryodhana, like a coward, had hidden himself in the water, breathing through a reed. The other three had also hidden themselves elsewhere. Seeing the bubbles in the water, the Pandavas discovered Duryodhana's hiding place and taunted him, telling him to come out and face his end like a hero. At this, Duryodhana emerged and magnanimously offered his kingdom to Yudhishthira. The Pandavas laughed at this generous offer from the defeated king and told him, as once before he had told Yudhishthira, that if he wanted to retain his kingdom he would have to fight for it.

Then Yudhishthira, in his usual quixotic fashion that sometimes bordered on foolishness, offered to give over the entire fortunes of the war to the winner of a duel between Duryodhana and one of his own brothers, quite forgetting the fact that Bhima had sworn to kill him. In his anxiety to be fair at all costs, he even told Duryodhana that he could choose one among them to fight with. The rest of the brothers were aghast at this astounding offer, but kept quiet even though they knew that this might well result in the collapse of all their hopes. But the cold war between Duryodhana and Bhima had continued too long for the former to even contemplate fighting with any of the others. His blood boiled when he thought of how Bhima had killed all his brothers and the gory scene of the killing of Dusshasana, his favorite brother, was fresh in his mind. His eyes became bloodshot and he looked scornfully at Yudhishthira, as if despising him for his weakness in having made such an offer. Then he turned his gaze on Bhima and the two glared at each other. They had many a score to settle and they both knew that the moment of reckoning had come. They had been looking forward to it.

They decided to fight this decisive battle on the banks of the Syamantakapanchaka lake. Silently, the seven of them marched toward the spot. Bhima took off his armor, as Duryodhana had none. Just as the battle was about to commence, Balarama returned from his pilgrimage, in time to witness the mighty battle between his two disciples. He warned them to observe the rules of fair play that he had taught them. The others made a circle around the two titans, who were ready to settle their lifelong feud once and for all. They were well matched. Bhima's blows were more powerful, but Duryodhana's body was like adamant as a result of his mother's look. The only time Gandhari had taken off the scarf around her eyes had been to instill strength into her eldest child when he had approached her and begged her to help him. She had told him to come to her naked and she would infuse the strength of a hundred elephants into him by the mere power of her gaze. But he had insisted on wearing a loin-cloth, and thus his thighs alone had not received the benefit of her powerful rays.

Duryodhana had been practicing on an iron effigy of Bhima for many years, preparing himself for this very day, so he was well acquainted with the length and girth of his opponent's body. For some time, they grappled without either of them being able to get the upper hand. At last, Duryodhana, selfish to the last, asked Bhima for his vulnerable spot. The latter truthfully pointed to his head and was immediately smitten down. Bhima fell like a log, but somehow he made a tremendous recovery just as Duryodhana pounced on his inert body. When he asked Duryodhana for his weak point, the latter pointed untruthfully at his own head. Bhima pounded on it with little effect, for his head was like iron. Actually, his weak point was his thighs and Bhima had sworn to smash them on that fatal day when Draupadi was humiliated in public. On that day, Duryodhana had bared his thigh to her, slapped it, and beckoned to her with vulgar gestures. In the heat of the fight and perhaps due to the blow on his head, Bhima had forgotten his oath.

The Lord, as usual, came to the rescue and reminded him of this by slapping his own thighs. Bhima saw this and the whole humiliating scene flashed before his eyes. Draupadi's piteous look of appeal to him and his utter helplessness then filled him with fury now. His eyes became red and bloodshot, and like an infuriated bull he charged at his tormentor. He should have smashed those thighs on that very day, but he had not been able to do so. Now, nothing could stop him, not even the thought that he was committing *adharma*. Is the question of *dharma* or *adharma* a simple one when dealing with one as low and unrighteous as Duryodhana, who had tried every mean and foul trick all through his association with the Pandavas to gain his own way?

Swinging up his mace, he pretended to be aiming another blow at his head. As Duryodhana nimbly jumped aside to avoid the blow, Bhima, summoning all the pent-up feelings of many years, brought the mace down with tremendous force on his adversary's thighs and broke them so that at last the villain fell, mortally wounded. Bhima roared the lion cry of victory. His anger unabated, he pressed his foot on Duryodhana's head, for he said a snake should be stamped on the head, but Yudhishthira intervened and restrained him. Bhima then knelt at his brother's feet and offered him the throne of the Kurus, which had been wrested from him by such unfair means.

At that moment Balarama, who had been a witness to the battle, rushed at Bhima with upraised plow to punish him for his unrighteous act. Krishna stopped him and asked him gently why he had not thought of restraining Duryodhana, when he had committed so many atrocities against the Pandavas. Balarama did not say a word and left for Dwaraka without waiting for the end. In spite of his agony, Duryodhana now burst out in a spurt of venom against Krishna.

The Lord calmly replied, "Think of the evil and suffering you have caused, the number of lives that have been lost only because of your refusal to see reason and listen to Me when I came for peace. All creatures get their just deserts. The wheel of Time turns slowly, but in the end it encompasses the destruction of all things."

Leaving Duryodhana to brood over his wrongs, the Pandavas returned to the enemy camp to take over. When they reached the spot, Krishna ordered Arjuna to dismount. Soon, to the amazement of everyone, the chariot burst into flames and was reduced to ashes.

Arjuna turned to Krishna with tears in his eyes, "My Lord," he said, "what is this I see? My chariot, which was given to me by Agni when he burned the Khandava forest, has been burned up before my very eyes. What is the reason for this?"

The Lord. replied "This chariot has withstood the powerful astras sent by Drona, Karna, and Ashvatthama only because I was sitting in it. It should have been burned up long ago. I have abandoned it now that you have achieved what you set out to achieve. So it is with everything in this world. Each thing is created for a purpose. The moment that purpose is achieved, it will perish. This is so even with men. Each man sets out on this strange journey called life. Each one has come with a definite purpose and once that is served, the earth has no more need of him and so he has to quit. This is the case even with Me. I have created Myself on this earth for a purpose. It is not yet over. But the moment it is fulfilled, I will also die and so will you and your dear brothers. But come, do not grieve. Let us be on to our next task." He then turned to Yudhishthira and congratulated him in formal terms.

All of them were deathly tired, both physically and mentally, and were ready to go to their camp and drop down on their beds, but Krishna forbade them to do so and insisted that it was customary for the victors to sleep outside. Thus, the five brothers, together with Satyaki, slept far away from their own camp, while the Lord Himself took on the thankless task of going to Hastinapura to comfort the parents of the Kauravas.

Sanjaya, who had been narrating the events of the battle to the blind King Dhritarashtra, had already informed him of the calamities that had overtaken his son. When Krishna came, Vidura was doing his best to console the weeping parents. The Lord's eyes filled with tears when He saw the condition of the old parents. He sat beside them and spoke gently and lovingly to them for a long time. Turning to Gandhari, He said, "Do you remember that on that day when I came to Hastinapura on a mission of peace, you told Duryodhana, 'Where there is righteousness there will be victory'? Mother, as you have said, so it has come to pass. You must not blame the Pandavas for this calamity You know how hard Yudhishthira tried to avert the war. If only Duryodhana had listened to all the advice everyone tried to give him, this catastrophe could have been averted. Now it is your duty to be kind to the children of Pandu. They have suffered so much in life. You must not turn your eyes in anger toward them."

Thus the Lord spent some time with them and left only after He had brought some measure of relief to their grief-stricken hearts. Krishna hurried back to Kurukshetra accompanied by Sanjaya, who wanted to pay his last respects to the Kuru king who was now in mortal agony. Even in his last hours, he was burning with thoughts of revenge. He felt no remorse for all he had done. After Sanjaya left, the other three, Ashvatthama, Kripa, and Kritavarma went to him and, in order to ease his pain a little, they offered to make a last attempt to annihilate the Pandavas. Duryodhana was delighted, made Ashvatthama their leader, and sent them off to do their worst.

The shades of night had fallen by now and as they rested under a tree, Ashvatthama noticed an owl silently coming and killing the baby crows while the birds were sleeping. A diabolical plan for revenge began to take shape in his maddened brain. He woke up the other two and detailed the plan to them. They refused to have anything to do with it, but Ashvatthama was determined and managed to persuade them to accompany him. The three planned a cold-blooded massacre of the sleeping Pandavas and their army. In the small hours of the night, the devilish trio silently slipped into the Pandava camp. Even the sentries were sleeping, since the war was supposedly over.

No one dreamed of such a horrifying sequel, except perhaps the Lord Himself and He, for some reason known only to the Cosmic Mind, refrained from saving any except the Pandavas. Perhaps the time had come for the chariots of their bodies to perish, as Arjuna's chariot had perished.

Leaving Kripa and Kritavarma to guard the exits and kill anyone who tried to escape, Ashvatthama slipped as silently as an owl into each of the tents to accomplish his hateful task and show his loyalty and love for Duryodhana. First he entered Drishtadyumna's tent and, despite his pleas to be killed quickly with a sword, he strangled him to death. Then he kicked Shikhandin violently until he died. He then mercilessly chopped off the heads of the five sleeping sons of the Pandava by Draupadi. To prevent anyone from escaping, Kripa set fire to all the tents.

There was complete pandemonium and the survivors rushed to the exits only to be mowed down by the three devils. Intoxicated with the blood oozing from his hands, Ashvatthama took the five heads of what he thought to be the Pandavas and presented them to the dying Duryodhana so that he could die in peace. The latter lovingly took them into his hands, gloated over them, and crushed them one by one with his dying hands. Suddenly he realized that Bhima's hard head could never be crushed so easily. He asked for a torch to be brought and in the flickering light he realized bitterly that fate had snatched the victory from beneath his nose once again. His gratitude now gave way to anger and he berated Ashvatthama with a stream of invective. The latter was already half demented and at this barrage of abuse he left in fury, not knowing what he should do.

At last, shaking with pain, rage, and frustration, Duryodhana, whose villainy has no parallel, gave up his life, unattended, unmourned, and alone except for the silent vultures that were circling him in the night sky.

News of the midnight massacre was taken to the Pandavas by Drishtadyumna's mortally wounded charioteer. Their grief at their hollow victory can be imagined. As the sun rose on the nineteenth morning, the scene was one of utter desolation and despair. Taking Draupadi with them, the Pandavas went to examine the horrific scene. Seeing the mangled bodies of their children, they fainted, Draupadi was the first to recover and she appealed to Bhima to wreak vengeance on the villain, Ashvatthama. He rushed off with Nakula as his charioteer. Krishna followed with Arjuna, for he well knew the power of Ashvatthama's *Brahmashirshastra*, which he would not hesitate to use if his own life were jeopardized.

Bhima found him hiding on the bank of the river. The last shreds of his sanity seemed to have left him. Not content with the massacre of innocent men and children for the sake of a man who had no gratitude to him and whom he knew to be a devil incarnate, Ashvatthama, the son of the great Dronacharya, who had already tarnished his caste and lineage by his actions, now condemned himself to a dreadful hell by taking up a blade of grass, invoking the *Brahmashirshastra*, and hurling it at Bhima and Arjuna with these words, "May the world be rid of the line of the Pandavas!"

The *Brahmashirshastra* was the most potent missile of that age and none of them had used it so far, since its consequences were far-reaching and devastating. Usually, it was not entrusted to one like Ashvatthama, who was morally incompetent to use it.

From the blade of grass there sprang a terrible flame that threatened to engulf the whole world. Krishna instructed Arjuna to counter it with his own *Brahmashirshastra*. The opposing missiles flashed through the air and, had they collided, there would have been universal destruction, but Vyasa and the celestial sage Narada came at the opportune moment and stopped the fiery onslaught by the power of their *tapasya*. Krishna asked Arjuna to recall his *astra* and he obeyed, but Ashvatthama, having lost his powers by his inhuman acts, was unable to recall the *astra*, which recoiled on him and would have destroyed him. He ran to the sages and begged them to save him. They did so out of consideration for his father and because they knew that it was too easy a death for him. Arjuna now bound the felon hand and foot and took him to Draupadi.

Krishna wanted to test her and said, "You may now pronounce the death sentence. How would you like him killed?"

But when the Lord chose to test His devotees, He generally gave them the strength to excel in the test and Draupadi, to her great glory, replied, "He is the cold-blooded murderer of my five sons as well as of my beloved brothers and so deserves the worst of deaths. But when I remember that he is the son of my husband's guru and that his mother, Kripi, is still alive, I do not feel like making another woman experience the pain which I am experiencing now. Moreover, his death will not bring to life my own sons. I do not want him killed."

The Lord was eminently pleased with her answer and said, "Instead of cutting off his head, we can take off his tuft of hair as well as the crest jewel adorning it. This is tantamount to death for a hero."

Draupadi agreed and Bhima cut off his hair in five places and took off his precious crest jewel, which had guarded him against all weapons, diseases, and hunger. But to crush a cobra without killing it is always unwise and the unrepentant villain crept away to nurse his grievance and make further plans. Devoid of mercy and completely deranged, he made a last, desperate attempt to exterminate the line of the Pandavas, for he realized that he could never kill the Pandavas themselves, who were divinely protected. Taking up another blade of grass, he discharged it with the potent *mantra* of the *Brahmashirshastra*, directed against any babies in the wombs of the Pandava wives, so that the line would become extinct. Uttara, the wife of Abhimanyu, was the only widow who was carrying a child in her womb and the missile came rushing at her. Her mother-in-law Subhadra, Lord Krishna's sister, took her to Him and begged Him to protect her. The Lord instantly dispatched his discus to counter the attack and saved her. He then went after the terrified Ashvatthama, who was fleeing for his life. Catching up with him, Krishna proceeded to punish him. The latter pleaded for death, but death at the hands of the Lord was too good for such a wretch.

In dire tones the Lord pronounced these fateful words, "May you live for thousands of years, condemned to wander over the world like a leper, shunned by all, afflicted with all sorts of diseases, your name itself a bane to all!"

Hearing this dreadful pronouncement, Ashvatthama fled from the scene to wander the world forever.

MUHAMMAD

c. 571–632

Born at Makkah in Arabia to a highly respected family, Muhammad was taken in by a kind uncle, Abu Talib, after both parents and a grandfather died. While on a trading mission a well-known Christian monk, Bahira, discerns the signs of God's prophethood in Muhammad. In the cave of Hira, Muhammad is greeted by the Angel Gabriel who conveys to him the word of God. Thus began his prophetic Mission and the revelation of the Holy Qur'an.

With divine consent, Prophet Muhammad, along with a band of his Muslim followers, emigrated to Madina on the invitation of its wise elders, who acknowledged him as the Prophet of God. He built a Mosque in Madina. This was also the beginning of the Islamic Hijra Calender. The first Islamic State was established by Muhammad in Madina.

In 632 Muhammad died at the age of sixty-three. Today Islam is widely considered to be the fastest growing religion in the world.

PREFACE

by Seyyed Hossein Nasr

THE PROPHET DOES NOT PLAY the same role in Islam that Christ does in Christianity. He is not God incarnate or the God-man. Rather, he is human (*al-bashar*), as asserted explicitly by the Qur'an, but unlike ordinary human beings in that he possesses the most perfect of natures, being, as a famous Arabic poem asserts, like a jewel among stones. The Prophet is seen by Muslims as the most perfect of all of God's creatures, the perfect man par excellence (*al-insan al-kamil*) and the beloved of God (*habib Allah*), whom the Qur'an calls an excellent model (*uswah hasanah*) to emulate. He represents perfect surrender to God combined with proximity (*qurb*) to Him, which makes him the best interpreter of God's message as well as its most faithful transmitter. God gave him the most perfect character and embellished his soul with the virtues of humility, generosity or nobility, and sincerity in the highest degree, virtues that characterize all

Islamic spirituality as it has become realized in the souls of Muslim men and women over the centuries. . . .

The prophet, who has many names and titles, including Muhammad, Ahmad, Mustafa, and Abu'l-Qasim, was born in the full light of history in the city of Mecca in Arabia in 570 A.D. in the powerful tribe of Qurayah and the branch of Banu Hashim. Mecca was at that time a major commercial and social center and also the religious heart of Arabia, for it was here that the various Arab tribes that had fallen into idolatry kept their idols at the Kabah, the shrine built by Abraham to commemorate the One God. Arabia lived at that time in the "Age of Ignorance" (*al-jahiliyyah*), having forgotten the message of Unity associated with the father of monotheism, Abraham, who had visited Mecca and who is the father of the Arabs through his son Ismail (Ishmael). Yet a number of those who preserved the primordial monotheism survived, the people the Qur'an calls the *hunafa* ("followers of the primordial religion"). The young Muhammad never practiced idolatry, but was always faithful to the One God even before he was chosen as prophet.

He lost both parents at an early, age and was brought up by his grandfather, 'Abd al-Muttalib, and uncle, Abu Talib, who was the father of Ali. He also spent some time among the bedouins in the desert outside Mecca. He soon gained the respect of everyone because of his great trustworthiness and came to be known as al-Amin, "the Trusted One." At the age of twenty-five, he married Khadijah, a wealthy businesswoman and widow some fifteen years older than he, who trusted him with guiding her caravans through the desert up to Syria. Khadijah, his first wife, bore him several children, including Fatimah, who married Ali and who is the mother of all the descendants of the Prophet, known as *sayyids* or *sharifs*. The Prophet had a very happy family life with Khadijah and did not marry any other woman as long as she was alive. She was to provide great comfort and support for him, especially when he received the call of prophecy and was confronted with the very harsh treatment and enmity of the Meccans, including members of his own tribe.

The great event of revelation occurred in the life of the Prophet when he was forty years of age. He had always been contemplative and would often retreat into the desert to fast and pray. Once, when he was performing one of these retreats in the cave of al-Hira outside Mecca, the archangel Gabriel appeared to him, bringing him the first verses of the revelation that changed his life and that of much of the world dramatically. The revelation continued for the next twenty-three years, until the end of his life.

The verses of the Qur'an descended on the Prophet at different times and under different conditions until the revelation was completed shortly before his death. At first he doubted the reality of his experience, but soon the true nature of what he had received became evident. His first converts were his wife, Khadijah, his revered friend, Abu Bakr, and his young cousin, Ali. Gradually his circle of followers expanded to include his uncle Hamzah and some of the most eminent personages of Mecca, such as Umar ibn al-Khattab. This success in turn increased the pressure of the Quraysh against him, for the new message implied nothing less than a complete change of their way of life, including the destruction of idols and idol worship, upon which their power rested. They finally decided to kill the Prophet, but God had planned otherwise. A delegation from a city to the north named Yathrib had come to Mecca and invited the Prophet to migrate (*al-hijrah*) to their city and become their ruler. The Prophet accepted their invitation and set out for that city in June 622. This date is so important for Islamic history that it marks the beginning of the Islamic calendar. It was in this city, soon to be named *Madinat al-nabi*, "the City of the Prophet," or simply Medina, that Islam was to become for the first time a social and political order, one that would eventually expand into one of the major civilizations of the world.

In Medina, the Prophet became the ruler of a community; he was at once statesman, judge, and military leader as well as the Prophet of God. The newly founded community was threatened by the Meccans, who attacked it on several occasions in battles of crucial significance for Islamic history. These battles — Badr, Khandaq, Khaybar, and others — were all won by the Muslims despite their being greatly outnumbered (the exception was the battle of Uhud, in which the Meccans left the field thinking that the Muslims had been completely defeated). Thereafter, the survival of the new community was assured. Meanwhile, tribes gradually came from all over Arabia to pay allegiance to the Prophet and accept the new religion, until finally the Meccans themselves could no longer resist. The Prophet marched into Mecca triumphantly in the year 8/630, forgiving all his enemies with great nobility and magnanimity. This episode marked, in a sense, the highlight of his earthly life — even his most ardent enemies embraced Islam. The Qur'an refers to this occasion in chapter 60:

> *In the Name of Allah, the Infinitely Good, the All-Merciful*
> *When Allah's succor, and triumph cometh and thou seest mankind entering the religion of Allah in troops, Then hymn the praise of thy Lord, and seek forgiveness of Him. Lo! He is ever ready to show mercy.*

The Prophet returned to Medina, from which he completed the Islamization of Arabia to the north. In the tenth year of the migration, he returned to Mecca to make the greater pilgrimage (*al-hajj*), instituting the rites of *hajj* that continue to be performed to this day. That was also to be his farewell pilgrimage, for on returning to Medina he soon fell ill and after three days of illness died on the thirteenth of Rabi al-awwal of the year 11/632. He was buried in the apartment of A'ishah, one of his wives whom he loved dearly, next to the mosque that was the first to be built in Islam. To this day his tomb stands at the center of the vast "mosque of the Prophet," and Medina remains the second holiest city of Islam, after Mecca.

In a twenty-three-year period, the Prophet succeeded in not only uniting Arabia under the banner of Islam, but also establishing a religious community of global extent, for which he remains always the ideal model of human behavior and action, and his biography (*al-Sirah*) has remained a spiritual and religious guide for Muslims throughout the centuries. His extraordinary life included almost every possible human experience, which he was able to sanctify and integrate into the Islamic perspective. He experienced poverty, oppression, and cruelty as well as power and dominion. He tasted great love as well as the tragedy of the death of his beloved wife Khadijah and his only son. He lived in great simplicity, yet ruled over a whole cosmic sector. He lived with a single wife much older than he was until the age of fifty and then contracted many marriages in his later years, which proves precisely that his multiple marriages had nothing to do with passions of the flesh. In fact, most of them were for political reasons, to unite various tribes within the Islamic community. They also represent the sacred character of sexuality in Islam and a perspective on sexuality very different from the one that identifies it with original sin.

The supreme inner experience of the Prophet occurred in Mecca when one night, shortly before his migration to Medina, he was taken miraculously by the archangel Gabriel to Jerusalem and from there to the Presence of God in what is known as the Nocturnal Ascension (*al-miraj*). This experience, mentioned in the Qur'an, constitutes the inner reality of the daily prayers and the model for all spiritual ascent and realization in Islam. When we think of the life of the Prophet in its totality, we must not only think of him as the leader of a human community, a father and head of a family, a man who married several wives, or a ruler who participated in battles or made social and political decisions for the preservation of Islam. We must also meditate on his inner life of prayer, vigil, and fasting and especially the *miraj*, for the Prophet and, with him, Islam came into the world to create a balance between the outward and the inward, the physical and the spiritual, and to establish an equilibrium on the basis of which human beings are able to realize the Unity, or *al-tawhid*, that is the goal of human life.

In the realization of this Unity, the model of the Prophet plays a basic role. That is why his wonts and deed, known in Arabic as *al-Sunnah*, are so central to the whole of Islam. The way he dressed and ate, the manner in which he treated his family and neighbors, his juridical and political deeds, and even his treatment of animals and plants constitute elements of his *Sunnah*, which is the most important source of Islam after the Qur'an. The *Sunnah* has been transmitted both orally and in written form over the centuries, and countless Muslims over the ages have sought to live and act in emulation of it. Its most direct expression is the *hadith*, or collection of sayings of the Prophet, which embrace practically every aspect of human life and thought.

MUHAMMAD

by Karen Armstrong

URING THE MONTH OF RAMADAN in 610 A.D., an Arab businessman had an experience that changed the history of the world. Every year at this time, Muhammad ibn Abdallah used to retire to a cave on the summit of Mount Hira, just outside Mecca in the Arabian Hijaz, where he prayed, fasted, and gave alms to the poor. He had long been worried by what he perceived to be a crisis in Arab society. In recent decades his tribe, the Quraysh, had become rich by trading in the surrounding countries. Mecca had become a thriving mercantile city, but in the aggressive stampede for wealth some of the old tribal values had been lost. Instead of looking after the weaker members of the tribe, as the nomadic code prescribed, the Quraysh were now intent on making money at the expense of some of the tribe's poorer family groupings, or clans. There was also spiritual restlessness in Mecca and throughout the peninsula.

Arabs knew that Judaism and Christianity, which were practiced in the Byzantine and Persian empires, were more sophisticated than their own pagan traditions. Some had come to believe that the High God of their pantheon, al-Lah (whose name simply meant "the God"), was the deity worshiped by the Jews and the Christians, but he had sent the Arabs no prophet and no scripture in their own language. Indeed, the Jews and Christians whom they met often taunted the Arabs for being left out of the divine plan. Throughout Arabia one tribe fought another, in a murderous cycle of vendetta and counter-vendetta. It seemed to many of the more thoughtful people in Arabia that the Arabs were a lost people, exiled forever from the civilized world and ignored by God himself. But that changed on the night of 17 Ramadan, when Muhammad woke to find himself overpowered by a devastating presence, which squeezed him tightly until he heard the first words of a new Arab's scripture pouring from his lips.

For the first two years, Muhammad kept quiet about his experience. He had new revelations, but confided only in his wife Khadijah and her cousin Waraqa ibn Nawfal, a Christian. Both were convinced that these revelations came from God, but it was only in 612 that Muhammad felt empowered to preach, and gradually gained converts: his young cousin Ali ibn Abi Talib, his friend Abu Bakr, and the young merchant Uthman ibn Affan from the powerful Umayyad family. Many of the converts, including a significant number of women, were from the poorer clans; others were unhappy about the new inequity in Mecca, which they felt was alien to the Arab spirit.

Muhammad's message was simple. He taught the Arabs no new doctrines about God: most of the Quraysh were already convinced that Allah had created the world and would judge humanity in the Last Days, as Jews and Christians believed. Muhammad did not think that he was founding a new religion, but that he was merely bringing the old faith in the One God to the Arabs, who had never had a prophet before. It was wrong, he insisted, to build a private fortune, but good to share wealth and create a society where the weak and vulnerable were treated with respect. If the Quraysh did not mend their ways, their society would collapse (as had other unjust societies in the past) because they were violating the fundamental laws of existence.

This was the core teaching of the new scripture, called the *qu'ran* (recitation) because believers, most of whom, including Muhammad himself, were illiterate, imbibed its teachings by listening to public readings of its chapters (*surahs*). The Qur'an was revealed to Muhammad verse by verse, *surah* by *surah* during the next twenty-one years, often in response to a crisis or a question that had arisen in the little community of the faithful. The revelations were painful to Muhammad, who used to say: "Never once did I receive a revelation, without thinking that my soul had been torn away from me." In the early days, the impact was so frightening that his whole body was convulsed; he would often sweat profusely, even on a cool day, experience a great heaviness, or hear strange sounds and voices. In purely secular terms, we could say that Muhammad had perceived the great problems confronting his people at a deeper level than most of his contemporaries, and that as he "listened" to events, he had to delve deeply and painfully into his inner being to find a solution that was not only politically viable but spiritually illuminating. He was also creating anew literary form and a masterpiece of Arab prose and poetry. Many of the first believers were converted by the sheer beauty of the Qur'an, which resonated with their deepest aspirations, cutting through their intellectual preconceptions in the manner of great art, and inspiring them, at a level more profound than the cerebral, to alter their whole way of life. One of the most dramatic of these conversions was that of Umar ibn al-Khattab, who was devoted to the old paganism, passionately opposed to Muhammad's message, and was determined to wipe out the new sect. But he was also an expert in Arabian poetry, and the first time he heard the words of the Qur'an he was overcome by their extraordinary eloquence. As he said, the language broke through all his reservations about its message: "When I heard the Qur'an my heart was softened and I wept, and Islam entered into me."

The new sect would eventually be called Islam (surrender); a *muslim* was a man or a woman who had made this submission of their entire being to Allah and his demand that human beings behave to one another with justice, equity, and compassion. It was an attitude expressed in the prostrations of the ritual prayer (*salat*) which Muslims were required to make three times a day. (Later this prayer would be increased to five times daily.) The old tribal ethic had been egalitarian; Arabs did not approve of the idea of monarchy, and it was abhorrent to them to grovel on the ground like slaves. But the prostrations were designed to counter the hard arrogance and self-sufficiency that was growing apace in Mecca. The postures of their bodies would re-educate the Muslims, teaching them to lay aside their pride and selfishness, and recall that before God they were nothing. In order to comply with the stern teaching of the Qur'an, Muslims were also required to give a regular proportion of their income to the poor in alms (*zakat*). They would also fast during Ramadan to remind themselves of the privations of the poor, who could not eat or drink whenever they chose.

Social justice was, therefore, the crucial virtue of Islam. Muslims were commanded as their first duty to build a community (*ummah*) characterized by practical compassion, in which there was a fair distribution of wealth. This was far more important than any doctrinal teaching about God. In fact the Qur'an has a negative view of theological speculation, which it calls *zannah*, self-indulgent whimsy about ineffable matters that nobody can ascertain one way or the other. It seemed pointless to argue about such abstruse dogmas; far more crucial was the effort (*jihad*) to live in the way that God had intended for human beings. The political and social welfare of the *ummah* would have sacramental value for Muslims. If the *ummah* prospered, it was a sign that Muslims were living according to God's will, and the experience of living in a truly *islamic* community, which made this existential surrender to the divine, would give Muslims intimations of sacred transcendence. Consequently, they would be affected as profoundly by any

misfortune or humiliation suffered by the *ummah* as
Christians by the spectacle of somebody blasphemously
trampling on the Bible or ripping the Eucharistic host
apart. This social concern had always been an essential
part of the visions of the great world religions, which had
developed during what historians have called the Axial Age
(c. 700 B.C. to 200 B.C.), when civilization, as we know it,
developed, together with the confessional faiths which have
continued to nourish humanity: Taoism and Confucianism
in China; Hinduism and Buddhism in the Indian subconti-
nent; monotheism in the Middle East; and rationalism in
Europe. These faiths all reformed the old paganism, which
was no longer adequate in the larger and more complex
societies that evolved once people had created a mercantile
economy capable of supporting this cultural effort. In the
larger states, people acquired broader horizons, and the old
local cults ceased to be appropriate; increasingly, the Axial
Age faiths focused on a single deity or supreme symbol of
transcendence. Each was concerned about the fundamental
injustice of their society. All pre-modern civilizations were
based economically upon a surplus of agricultural produce;
they therefore depended upon the labor of peasants who
could not enjoy their high culture, which was only for an
elite. To counter this, the new faiths stressed the importance of compassion. Arabia had remained outside the civilized world. Its intractable climate meant that the Arabs
lived on the brink of starvation; there seemed no way that
they could acquire an agrarian surplus that would put them
on a footing with Sassanid Persia or Byzantium. But when
the Quraysh began to develop a market economy their per-

spective began to change. Many were still happy with the old paganism, but there was a growing tendency to worship only one God; and there was, as we have seen, a growing unease about the inequity of the new civilization that was developing in Mecca. The Arabs were now ready for an Axial Age faith of their own.

But that did not mean a wholesale rejection of tradition. The Axial Age prophets and reformers all built on the old pagan rites of their region, and Muhammad would do the same. He did demand that they ignore the cult of such popular Arabian goddesses as Manat, al-Lat, and al-Uzzah, however, and worship Allah alone. The pagan deities are said in the Qur'an to be like weak tribal chiefs, who were a liability for their people, because they could not give them adequate protection. The Qur'an did not put forward any philosophical arguments for monotheism; its approach was practical, and, as such, it appealed to the pragmatic Arabs. The old religion, the Qur'an claimed, was simply not working. There was spiritual malaise, chronic and destructive warfare, and an injustice that violated the best Arab traditions and tribal codes. The way forward lay in a single God and a unified *ummah*, which was governed by justice and equity.

Radical as this sounded, the Qur'an insisted that its message was simply a "reminder" of truths that everybody knew. This was the primordial faith that had been preached to the whole of humanity by the prophets of the past. God had not left human beings in ignorance about the way they should live: he had sent messengers to every people on the face of the earth. Islamic tradition would later assert that there had been 124,000 such prophets, a symbolic number suggesting infinity. All had brought their people a divinely inspired scripture; they might express the truths of God's religion differently, but essentially the message was always the same. Now at last God had sent the Quraysh a prophet and a scripture. Constantly the Qur'an points out that Muhammad had not come to cancel the older religions, to contradict their prophets, or to start a new faith. His message is the same as that of Abraham, Moses, David, Solomon, or Jesus. The Qur'an mentions only those prophets who were known to the Arabs, but today Muslim scholars argue that had Muhammad known about the Buddhists or the Hindus, the Australian Aborigines or the Native Americans, the Qur'an would have endorsed their sages too, because all rightly guided religion that submitted wholly to God, refused to worship manmade deities, and preached that justice and equality came from the same divine source. Hence Muhammad never asked Jews or Christians to accept Islam, unless they particularly wished to do so, because they had received perfectly valid revelations of their own. The Qur'an insists strongly that "there shall be no coercion in matters of faith," and commands Muslims to respect the beliefs of Jews and Christians, whom the Qur'an calls *ahl al-kitab*, a phrase usually translated "People of the Book" but which is more accurately rendered "people of an earlier revelation:"

> *Do not argue with the followers of earlier revelation*
> *otherwise than in a most kindly manner — unless it be*

*such of them as are bent on evil-doing — and say: "We
believe in that which has been bestowed from on high
upon us, as well as that which has been bestowed upon
you; for our God and your God is one and the same,
and it is unto Him that we [all] surrender ourselves."*

It is only our more modern culture that can afford to prize
originality and jettison tradition wholesale. In pre-
modern society, continuity was crucial. Muhammad did
not envisage a violent rupture with the past or with other
faith communities. He wanted to root the new scripture
in the spiritual landscape of Arabia.

Hence Muslims continued to perform the customary
rituals at the Kabah, the cube-shaped shrine in the heart
of Mecca, the most important center of worship in Arabia.
It was extremely ancient even in Muhammad's time, and
the original meaning of the cult associated with it had
been forgotten, but it was still loved by the Arabs, who
assembled each year for the *hajj* pilgrimage from all over
the peninsula. They would circle the shrine seven times,
following the direction of the sun around the earth; kiss
the Black Stone embedded in the wall of the Kabah, which
was probably a meteorite that had once hurtled to the
ground, linking the site to the heavenly world. These rites
(known as the *umrah*) could be performed at any time,
but during the *hajj* pilgrims would also run from the steps
of al-Safa beside the Kabah across the valley to al-
Marwah, where they prayed. They then moved to the
environs of Mecca: on the plain of Arafat, they stood all
night in vigil; they rushed in a body to the hollow of

Muzdalifah; hurled pebbles at a rock in Mina, shaved their heads, and on the Id al-Adha, the final day of the pilgrimage, they performed an animal sacrifice.

The ideal of community was central to the cult of the Kabah. All violence was forbidden in Mecca and the surrounding countryside at all times. This had been a key factor in the commercial success of the Quraysh, since it enabled Arabs to trade there without fearing the reprisals of vendetta warfare. During the *hajj* pilgrims were forbidden to carry arms, to argue, to kill game or even to kill an insect or speak a cross word. All this was clearly congenial to Muhammad's ideal for the *ummah*, and he was himself devoted to the shrine, often made the *umrah*, and liked to recite the Qur'an beside the Kabah. Officially, the shrine was dedicated to Hubal, a Nabatean deity, and there were 360 idols arranged around the Kabah, probably representing the days of the year. But by Muhammad's day, it seems that the Kabah was venerated as the shrine of Allah, the High God, and it is a mark of the widespread conviction that Allah was the same as the deity worshiped by monotheists that those Arabs in the northern tribes on the borders of the Byzantine Empire who had converted to Christianity used to make the *hajj* alongside the pagans. Yet for all this, in the early days of his mission, Muhammad still made the Muslims perform the *salat* prayer facing Jerusalem, the holy city of the *ahl alkitab*, turning their backs on the pagan associations of the Kabah. This expressed his longing to bring the Arabs into the monotheistic family.

Muhammad acquired a small following and eventually some seventy families had converted to Islam. At first, the most powerful men in Mecca ignored the Muslims, but by 616 they had become extremely angry with Muhammad who, they said, reviled the faith of their fathers, and was obviously a charlatan, who only pretended to be a prophet. They were particularly incensed by the Qur'an's description of the Last Judgment, which they dismissed as primitive and irrational. Arabs did not believe in the afterlife and should give no credence to such "fairy tales." But they were especially concerned that in the Qur'an this Judaeo-Christian belief struck at the heart of their cut-throat capitalism. On the Last Day, Arabs were warned that the wealth and power of their tribe would not help them; each individual would be tried on his or her own merits: why had they not taken care of the poor? Why had they accumulated fortunes instead of sharing their money? Those Quraysh who were doing very well in the new Mecca were not likely to look kindly on this kind of talk, and the opposition grew, led by Abu al-Hakam (who is called Abu Jahl, "Father of Lies," in the Qur'an), Abu Sufyan, an extremely intelligent man, who had once been a personal friend of Muhammad, and Suhayl ibn Amr, a devout pagan. They were all disturbed by the idea of abandoning the faith of their ancestors; all had relatives who had converted to Islam; and all feared that Muhammad was plotting to take over the leadership of Mecca. The Qur'an insisted that Muhammad had no political function but that he was simply a *nadhir*, a "warner," but how long would a man who claimed to receive instructions from Allah accept the rulings of more ordinary mortals like themselves?

Relations deteriorated sharply. Abu Jahl imposed a boycott on Muhammad's clan, forbidding the Quraysh to marry or trade with the Muslims. This meant that nobody could sell them anyy food. The ban lasted for two years, and the food shortages may well have been responsible for the death of Muhammad's beloved wife Khadijah, and it certainly ruined some of the Muslims financially. Slaves who had converted to Islam were particularly badly treated, tied up, and left to burn in the blazing sun. Most seriously, in 619, after the ban had been lifted, Muhammad's uncle and protector (*wali*) Abu Talib died. Muhammad was an orphan; his parents had died in his infancy. Without a protector who would avenge his death, according to the harsh vendetta lore of Arabia, a man could be killed with impunity, and Muhammad had great difficulty finding a Meccan chieftain who would become his patron. The position of the *ummah* was becoming untenable in Mecca, and a new solution clearly had to be found.

Muhammad was, therefore, ready to listen to a delegation of chiefs from Yathrib, an agricultural settlement some 250 miles north of Mecca. A number of tribes had abandoned the nomadic way of life and settled there, but after centuries of warfare on the steppes found it impossible to live together peacefully. The whole settlement was caught up in one deadly feud after another. Some of these tribes had either converted to Judaism or were of Jewish descent, and so the people of Yathrib were accustomed to monotheistic ideas, were not in thrall to the old paganism, and were desperate to find a new solution that would enable their people to live together in a single community. The envoys from Yathrib, who approached Muhammad during the *hajj* in 620, converted to Islam and made a pledge with the Muslims: each vowed that they would not fight each other, and would defend each other from common enemies. Eventually, in 622, the Muslim families slipped away, one by one, and made the migration (*hijrah*) to Yathrib. Muhammad, whose new protector had recently died, was almost assassinated before he and Abu Bakr were able to escape.

The *hijrah* marks the start of the Muslim era, because it was at this point that Muhammad was able to implement the Qur'anic ideal fully and that Islam became a factor in history. It was a revolutionary step. The *hijrah* was no mere change of address. In pre-Islamic Arabia the tribe was a sacred value. To turn your back on your blood-group and join another was unheard of; it was essentially blasphemous, and the Quraysh could not condone this defection. They vowed to exterminate the *ummah* in Yathrib. Muhammad had become the head of a collection of tribal groups that were not bound together by blood but by a shared ideology, an astonishing innovation in Arabian society. Nobody was forced to convert to the religion of the Qur'an, but Muslims, pagans, and Jews all belonged to one *ummah*, could not attack one another, and vowed to give one another protection. News of this extraordinary new "supertribe" spread, and though at the outset nobody thought that it had a chance of survival, it proved to be an inspiration that would bring peace to Arabia before the death of the Prophet in 632, just ten years after the *hijrah*.

Yathrib would become known as al-Medinah (*the City*), because it became the pattern of the perfect Muslim society. When Muhammad arrived in Medina one of his first actions was to build a simple mosque (*masjid*: literally, place of prostration). It was a rough building, which expressed the austerity of the early Islamic ideal. Tree trunks supported the roof, a stone marked the *qiblah* (the direction of prayer), and the Prophet stood on a tree trunk to preach. All future mosques would, as far as possible, be built according to this model. There was also a courtyard, where Muslims met to discuss all the concerns of the *ummah* — social, political, and military as well as religious. Muhammad and his wives lived in small huts around the edge of the courtyard. Unlike a Christian church, which is separated from mundane activities and devoted only to worship, no activity was excluded from the mosque. In the Qur'anic vision there is no dichotomy between the sacred and the profane, the religious and the political, sexuality and worship. The whole of life was potentially holy, and had to be brought into the ambit of the divine. The aim was *tawhid* (making one), the integration of the whole of life in a unified community, which would give Muslims intimations of the Unity which is God.

Muhammad's numerous wives have occasioned a good deal of prurient interest in the West, but it would be a mistake to imagine the Prophet basking decadently in sensual delight, like some of the later Islamic rulers. In Mecca, Muhammad had remained monogamous, married only to Khadijah, even though polygamy was common in Arabia. Khadijah was a good deal older than he, but bore him at least six children, of whom only four daughters survived. In Medina, Muhammad became a great *sayyid* (chief), and was expected to have a large harem, but most of these marriages were politically motivated. As he formed his new supertribe, he was eager to forge marriage ties with some of his closest companions, to bind them closer together. His favourite new wife was Aisha, the daughter of Abu Bakr, and he also married Hafsah, the daughter of Umar ibn al-Khattab. He married two of his daughters to Uthman ibn Affan and Ali ibn Abi Talib. Many of his other wives were older women, who were without protectors or were related to the chiefs of those tribes who became the allies of the *ummah*. None of them bore the Prophet any children. His wives were sometimes more of a hindrance than a pleasure. On one occasion, when they were squabbling about the division of booty after a raid, the Prophet threatened to divorce them all unless they lived more strictly in accordance with Islamic values. But it is still true that Muhammad was one of those rare men who truly enjoy the company of women. Some of his male companions were astonished by his leniency toward his wives and the way they stood up to him and answered him back. Muhammad scrupulously helped with the chores, mended his own clothes, and sought out the companionship of his wives. He often liked to take one of them on an expedition, and would consult them and take their advice seriously. On one occasion his most intelligent wife, Umm Salamah, helped to prevent a mutiny.

The emancipation of women was a project dear to the

Prophet's heart. The Qur'an gave women rights of inheritance and divorce centuries before Western women were accorded such status. The Qur'an prescribes some degree of segregation and veiling for the Prophet's wives, but there is nothing in the Qur'an that requires the veiling of *all* women or their seclusion in a separate part of the house. These customs were adopted some three or four generations after the Prophet's death. Muslims at that time were copying the Greek Christians of Byzantium, who had long veiled and segregated their women in this manner; they also appropriated some of their Christian misogyny. The Qur'an makes men and women partners before God, with identical duties and responsibilities.

The Qur'an also came to permit polygamy; at a time when Muslims were being killed in the wars against Mecca, and women were left without protectors, men were permitted to have up to four wives provided that they treat them all with absolute equality and show no signs of favouring one rather than the others. The women of the first *ummah* in Medina took full part in its public life, and some, according to Arab custom, fought alongside the men in battle. They did not seem to have experienced Islam as an oppressive religion, though later, as happened in Christianity, men would hijack the faith and bring it into line with the prevailing patriarchy.

In the early years at Medina there were two important developments. Muhammad had been greatly excited by the prospect of working closely with the Jewish tribes, and had even, shortly before the *hijrah*, introduced some practices (such as communal prayer on Friday afternoons, when Jews would be preparing for the Sabbath, and a fast on the Jewish Day of Atonement) to align Islam more closely with Judaism. His disappointment, when the Jews of Medina refused to accept him as an authentic prophet, was one of the greatest of his life. For Jews, the era of prophecy was over, so it was not surprising that they could not accept Muhammad, but the polemic with the Jews of Medina occupies a significant proportion of the Qur'an and shows that it troubled Muhammad. Some of the Qur'anic stories about such prophets as Noah or Moses were different from those of the Bible. Many of the Jews used to scoff when these were recited in the mosque.

The three main Jewish tribes also resented Muhammad's ascendancy; they had formed a powerful bloc before his arrival in the settlement, and now felt demoted and determined to get rid of him.

But some of the Jews in the smaller clans were friendly and enhanced Muhammad's knowledge of Jewish scripture. He was especially delighted to hear that in the Book of Genesis Abraham had two sons: Isaac and Ishmael (who became Ismail in Arabic), the child of his concubine Hagar. Abraham had been forced to cast Hagar and Ismail out into the wilderness, but God had saved them and promised that Ismail too would be the father of a great nation, the Arabs. Local tradition had it that Hagar and Ismail had settled in Mecca, that Abraham had visited them there and that together Abraham and Ismail had rebuilt the Kabah (which had originally been erected by Adam but had fallen into disrepair). This was music to Muhammad's ears. It seemed that the Arabs had not been left out of the divine plan after all, and that the Kabah had venerable monotheistic credentials.

By 624 it was clear that most of the Jews of Medina would never be reconciled with the Prophet. Muhammad had also been shocked to learn that the Jews and Christians (whom he had assumed to belong to a single faith) actually had serious theological differences, even though he appears to have thought that not all the *ahl al-kitab* condoned this disgraceful sectarianism. In January 624 he made what must have been one of his most creative gestures. During the *salat* prayer, he told the congregation to turn around, so that they prayed in the direction of Mecca rather than Jerusalem. This change of *qiblah* was a declaration of independence. By turning away from Jerusalem toward the Kabah, which had no connection with Judaism or Christianity, Muslims tacitly demonstrated that they were reverting to the original pure monotheism of Abraham, who had lived before either Torah or the Gospel and, therefore, before the religion of the one God had been split into warring sects. Muslims would direct themselves to God alone: it was idolatrous to bow before a human system or an established religion rather than before God himself:

> *Verily, as for those who have broken the unity of their faith and become sects — thou has nothing to do with them... Say: "Behold, my Sustainer has guided me to a straight way through an ever-true faith — in the way of Abraham, who turned away from all that is false, and was not of those who ascribe divinity to aught beside Him." Say: "Behold,*

*my prayer, and [all] my acts of worship, and my liv-
ing and dying are for God alone."*

The change of *qiblah* appealed to all Arab Muslims, especially to the emigrants who had made the *hijrah* from
Mecca. Muslims would no longer tag lamely behind those
Jews and Christians who ridiculed their aspirations, but
would take their own direct route to God.

The second major development occurred shortly after
the change of the *qiblah*. Muhammad and the emigrants
from Mecca had no means of earning a living in Medina;
there was not enough land for them to farm, and, in any
case, they were merchants and businessmen not agricul-
turalists. The Medinese, who were known as the *ansar*
(the helpers), could not afford to keep them *gratis*, so the
emigrants resorted to the *ghazu*, the "raid," which was a
sort of national sport in Arabia, as well as being a rough-
and-ready means of redistributing resources in a land
where there was simply not enough to go round. Raiding
parties would attack a caravan or contingent from a rival
tribe and carry off booty and livestock, taking care to
avoid killing people since this would mean a vendetta. It
was forbidden to conduct a raid against a tribe that had
become an ally or "client" (a weaker tribal group who had
sought protection from one of the more powerful tribes).
The emigrants, who had been persecuted by the Quraysh
and forced to leave their homes, began to conduct *ghazu*
against the rich Meccan caravans, which brought them an
income, but to conduct a *ghazu* against one's *own* tribe
was a serious breach in precedent. The raiding parties

enjoyed some initial success, but in March 624 Muhammad led a large band of migrants to the coast to intercept the largest Meccan caravan of the year. When they heard of this outrage, the Quraysh dispatched an army to defend the caravan, but, against the odds, the Muslims inflicted a stunning defeat on the Meccans at the well of Badr. Even though the Meccans were superior in terms of numbers, they fought in the old Arab style with careless bravado, each chief leading his own men. Muhammad's troops, however, were carefully drilled and fought under his unified command. It was a rout that impressed the Bedouin tribes, some of whom enjoyed the spectacle of seeing the mighty Quraysh brought low.

There then ensued desperate days for the *ummah*. Muhammad had to contend with the hostility of some of the pagans in Medina, who resented the power of the Muslim newcomers and were determined to expel them from the settlement. He also had to deal with Mecca, where Abu Sufyan now directed the campaign against him, and had launched two major offensives against the Muslims in Medina. His object was not simply to defeat the *ummah* in battle, but to annihilate all the Muslims. The harsh ethic of the desert meant that there were no half-measures in warfare: if possible, a victorious chief was expected to exterminate the enemy, so the *ummah* faced the threat of total extinction. In 625 Mecca inflicted a severe defeat on the *ummah* at the Battle of Uhud, but two years later the Muslims trounced the Meccans at the Battle of the Trench, so called because Muhammad protected the settlement by digging a ditch around Medina, which threw the Quraysh, who still regarded war rather as a chivalric game and had never heard of such an unsporting trick, into confusion, and rendered their cavalry useless. Muhammad's second victory over the numerically superior Quraysh (there had been ten thousand Meccans to three thousand Muslims) was a turning point. It convinced the nomadic tribes that Muhammad was the coming man, and made the Quraysh look decidedly *passé*. The gods in whose name they fought were clearly not working on their behalf. Many of the tribes wanted to become the allies of the *ummah*, and Muhammad began to build a powerful tribal confederacy, whose members swore not to attack one another and to fight each other's enemies. Some of the Meccans also began to defect and made the *hijrah* to Medina; at last, after five years of deadly peril, Muhammad could be confident that the *ummah* would survive.

In Medina, the chief casualties of this Muslim success were the three Jewish tribes of Qaynuqah, Nadir, and Qurayzah, who were determined to destroy Muhammad and who all independently formed alliances with Mecca. They had powerful armies, and obviously posed a threat to the Muslims, since their territory was so situated that they could easily join a besieging Meccan army or attack the *ummah* from the rear. When the Qaynuqah staged an unsuccessful rebellion against Muhammad in 625, they were expelled from Medina, in accordance with Arab custom. Muhammad tried to reassure the Nadir, and made a special treaty with them, but when he discovered that they had been plotting to assassinate him they too were sent into exile, where they joined the nearby Jewish settlement of Khaybar, and drummed up support for Abu Sufyan among the northern Arab tribes. The Nadir proved to be even more of a danger outside Medina, so when the Jewish tribe of Qurayzah sided with Mecca during the Battle of the Trench, when for a time it seemed that the Muslims faced certain defeat, Muhammad showed no mercy. The seven hundred men of the Qurayzah were killed, and their women and children sold as slaves.

The massacre of the Qurayzah was a horrible incident, but it would be a mistake to judge it by the standards of our own time. This was a very primitive society: the Muslims themselves had just narrowly escaped extermination, and had Muhammad simply exiled the Qurayzah they would have swelled the Jewish opposition in Khaybar and brought another war upon the *ummah*. In seventh-century Arabia an Arab chief was not expected to show mercy to traitors like the Qurayzah. The executions sent a grim message to Khaybar and helped to quell the pagan opposition in Medina, since the pagan leaders had been the allies of the rebellious Jews. This was a fight to the death, and everybody had always known that the stakes were high. The struggle did not indicate any hostility toward Jews in general, but only toward the three rebel tribes. The Qur'an continued to revere Jewish prophets and to urge Muslims to respect the People of the Book. Smaller Jewish groups continued to live in Medina, and later Jews, like Christians, enjoyed full religious liberty in the Islamic empires. Anti-semitism is a Christian vice. Hatred of the Jews became marked in the Muslim world only after the creation of the state of Israel in 1948 and the subsequent loss of Arab Palestine. It is significant that Muslims were compelled to import anti-Jewish myths from Europe, and translate into Arabic such virulently anti-semitic texts as the *Protocols of the Elders of Zion*, because they had no such traditions of their own. Because of this new hostility toward the Jewish people, some Muslims now quote the passages in the Qur'an that refer to Muhammad's struggle with the three rebellious Jewish tribes to justify their prejudice. By taking these verses out of context, they have distorted both the message of the Qur'an and the attitude of the Prophet, who himself felt no such hatred of Judaism.

Muhammad's intransigence toward the Qurayzah had been designed to bring hostilities to an end as soon as possible. The Qur'an teaches that war is such a catastrophe that Muslims must use every method in their power to restore peace and normality in the shortest possible time. Arabia was a chronically violent society, and the *ummah* had to fight its way to peace. Major social change of the type that Muhammad was attempting in the peninsula is rarely achieved without bloodshed. But after the Battle of the Trench, when Muhammad had humiliated Mecca and quashed opposition in Medina, he felt it was time to abandon the *jihad* and begin a peace offensive. In March 628 he set in train a daring and imaginative initiative that brought the conflict to a close. He announced that he was going to make a *hajj* to Mecca, and asked for volunteers to accompany him. Since pilgrims were forbidden to carry arms, the Muslims would be

walking directly into the lions' den and putting themselves at the mercy of the hostile and resentful Quraysh.
Nevertheless, about a thousand Muslims agreed to join
the Prophet and set out for Mecca, dressed in the traditional white robes of the *hajji*. If the Quraysh forbade
Arabs to approach the Kabah or attacked bona fide pilgrims they would betray their sacred duty as the
guardians of the shrine. The Quraysh did, however, dis-
patch troops to attack the pilgrims before they reached
the area outside the city where violence was forbidden,
but the Prophet evaded them and, with the help of some
of his Bedouin allies, managed to reach the edge of the
sanctuary, camped at Hudaybiyyah and awaited developments. Eventually the Quraysh were pressured by this
peaceful demonstration to sign a treaty with the *ummah*.
It was an unpopular move on both sides. Many of the
Muslims were eager for action, and felt that the treaty
was shameful, but Muhammad was determined to achieve
victory by peaceful means.

Hudaybiyyah was another turning point. It impressed
still more of the Bedouin, and conversion to Islam
became even more of an irreversible trend. Eventually in
630, when the Quraysh violated the treaty by attacking
one of the Prophet's tribal allies, Muhammad marched
upon Mecca with an army of ten thousand men. Faced
with this overwhelming force and, as pragmatists, realizing what it signified, the Quraysh conceded defeat,
opened the city gates, and Muhammad took Mecca without shedding a drop of blood. He destroyed the idols
around the Kabah, rededicated it to Allah, the one God,

and gave the old pagan rites of the *hajj* an Islamic significance by linking them to the story of Abraham, Hagar,
and Ismail. None of the Quraysh was forced to become
Muslim, but Muhammad's victory convinced some of his
most principled opponents, such as Abu Sufyan, that the
old religion had failed. When Muhammad died in 632, in
the arms of his beloved wife Aisha, almost all the tribes of
Arabia had joined the ummah as Confederates or as converted Muslims. Since members of the *ummah* could not,
of course, attack one another, the ghastly cycle of tribal
warfare, of vendetta and counter-vendetta, had ended.
Single-handedly, Muhammad had brought peace to war-
torn Arabia. . . .

When Muhammad had made the *hijra* in 622 the little
Islamic community had taken its first step forward to
political power: ten years later it dominated almost the
whole of Arabia and had laid the foundations for a new
Arab polity which would enable Muslims to govern a
huge empire for over a thousand years. This political success had involved continuous strain and effort and the
tumultuous years at Medina had shown how difficult and
dangerous it could be to undertake the reconstruction of
human society according to God's plan. Muhammad
experienced the strain of translating the ineffable Word
of God into human language, which had sometimes
seemed to crack and splinter under the divine impact.
The struggle to incarnate the Word of God in human
society had also taken Muslims to the limits of their
endurance and perception, so that they had sometimes

been on the brink of despair and sometimes on the point of abandoning Muhammad altogether. But his success proved to be the best argument for his extraordinary and controversial policies. When Muhammad had made the decision to fight at Badr, to expel or massacre the Jewish tribes or to make the treaty at Hudaybiyah, he had not been inspired directly by God but had had to ask for help and advice and use his own native wit. The Qur'an did not expect Muslims to abandon their natural common sense or to sit back and wait for God to save them by means of a miracle. Islam was a practical and realistic faith, which saw human intelligence and divine inspiration working harmoniously side by side. By the year 632 it seemed as though God's will was really about to be done in Arabia. Unlike so many of the earlier prophets, Muhammad had not only brought individual men and women a new per-sonal vision of hope, but he had undertaken the task of redeeming human history and creating a just society which would enable men and women to fulfill their true potential. The political success of the *ummah* had almost become a sacrament for the Muslims: it was an outward sign of God's invisible presence in their midst. Political activity would continue to be a sacred responsibility and the later success of the Muslim empire a "sign" that mankind as a whole could be redeemed.

Instead of wandering in unworldly fashion round the hills of Galilee preaching and healing, like the Jesus of the Gospels, Muhammad had had to engage in a grim politi-cal effort to reform his society, and his followers were pledged to continue this struggle. Instead of devoting all their efforts to restructuring, their own personal lives within the context of the *pax Romana*, like the early Christians, Muhammad and his companions had undertaken the redemption of their society, without which there could be no moral or spiritual advance. The Qur'an is clear that the eternal fate of the individual is of paramount importance and takes precedence over the social duties of Muslims. History and political activity is never an end in itself but is overshadowed and qualified by a transcendent divine order: the eternal fate of the individual is more important than social reform, as the constant Qur'anic symbolism of Judgment, Hell, and Heaven makes clear. In this the Qur'an responds to the new spirit of individualism which was beginning to make itself felt in Arabia, and its social legislation reflects this concern. Despite the decline of the tribal system, old communal ideals were still normative and Muhammad could not ignore this fact and produce a full-blown individualism to satisfy our present Western liberal ideals — but he had made a start. Yet the salvation of the individual could not be achieved if the endless cycle of bloodshed and exploitation continued in Arabia: a corrupt or disintegrating society inevitably breeds immorality, malaise, and despair in all but the truly heroic, so the conditions of seventh-century Arabia demanded a social as well as an individual plan of salvation.

Muhammad had managed to create a community in Medina which was strong and independent of the surrounding chaos. Other tribal groups were beginning to join it, though they were not as yet all committed to his religious vision. In order to survive, the *ummah* had to be strong and powerful, yet Muhammad's chief aim had not been political strength but to create a *good* society.

Muhammad's success seemed to vindicate the Qur'anic claim that societies which refused this order were bound to perish. But the struggle was not over. When the Muslims had returned from Tabuk, some had put away their swords, but Muhammad is said to have told them that the fighting was not over and that they should prepare for a new effort. The challenge of realizing God's will in human history would never end: there would always be new dangers and problems to overcome. Sometimes Muslims would have to fight; at other times they could live in peace. But they had embarked on the project of redeeming history as well as the individual, to make what *ought* to happen a living reality in the world. To the present day, Muslims have taken this vocation very seriously.

The grudging submission of Taif showed that many of the Arabs were reluctant to embrace the new order. The Bedouin allies had only a superficial loyalty to Muhammad, yet he had a core of dedicated Muslims who may not always have understood fully what he was trying to do yet who would later show that they had grasped the essential message. Abu Bakr, Umar, and Uthman ibn Affan had become members of their Prophet's family by marriage and this had reaffirmed their spiritual kinship with him. They understood that religion was a priority: first the Arabs had to reform themselves by practicing the "pillars" of Islam which taught them to put God at the center of their lives and look after the vulnerable members of society.

The fourth close disciple of Muhammad was his ward Ali, who was younger than the others and sometimes impatient of the older men. But by 632 he was one of the only members of Muhammad's immediate household left. Umm Kulthum had died during the expedition to Tabuk and this meant that Fatimah (Ali's wife) was the only surviving child of Khadijaj. Muhammad was devoted to Ali's two sons, Hasan and Husayn. He used to let them climb on his back and ride him like a horse. But Muhammad also had a new baby son by his concubine Maryam the Egyptian. He used to love carrying little Ibrahim around Medina. Aisha, however, refused to be impressed. "Don't you think he is like me?" he would ask. "I see no likeness," retorted Aisha. "Look how plump he is and see his beautiful complexion!" enthused the Prophet. "Anyone fed on sheep's milk is bound to be plump and fair," Aisha replied tartly, probably annoyed that special milk was delivered to Ibrahim's foster-mother every day. Despite this care, the baby fell ill at the beginning of 632 and it was clear that he would not recover. Muhammad was with his son when he died and, weeping bitterly, took him into his arms at the last moment. He comforted himself that it would not be long before they were reunited.

Muhammad became increasingly conscious of his approaching death during the tenth yeak after the *hijra*. He always liked to make a retreat during Ramadan if he was able to spend it in Medina and this year he asked his Companions to make a longer retreat than usual, confiding to Fatimah that he thought his time had come. So in the Dhu al-Hijja, the traditional month for the *hajj*, Muhammad announced that he would lead the pilgrimage himself that year. It would be the first time that these ancient rites around the Kabah and the shrines around Mount Arafat had been performed only by the worshippers of the One God, and Muhammad was determined to root his new religion into the sacred traditions of the Arabs. He set out at the end of February 632 with all his wives and a huge crowd of pilgrims, arriving outside Mecca on 5 Dhu al-Hijja, 3 March. He began to utter the ancient cry of the pilgrims: "Here I am at your service, O God." Then he began to lead them through the old pagan rituals, so dear to the hearts of the Arabs, giving them a new significance at the same time as he was assuring an essential and creative continuity with the past.

Every Muslim should try to make the *hajj* at least once in a lifetime, provided that his or her circumstances permit. To an outsider these rites seem bizarre — as do any alien religious or social rituals — but they are still able to inspire an intense religious experience and Muslims often find that the *hajj* is the climax of their spiritual lives, both as individuals and as members of the *ummah.* The communal and personal aspects of Islamic spirituality are perfectly enshrined in the rites and practices of the *hajj.* Today many of the thousands of pilgrims who assemble each year in Mecca to make the pilgrimage together are not Arabs, but they have been able to make these ancient Arabian rituals their own. As they converge on the Kabah, clad in the traditional pilgrim dress that obliterates all distinctions of race or class, they feel that they have been liberated from the egotistic limitations of their daily lives and have been caught up into a community that has one focus and one orientation. The circumambulations around the Kabah recently inspired the late Iranian philosopher Ali Shariati:

> *As you circumambulate and move closer to the Ka'aba, you feel like a small stream merging with a big river. Carried by a wave you lose touch with the ground. Suddenly, you are floating, carried on by the flood. As you approach the centre, the pressure of the crowd squeezes you so hard that you are given a new life. You are now part of the People; you are now a Man, alive and eternal. . . . The Ka'aba is the world's sun whose face attracts you into its orbit. You have become part of this universal system. Circumambulating around Allah, you will soon forget yourself. . . . You have been transformed into a particle that is gradually melting and disappearing. This is absolute love at its peak.*

Jews and Christians have also emphasized the spirituality of the community: St Paul's extended image of the Body of Christ also argues that the unity of the Church and the communion of its members is a revelation of the highest love. The *hajj* offers each individual Muslim the experience of personal integration in the context of the *ummah*, with God at its center.

In one sense the *hajj* gives Muslims an image of the ideal

community, in attitude and orientation. In most religions, peace and harmony are important pilgrimage themes and once the pilgrims have entered the Sanctuary all violence of any kind is forbidden: pilgrims may not even kill an insect or speak an impatient word. Hence the outrage throughout the Muslim world when the *hajj* of 1987 was violated by Iranian pilgrims who instigated a riot in which 402 people were killed and 649 injured.

The Qur'an constantly speaks of the Return to God which all creatures must inevitably make, and the *hajj* is a powerful expression of the Muslims' voluntary journey back to God, from whence they came. The pilgrim cry, which they all shout in unison, reminds them that as individuals and as *ummah* they have dedicated themselves wholly to God's service and for the days of the *hajj* they are able to live this commitment more intensely than usual, turning their back on all other concerns: When Muhammad had led his pilgrim body of Emigrants, Helpers, and Bedouin to the Kabah in 632 they must all have felt that this was a return journey in a profound sense. Most pilgrimages to holy places are seen as some kind of approach to the roots of one's being or to the beginning of the world, and the Emigrants must have felt a special sense of homecoming. But Muhammad was reminding all the Arabs that they were returning to their roots because Abraham and Ishmael, the fathers of the Arabs, were said to have built the shrine. Today also Muslims experience a sense of returning to the roots of their Muslim identity. They naturally remember Muhammad, but the rites of the pilgrimage are primarily designed to recall Abraham and Ishmael, the fathers of all true believers. Thus when they run seven times between Safa and Marwah, they remember how Hagar ran frantically backward and forward in search of water for the little Ishmael, after Abraham had left them in the desert. Later they go even further back to their common origins when they stand on the slopes of Mount Arafat, sixteen miles outside Mecca, and recall the original covenant God made with Adam, the first prophet and founder of the human race. At Mina they throw stones at the three pillars as a reminder of the constant struggle with temptation that the *jihad* in God's service requires. Then they sacrifice a sheep or a goat in memory of Abraham's animal sacrifice after he had offered his own son to God. All over the world, Muslims who have not made the *hajj* that year perform this rite at the appointed time, so that the whole *ummah* demonstrates its readiness to sacrifice everything, even the things that are dearest to them, in God's service.

Today the mosque of Namira stands near Mount Arafat on the spot where Muhammad is believed to have preached his Farewell Sermon to the pilgrims of 632. He reminded them to deal justly with one another, to treat women as kindly as possible, and to abandon all the blood-feuds for offences committed in the pagan period. The *ummah* was one: "Know that every Muslim is a Muslim's brother, and that the Muslims are brethren. It is only lawful to take from a brother what he gives you willingly, so wrong not yourselves. O God, have I not told you?" This commandment may sound minimal compared with the Sermon on the Mount or St Paul's hymn to charity, but Muhammad was a realist and knew that what he was asking was revolutionary. Instead of being members of distinct tribes, the Arab Muslims were now one community, just as the God of the Kabah was One.

When he returned to Medina after the Farewell Pilgrimage, Muhammad began to experience incapacitating headaches. Aisha remembered that one day she was lying in her apartment with a headache herself. "O my head!" she moaned when Muhammad came in. "Nay, Aisha," he replied, "it is O *my* head." But at this stage he was still able to tease her gently. How would Aisha like to die before he did? It would give him the chance to take her into his arms at the graveside and give her a lovely funeral. Aisha replied with her usual asperity: after the funeral he would go straight off to sleep with one of his other wives! "Nay, Aisha," Muhammad said as he left the apartment, "it is O *my* head."

The pain got worse and he also seems to have suffered from fainting fits, but he never retired permanently to bed. He would often wrap a cloth round his aching temples and go to the mosque to lead the prayers or to address the people. But one morning he seemed to pray for a specially long time in honour of the Muslims who had died at Uhud and added: "God has given one of his servants the choice between this world and that which is with God and he has chosen the latter." But the only person who seems to have understood this reference to Muhammad's death was Abu Bakr, who began to weep bitterly. "Gently, gently, Abu Bakr," Muhammad said tenderly. But eventually the Prophet collapsed in Maymunah's hut. His wives hung lovingly over him and noticed that he kept asking: "Where shall I be tomorrow? Where shall I be tomorrow?" Realizing that he wanted to know when he could be with Aisha, they unanimously agreed that he should be moved to her hut and be nursed there.

Muhammad lay there quietly with his head in Aisha's lap, but people seemed to have considered it a mere temporary indisposition, because he still attended the public prayers in the mosque. The *ummah* appears to have found the idea of his death so unbearable and frightening that it failed to read the signs correctly, though Abu Bakr warned Aisha that Muhammad was not long for this world. What he had achieved in Arabia was unique and unprecedented, so life without him in the new order seemed inconceivable. People snatched at any straw of hope, as when Muhammad staggered to the mosque one day to reassure them that Usamah, Zayd's young son, was quite able and experienced enough to lead an expedition to the north. When he got too ill, he asked Abu Bakr to lead the prayers for him, and even Aisha seems to have resisted this decision. Eventually Muhammad had to speak to them sharply to get them to obey him. Aisha later said that she had objected not because she felt that her father was unworthy of this honour, but because she was afraid that people would hate him for doing Muhammad's job. But still Muhammad gave them grounds for hope, because he would sometimes attend the prayers even though he was too ill to recite them himself, sitting quietly beside Abu Bakr.

On 12 Rabi (8 June 632) Abu Bakr noticed during prayers that the attention of the people was wavering and that they were looking toward the entrance of the mosque. He knew at once that Muhammad must have come in because nothing else would have distracted the congregation in this way. Muhammad looked much better; indeed, somebody said that they had never seen him looking so radiant, and a wave of joy and relief filled the mosque. Abu Bakr instantly made ready to stand down, but Muhammad put his hands on his shoulders and pushed him gently back to the head of the congregation and sat down beside him until the service was over: Afterward he went back to Aisha's hut and lay quietly with his head in her lap. He seemed so much better that Abu Bakr asked leave to visit a wife he had recently married, who still lived on the other side of Medina. During the afternoon, Ali and Abbas both looked in and spread the good news that the Prophet seemed to be on the mend, and when Abd al-Rahman dropped in to visit, Muhammad noticed that he was holding a toothpick and made it clear that he wanted to use it. Aisha softened it for him and noticed that he used the implement more vigorously than ever before. But not long afterward Aisha felt that he was lying more heavily in her lap and that he seemed to be losing consciousness. Still she did not realize what was happening. As she said later, "It was due to my ignorance and extreme youth that the apostle died in my arms." She heard him murmur the words, "Nay, the most Exalted Companion in paradise," and then discovered that he had gone. Carefully she laid his head on the pillow and began to beat her breast, slap her face, and cry aloud in the time-honoured Arab way.

When the people heard the women lamenting the dead, they hurried ashen-faced to the mosque. The news travelled quickly through the oasis and Abu Bakr hurried back to the "city." He took one look at Muhammad, kissed his face, and bade him farewell. Then he went into the mosque, where he found Umar addressing the crowds. Umar absolutely refused to believe that Muhammad was dead: his soul had just left his body temporarily, he argued, and he would certainly return to his people. He would be the last of them all to die. There must have been a hysterical note in Umar's compulsive harangue, because Abu Bakr murmured, "Gently, Umar," but Umar could not stop talking. All that Abu Bakr could do was to step forward quietly, and the expression on his face and his composure must have impressed the people, because they gradually stopped listening to Umar's tirade and clustered round him.

Abu Bakr reminded them that Muhammad had dedicated his whole life to preaching the unity of God. The Qur'an had warned them incessantly that they must not give to any mere creature the honour due to God alone. Constantly Muhammad had warned them against honoring him in the same way as the Christians honored Jesus; he was only a mere mortal like themselves. To refuse to admit that Muhammad had died, therefore, was to deny the basic truth about Muhammad. But as long as the Muslims remained true to the belief that God alone was worthy of worship, Muhammad would live on. "O men, if anyone worships Muhammad, Muhammad is dead," he ended eloquently. "If anyone worships God, God is alive, immortal." Finally, he quoted the verse that had been revealed to Muhammad after the battle of Uhud, when so many of the Muslims had been overwhelmed by the rumour that the Prophet had been killed:

> *Muhammad is naught but a Messenger; Messengers*
> *have passed away before him. Why, if he should die*
> *or is slain, will you turn upon your heels?*
> *If any man should turn about on his heels, he will*
> *not harm God in any way; and God will recompense*
> *the thankful.*

These verses made such an impression on the people that it was as though they had never heard them before. Umar was completely devastated: "By God, when I heard Abu Bakr recite those words I was dumbfounded, so that my legs would not bear me and I fell to the ground knowing that the apostle was indeed dead."

The shock of Muhammad's death was one of the gravest crises that the Muslim community had ever had to face. Until this moment, Muhammad had guided their every step, so how would they continue without him? Were they supposed to continue? Some of the Bedouin tribes, whose commitment had been merely political, broke away from the *ummah* thinking that the death of Muhammad had abrogated their pact. There was a real danger that Arabia would lapse into its old tribal divisions. Some of the more committed Muslims may also have wondered whether Muhammad's death meant the end of the Muhammadan venture, and those who wanted to appoint a successor split immediately into rival camps; these probably reflected the divisions in the community that had worried Muhammad during his last years.

Most of the Emigrants supported the claim of Abu Bakr, who had been Muhammad's close friend from the very beginning of his mission. Umar also supported this claim. But the Helpers naturally wanted Sa'd ibn Ubadah, one of their own number, to be the first Caliph or Representative of Muhammad; and, the Prophet's immediate family believed that he would have wanted Ali to succeed him. Abd Bakr eventually carried the day, largely because his calm grasp of the crisis had impressed the whole *ummah*. After he had been elected, Abu Bakr addressed the community, laying down the principles that should henceforth apply to all Muslim rulers:

I have been given authority over you but I am not the best of you. If I do well, help me, and if I do ill, then put me right. Truth consists in loyalty and falsehood in treachery. The weak among you shall be strong in my eyes until I secure his right if God will; and the strong among you shall be weak in my eyes until I wrest the right from him. If a people refrain from fighting in the way of God, God will smite them with disgrace. Wickedness is never widespread in a people but God brings calamity upon them all. Obey me as long as I obey God and His apostle, and if I disobey them you owe me no obedience. Arise to prayer. God have mercy on you.

At first Ali held aloof from Abu Bakr, but later he made his submission. Abu Bakr died after only two years and was succeeded by Umar, then by Uthman; finally in 656 Ali became the Fourth Caliph. They were known as the *rashidun*, the Rightly Guided caliphs, because they governed in accordance with Muhammad's principles. Ali in particular emphasized that a Muslim ruler must not be tyrannical. He was, under God, on a par with his subjects and must take care to lighten the burden of the poor and destitute. That is the only way for a regime to survive:

> *So if your subjects complain of burden, of blight, of the cutting off of irrigation water, of lack of rain, or of the transformation of the earth through its being inundated by a flood or ruined by drought, lighten their burden to the extent you wish your affair to be rectified. And let not anything by which you have lightened their burden weigh heavily against you, for it is a store which they will return to you by bringing about prosperity in your land and establishing your rule. . . . Truly the destruction of the earth only results from the destitution of its inhabitants, and its inhabitants become destitute only when rulers concern themselves with amassing wealth, when they have misgivings about the endurance of their own rule and when they profit little from warning examples.*

A ruler must not separate himself from his people in splendid isolation. He must share their burdens, be available to listen to their problems, and take their advice.

Not all Muslim rulers have lived up to these high standards. Indeed, the fact that Muslims look back to the period of the *rashidun* as a Golden Age shows that later caliphs and sultans did not adhere with the same passion to the principles of egalitarianism and justice. But sometimes a Muslim would be able to build an empire by showing that he was living and ruling by these principles. As we have seen, at the time of the Crusades both Nur ad-Din and Saladin went out of their way to give to the poor, reform taxation on Islamic lines, and to be accessible to the people. In our own day we have seen Muslims bringing down rulers like the Shah of Iran and President Sadat of Egypt because their governments were unIslamic. The ideals that had inspired Muhammad and the *rashidun* have continued to be a powerful force in Muslim society, and a ruler ignores them at his peril.

Christianity has had a passion for theological discussion, and the major divisions in Christendom have been brought about by doctrinal disputes. Like Judaism, Islam has no similar concept of theological "heresy." Its most formative disputes and most crucial divisions have been caused by political differences. The unity of the *umma*, which had been so important to Muhammad, was broken when a split developed between the main body of the Muslims, known as the Sunnah, and the *Shiah-i Ali*, the party of Ali, who believed that only one of Ali's descendants should govern the *ummah*. As a minority party, the Shiah developed a piety of protest which was typified by Muhammad's grandson Husayn, who had refused to accept the Ummayad caliphate and was cruelly killed with his small band of companions at the battle of Kerbala by the Caliph Yazid. The intense disputes between the various Shiite and Sunni groups about who should lead the Muslim community and what kind of society it should be have been as formative and important as the great Christological debates in Christianity. This in itself shows that the political reality of the *ummah* has been a sacred value in Islam. There are no doctrinal differences between Shiites and Sunnis, though each has developed a distinctive type of piety. We have seen that the Qur'an regards such theological divisions as disedifying and futile. But politics has been important in Islam not simply because Muslim rulers have used it to further their own political power, but because the Islamic venture has been a dynamic attempt to redeem history from the disintegration and chaos that must ensue if society is not governed by just and equitable laws. The political effort is not extrinsic to a Muslim's personal spiritual life, but the *ummah* is of sacramental importance. It could be considered to hold rather the same place as a particular theological option (Catholic, Protestant, Methodist, Baptist) has in the spiritual lives of each Christian.

After Muhammad's death, the continuing success of the Muslim venture vindicated the political effort, and seemed to demonstrate that if a society was reorganized according to God's will it would prevail. The Arab armies had quickly established an empire which spread from the Himalayas to the Pyrenees. Originally this was inspired less by the Qur'an than by Arab imperialism. There was no attempt to force the new religion on their new subjects. Islam continued to be seen as the religion of the Arabs, just as Judaism was the religion of the sons of Israel; there was even a brief period in about 700 when conversions were forbidden by law. But about a hundred years after Muhammad's death the caliphs did begin to encourage conversions and people began to flock into Islam, proving that the Qur'an answered a religious need for the people of the Middle East and North Africa. It was able to assimilate the wisdom of other ancient cultures and quickly established its own distinctive cultural tradition. Islam was not a threatening divisive force but proved able to integrate society.

Muslim jurists developed a theology of the *jihad* to meet the new conditions. They taught that, because there was only one God, the whole world should be united in one polity and it was the duty of all Muslims to engage in a continued struggle to make the world accept the divine principles and create a just society. The *umma*, the House of Islam, was the sacred area where the will of God had been imposed; the rest of the world, the House of War, was the profane area which should be made to surrender to God's rule. Until this had been achieved, Islam must engage in a perpetual warlike effort. But this martial theology was laid aside in practice and became a dead letter once it was clear that the Islamic empire had reached the limits of its expansion about a hundred years after Muhammad's death, and Muslims developed normal diplomatic and economic links with their neighbors in the House of War. There was no pressure on Jews, Christians, or Zoroastrians to convert to Islam; Muslims continued to uphold the old religious pluralism of the

Middle East and learned to coexist with members of other religions, which, according to the Qur'an, were perfectly valid earlier revelations.

The rise and fall of the various dynasties and empires, the further expansion of Islam into India and Indonesia, and the development of new and different moods and ways of interpreting the Qur'an can all be seen as a continuation of the Islamic dialogue with history. Muslims continued to respond creatively to the challenge of modernity until relatively recently. They were able to respond to catastrophes like the Mongol devastations in the thirteenth century and rise again to new power and achievement. The Qur'an continued to give people of many different races and times the means of surmounting disaster and finding the courage to carry on. Sometimes the new effort would be a specifically spiritual response. Thus the great mystic Jalaluddin Rumi produced the *Mathnawi*, which is perhaps the greatest classic of the Sufi tradition, a few years after the destruction of Baghdad, the capital of the Islamic empire, by the Mongol hordes. The Sufis show how deeply the political and social element of Islam affects Muslim spirituality. Devotion to the *ummah* has always been an important component of the mystic vocation. As Louis Massignon, the great expert on Sufi mysticism, has explained: "The mystic call is as a rule the result of an inner rebellion of the conscience against social injustices, not only those of others but primarily and particularly against one's own faults: with a desire intensified by inner purification to find God at any price." The Sufi vocation is primarily ascetic: they engage in a campaign of spiritual effort which they call the "greater *jihad*' (as opposed to the "lesser *jihad*" of physical combat). To the present day, however, an intense spirituality modulates easily into political activism in the Muslim world. Sufis have been in the forefront of many reform movements or in the van of opposition to anything that threatens the *ummah*, whether this is an external enemy like the Mongol army or a ruler who is failing to govern in accordance with Islamic principles. Sufis do not withdraw from the world like Christian monks: the world is the theater of their campaign to find God.

This spirituality is based on the example of the Prophet himself, who did not retire from the world but worked incessantly to reorganize his society. Instead of waiting for utopia or a messianic fulfillment, Muhammad had tried to create his own ideal society himself at Medina. From the first, Muslims modelled themselves on the pattern of his own life: his hijra had been a prelude to a political campaign and from the time of the Kharaji sect, who broke away from the main *ummah* during the seventh century, to the group known as the *takfir wa'l hijra* in Sadat's Egypt, Muslims who want to reform the *ummah* have withdrawn from what they see as a corrupt society and waged war against the establishment. Abu Bakr had told Muslims that it was their duty to depose him if he failed to rule correctly, and Muslims take this very seriously. The welfare of the *ummah* is so integral to their spiritual lives that they do not regard a retreat from the world as the highest spiritual duty. They must engage in the *jihad*, not in a spirit of atavistic or fanatical rage, but in a spirit of self-sacrifice, courage, and endurance. As the late Ali Shariati explained to the people of Iran during the rule of the Shah, death to self was not the solitary discipline of monasticism, but the dedicated struggle to defend the people of God, even if this meant suffering and death:

> . . . *Your monasticism is not in a monastery, but in society; self-sacrifice, sincerity, self-negation, bearing bondages, deprivations, tortures, anguishes and accepting dangers in the arenas of clashes and for the sake of the people that you reach God. The Prophet has said, "Every religion has a kind of monasticism and the monasticism of my religion is the 'jihad.'"*

Each religion has its own special emphasis, but this social concern is important to the spirituality of all three monotheistic traditions. If Christians find the Muslims' conception of their essentially political vocation abstruse theological formulations of ineffable truths seem equally bizarre to Muslims and Jews.

One of the chief ways in which Muslims have built this deep sense of brotherhood and solidarity has been through devotion to the Prophet Muhammad. Muslims have continued to emphasize that Muhammad is merely an ordinary man like themselves, but over the centuries they have added a qualification. Yes, Muhammad is a man like other men, but he is "like a precious gem among stones." Where ordinary stones are opaque and heavy, a, jewel is translucent, shot through with the transfiguring element of light. Muhammad's life has become a "sign" like the other signs that the Qur'an urges Muslims to see in the natural world. His prophetic career was a symbol, a theophany, which not only shows God's activity in the world, but illustrates the perfect human surrender to God. The development of the ideal of Muhammadan sanctity has been an imaginative attempt; to penetrate the meaning of his life and apply it to the circumstances of daily life. Christians also developed an image of Jesus the man, who is also the Logos, the blueprint of God's plan for creation. Unlike the devotion to Jesus, however, the Muslim devotion to Muhammad is not to the personal, historical character but to a symbol or sacrament which, like the symbolism of great art, illuminates life and gives it a new meaning by pointing to another dimension of reality beyond itself.

Christians do not have anything equivalent to either the Torah or the *shari'a* and tend to think that this minute observance must be burdensome and prohibitive. It is a type of spirituality that has been given a very bad press in the New Testament, where Paul inveighs against the Torah as part of his polemic against the Jewish Christians who wanted to keep the religion of Jesus a strict sect of Judaism. But neither Muslims nor Jews regard the Law as a burden. Muslims see the *sunnah* as a type of sacrament: they help them to develop that God-consciousness prescribed by the Qur'an in the interstices of their daily lives. By modelling themselves as closely as possible on the

Prophet, they are not only internalizing him at a very deep level but they are also trying to cultivate the inner attitude of Muhammad and draw close to the God that they find in the depths of their beings. Some of the hadith are actually sayings of God Himself which have been put on to the lips of the Prophet. These *hadith qudsi*, sacred traditions, emphasize that God is not a metaphysical Being "out there" but is in some sense mysteriously identified with the ground of their being. This famous tradition lists the stages whereby one apprehends this inner presence: you must begin by observing the commandments and then progress to voluntary acts of piety:

> *My servant draws near to me by means of nothing dearer to me than that which I have established as a duty for him. And my servant continues drawing nearer to me through supererogatory acts until I love him: and when I love him, I become his ear through which he hears, his eye with which he sees, his hand with which he grasps, and his foot with which he walks.*

The external actions, like the physical elements of the Christian sacraments, are the outward signs of this inward grace and must be observed and guarded with reverence. This concern means that Muslims all over the world share a particular lifestyle and whatever their other differences have acquired a very clear Muslim identity which instantly draws them together. The way they pray or wash, their table manners or personal hygiene follow a common, distinctive pattern. Muslims from China, Indonesia, and the various parts of the Middle East will for example perform the prostrations of *salat* in exactly the same way, taking precisely the same number of seconds.

Muslims who revere Muhammad in this symbolic manner will not be particularly interested in the quest for the historical Muhammad, any more than Christians who have made a similar imaginative commitment to Christ will be disturbed by current research into Jesus' mundane life. But the Salman Rushdie affair has shown that what is perceived as an attack on the Prophet has violated a sacred area of the Muslim psyche throughout the world. It was always a capital offence in the Islamic empire to denigrate Muhammad or his religion, but it has particular power to wound Muslims today because of the humiliation of the *ummah* at the hands of the Western world. During the eighteenth century, the Islamic empire began to decline, and this time it found it particularly difficult to rise again to new life. Its decline and fall coincided with the rise of the West with a type of society which had never been achieved in the world before and which was, therefore, difficult to combat. This has not just been a political humiliation but has touched the core of the Muslim identity. If Islam is, for the first time in its history, no longer successful how can its claims be true? The Qur'anic social prescriptions had hitherto proved infallible, but if Muslim society fell apart even though the *umma* was doing its best to implement the divine plan something had gone radically wrong with Islamic history.

Again, it must be emphasized that the success of the

ummah has a central and quasi-sacramental importance in the personal religious life of each Muslim. It has produced a religious crisis in the Islamic world similar in gravity to that experienced in Europe when the scientific discoveries of Lyell and Darwin seemed to undermine the foundations of the Christian faith. The despair of a poem like Matthew Arnold's "Dover Beach" and the desolation of Alfred Lord Tennyson's *In Memoriam* may give us some insight into the dread and dismay that some Muslims are experiencing today. How to explain the apparent impotence of Islam before the West and its triumphant secularism? The essence of the social teaching of the Qur'an had been that a society founded on the right principles could not fail, because it was in harmony with the way things ought to be. The success of the *ummah* under Muhammad and his successors had proved that such a society worked; its success had sacramental value. Christianity has usually been at its best during times of adversity; Islam has the opposite problem.

When we consider the Western view of Muhammad, we look briefly at the rage and despair of the martyrs of Cordova in the ninth century. In the Islamic world today, many people are turning to a new radical form of Islam that is sometimes fuelled by a similar dread. Like the Cordovans, many Muslims are trying to discover a new identity and to return to their own roots. This has been a theme in the so-called fundamentalist movements in recent years. Not only have Muslims felt humiliated and degraded before the external power of the West, but they have felt disoriented and lost because their own traditions seem to be swamped by the dominant Western culture. The secularism which we have cultivated carefully in the West has sprung from our own traditions, but in the Islamic countries it seems alien and foreign — of negative rather than positive import. A generation of people has grown up in the Islamic world at home neither in the East nor in the West, and the answer that many people have found has been a return to their Islamic roots. Just as Muhammad sought to embed his religion in the sacred traditions of Arabia when he redefined the meaning of the *hajj*, radical Muslims have sought to root themselves more securely in their Islamic past.

Another theme of the new fundamentalism has been an attempt to get Islamic history back on the right tack and to make the *ummah* effective and strong once again. The Iranian revolution was not just an atavistic return to the past, but was an attempt to impose decent values in Iran again. The ideal of the Islamic state in Pakistan and Iran roused deep hopes that seemed strange to Westerners, who have developed a secular ideal of government, but both represented a profound religious and cultural imperative and a chance to make Islam work effectively once more. The history of both efforts shows how problematic and fraught with insuperable difficulties such an attempt to incarnate God's Word is proving to be in the twentieth century. Whereas in the past Muslims were able to rise again after their various disasters and crises — the death of the Prophet, the Mongol devastations and so forth — this time it is proving to be a great deal harder, and a certain frantic despair has entered the religion.

The phenomenon of Islamic fundamentalism is complex; it has sprung from great pain and enshrines a desperate need on the part of many Muslim people to take their destiny into their own hands again, in the time-honored Islamic way. Some of these new radical forms of Islam do not seem healthy, but seem full of the insecurity and dismay that fuelled the suicidal cult of the martyrs of Cordova, who were fired by many of the same needs and fears. We have seen that at the time of the Suez crisis the Islamic scholar Wilfred Cantwell Smith wrote that a healthy and functioning Islam was crucial because it had helped Muslim people to cultivate decent values and ideals which we in the West also share because they spring from a common tradition. Since Suez, the West has alienated the people of the Middle East even more and has discredited the liberal secularism that it is so anxious to spread. We in the West have never been able to cope with Islam: our ideas of it have been crude and dismissive and today we seem to belie our own avowed commitment to tolerance and compassion by our contempt for the pain and inchoate distress in the Muslim world. Islam is not, going to disappear or wither away; it would have been better if it had remained healthy and strong. We can only hope that it is not too late.

People in the Islamic world have many problems in the late twentieth century, but, as Wilfred Cantwell Smith pointed out in 1956, the West also has a problem. The fundamental weakness of both Western civilization and Christianity in the modern world:

is their inability to recognize that they share the planet not with inferiors but with equals. Unless Western civilisation intellectually and socially, politically and economically, and the Christian church theologically, can learn to treat other men with fundamental respect, these two in their turn will have failed to come to terms with the actualities of the twentieth century. The problems raised in this are, of course, as profound as anything that we have touched on for Islam.

The reality is that Islam and the West share a common tradition. From the time of the Prophet Muhammad, Muslims have recognized this, but the West cannot accept it. Today some Muslims are beginning to turn against the cultures of the People of the Book, which have humiliated and despised them. They have even begun to Islamize their new hatred. The beloved figure of the Prophet Muhammad became central to one of the latest clashes between Islam and the West during the Salmon Rushdie affair. If Muslims need to understand our Western traditions and institutions more thoroughly today, we in the West need to divest ourselves of some of our old prejudice. Perhaps one place to start is with the figure of Muhammad: a complex, passionate man who sometimes did things that it is difficult for us to accept, but who had genius of a profound order and founded a religion and a cultural tradition that was not based on the sword — despite the Western myth — and whose name "Islam" signifies peace and reconciliation.

RUMI

c. 1207–1273

Jalaluddin Rumi, Persian lyric poet and mystic, was born in Balkh, modern Afghanistan. He settled at Iconium (Konya) in 1226 and founded a sect that, after his death, was known in the West as the Whirling Dervishes. He wrote a great deal of lyrical poetry, including a long epic on Sufi mystical doctrine called Masnavi-ye Manavi *("Spiritual Couplets")*

After meeting and embarking on a deep friendship with a wandering dervish — holy man — named Shams ad-Din (Sun of Religion), Rumi's disciples and family became jealous and Shams was murdered. To cope with the grief of losing his beloved friend, Rumi turned to writing poetry. His mystical poems — about 30,000 verses and a large number of ruba'iyat ("quatrains") — reflect the different stages of his love and grieving for Sham.

Rumi died at sunset on December 17, 1273. His tomb in Konya is still visited by thousands each month.

PREFACE

by Huston Smith

T HRICE IN FOURTEEN CENTURIES of deeply
troubled political relationships, the West has
opened its heart to Islam and been touched by
its soul.

First there was *The Ruba'iyat of Omar Khayyam*,
which, in Edward FitzGerald's translation, created something of a cult in the West. Its best-known stanza still
rings in our ears:

A book of Verse underneath the Bough,
A jug of Wine, a Loaf of bread — And Thou
Beside me singing in the Wilderness —
O, Wilderness were Paradise enow!

Then came T. E. Lawrence, whose adventures gave rise to
the motion picture extravaganza *Lawrence of Arabia*,
based on his autobiographical *The Seven Pillars of*

Wisdom. And now we have Jalaluddin Rumi, who, eight centuries after his death, has been for almost a decade the best-selling poet in America. It is not difficult to account for these romances, which are reminiscent of the West's romance with Zen following World War II. In the *Ruba'iyat*, poetry holds the key, for it speaks a universal language. In Lawrence's case the common objective of overthrowing the Ottoman Empire brought England and Arabia together for a time. As for Rumi, poetry again enters, but this time with mysticism added. This is a winning combination, for poetry and mysticism are both universal languages of the human soul and nowhere do they reenforce each other more than in the life and legacy of Jalaluddin Rumi. His name literally means Majesty of Religion (*jalal*, majesty; *din*, religion).

Sufism, which Westerners have almost come to equate with Rumi, is in fact the mystical dimension of Islam as a whole. Its name derives primarily from the coarse woolen garments its early adherents wore, and (though the adjective sounds odd here) it is not misleading to think of the Sufis as *impatient* Muslims. Every upright Muslim expects to see God after death, but the Sufis want Allah now, moment by moment at the very center of their lives. This takes doing, and those who were willing to make the effort attracted followers who (recognizing their attainments) considered them their *shaikhs*, or masters, and formed Sufi Orders around them. Rumi's father was such a shaikh in Konya, now in Turkey, and when he died his son succeeded him. However, Rumi's own creativity and spiritual attainment proved to be too great to fit the existing mold, and gave rise to a new lineage, the Mevlevi Order. The word *mevlevi* means "our lord," the title that Rumi's followers addressed him by, and etymologists have also conjectured that it carries traces of the word *tevellu,* which appears in a Qur'anic dictum Sufis make much of, "Wheresoe'er one turns, there is the face of Allah." In any case, the Order became famous for the sacred dance that was its central practice. . . . Rumi often found himself drawn to circle a pillar in his mosque; with one hand cupped around the pillar, he would lean back from it while he gyrated. The symbolism of planets circling their sun may have contributed to the fact that the movement elevated him and caused torrents of ecstatic poetry to pour from his lips. His disciples came to mimic this movement when they gathered for their ritual meetings. In their case they circled not a pillar, but (for the first half of the dance) a red sheepskin in the center of the hall representing Rumi's teacher, the wandering *dervish* Shams of Tabriz, and for the second half, their Rumi himself when he entered the hall. From this practice, the *mevlevis* came to be known as Whirling Dervishes, *darvish* being the Persian word for "poor in spirit," or humility. . . . The Mevlevi Order acquired such strength that it came to span the two main branches of Islam: its larger, "traditional" Sunni branch (*sunnah* means traditional), and the Shiite branch, which centers in what was formerly Persia. The word *shia* literally means "partisan," and refers here to the Partisans of Ali, Muhammad's son-in-law, whom Shiites believe should have been named Muhammad's successor but was unfairly passed over. In the course of time the Mevlevi dance took on the colorations of its respective hosts and the objective of the dance came to differ somewhat according to which branch of Islam it is performed in. In Shiism (the more emotionally inclined of the two sects) the whirling of the ritual dance aims to induce God-intoxicated ecstasy, whereas among Sunnis it serves more as the means for encircling and approaching the divine lover who is Allah himself.

A second distinctive feature of the Mevlevi Order is its emphasis on music. Other orders tend to be suspicious of music, fearing the emotionalism it can easily induce, but the Mevlevis regard it as an approach to God. Novices are required to learn a ritually approved instrument or join a chorus, and these requirements made the Mevlevi Order something like a school of Music for the Ottoman Empire. As might be expected, calligraphy figures somewhere on most of these pages. Personally, I have never been able to decide whether Chinese or Islamic calligraphy is more beautiful, and I am glad that I cannot, because it allows me to honor both equally. Beyond its calligraphy, the blending of organic and geometric forms is a distinctive feature of Islamic art.

Geometry, the symbol and evidence of order in the universe, appears in straightforward polygonal forms, but as often as not it is hidden in the foliage of a leafy arabesque, a word that openly announces its Arabic origin. Rhythmically repeated patterns remind us of infinity and a world of unity beyond forms. Conveying this message of unity is the ultimate function of Islamic art, and the selections in this volume realize that purpose impressively. The text [here] uses primarily the six books of the *Mathnawi* — one of the two enormous compendia of Rumi's poems and teaching tales — as its organizer. The verses of the *Mathnawi* represent a highly accomplished spiritualization of Sufism while remaining completely true to Islamic orthodoxy. Their persistent themes are the longing for the eternal, the reuniting with Allah, enlightenment through love, and the merging of one's self with the universal spirit of the world. To add one of my favorite passages, it reads:

> *The senses and thoughts are like weeds on the clear water's surface.*
> *The hand of the heart sweeps the weeds aside: then the water is revealed to the heart.*
> *Unless Allah loose the hand of the heart, the weeds on our water are increased by worldly desires.*
> *When piety has chained the hands of desire, Allah looses the hands of the heart.*

We have it from Plotinus that to behold the beautiful is to become beautiful. If he was right, this wonderfully conceived and executed volume should help the project along.

RUMI

by Coleman Barks

THE THIRTEENTH CENTURY in the Near East
was a time of tremendous political turmoil and
war: the Christian military expeditions called
crusades continued to set out from the European west
across the Anatolian peninsula, and from the east the
inexorable Mongol armies rode down from the Asian
steppes.

It was also a time of brilliant mystical awareness,
when the lives of three of the world's great lovers of God's
presence in humanity, and in existence itself, overlapped:
Francis of Assisi (c. 1182–1226) at the beginning of the century, Meister Eckhart (c. 1260–1328) at the end; and
Jelaluddin Rumi (1207–73) at the center. They were all
magnificently surrendered souls, and wonderful creators
with language.

Rumi was born near the city of Balkh, in what is now
Afghanistan, then the eastern edge of the Persian empire,

on September 30, 1207. He was the descendant of a long line of Islamic jurists, theologians, and mystics. His father, Bahauddin Walad, wrote an intimate spiritual diary, the *Ma'arif* ("Love Notes of Self to Soul"), which Rumi treasured.

When Rumi was still a young man, his family fled from Balkh just ahead of the invading armies of Genghis Khan, who was extending his Mongol empire through Persia and would eventually reach all the way to the Adriatic Sea. Rumi and his family traveled to Damascus and on to Nishapur, where they met the poet and teacher Fariduddin Attar, who recognized the teenaged boy Rumi as a great spirit. He is reported to have said, as he saw Bahauddin walking toward him with the young Rumi a little behind, "Here comes a sea, followed by an ocean!" To honor this insight, Attar gave Rumi his book, the *Ilahinama* ("The Book of God").

Rumi's family eventually settled in Konya, in south-central Turkey, where Bahauddin resumed his role as the head of the dervish learning community, or *medrese*. Several years later, when Rumi was still in his twenties, his father died, and Rumi assumed the position, directing the study of theology, poetry, music, and other subjects and practices related to the growth of the soul, including cooking and the husbandry of animals. Rumi gained a wide reputation as a devout scholar, and his school numbered over ten thousand students.

The work of the dervish community was to open the heart, to explore the mystery of union, to fiercely search for and try to say truth, and to celebrate the glory and difficulty of being in a human incarnation. To these ends, they used silence and song, poetry, meditation, stories, discourse, and jokes. They fasted and feasted. They walked together and watched the animals. Animal behavior was a kind of scripture they studied. They cooked, and they worked in the garden. They tended orchards and vineyards.

The great human questions arose. What is the purpose of desire? What is a dream? A song? How do we know the depth of silence in another human being? What is the heart? What is it to be a true human being? What is the source of the universe and how do these individual awarenesses connect to that? They asked the Faustian question in many guises: What is it at bottom that holds the world together? How do we balance surrender and discipline? This high level of continuous question-and-answer permeated the poetry and music, the movement, and each activity of the community. They knew that answers might not come in discursive form, but rather in music, in image, in dream, and in the events of life as they occur.

There was also more practical inquiry. How should I make a living? How do I get my relatives out of my house? Could you help me postpone payment of this loan? The dervishes had jobs in the workday world: mason, weaver, bookbinder, grocer, hatmaker, tailor, carpenter. They were craftsmen, and women, not renunciates of everyday life, but affirmative makers and ecstatics. Some people call them *sufis*, or mystics. I say they're on the way of the heart.

At about this time Burhan Mahaqqiq, a meditator in

the remote mountain regions north and east of Konya, returned, not knowing that his teacher, Rumi's father, had died. Burhan decided to devote the rest of his life to the training of his teacher's son. For nine years he led Rumi on many — sometimes consecutive — forty-day fasts (*chillas*). Rumi became a deep and radiant adept in the science. of that mystical tradition. He taught students to open their hearts, and he wrote poetry that encouraged the process. By *mystical* I do not mean to refer to a secret lineage or to anything esoteric. It is a vague and imprecise word in English, like *spiritual*, which I also try to avoid using, unsuccessfully. The area of experience that "mystical" and "spiritual" refer to is often not empirically verifiable; that is, a camera can't photograph it, a scale can't weigh it nor can words do much to describe it. It is not exclusively physical, emotional, or mental, though it may partake of those three areas. Like the depths of our loving, mystical experience can be neither proven, *nor denied*. It does happen, and it is the region of human existence Rumi's poems inhabit.

Rumi married twice (his first wife died), and he raised four children. We do have some sense of Rumi's daily life at this time, because his oldest son, Sultan Velad, saved 147 of Rumi's personal letters. In them we learn how closely he was involved in the community's life. In one letter he begs a man to put off collecting money owed to another man for fifteen days. He asks a wealthy nobleman to help out a student with a small loan. Someone's relatives have moved into the hut of a devout old woman he asks if the situation can be remedied. Sudden lines of poetry are scattered throughout the letters. Rumi was a practical worker in the world as well as an ecstatic.

In late October 1244 the meeting with Shams of Tabriz occurred. It was to become the central event in Rumi's life and the one that galvanized him into becoming perhaps the planet's greatest mystical poet. Shams was a fierce God-man, man-God. He wore an old black cloak. Sufi stories tell of his wandering in search of a friend, someone who could endure the rigors and depth of his presence. Shams would alternate between periods of ecstatic soul trance and days of physical labor as a mason. Whenever students would gather around him, as they inevitably did, he would wrap his black robe around his shoulders, excuse himself, and be gone.

Shams had one continuous internal question, "Is there no friend for me?"

Finally a voice came, "What will you give?"

"My head."

"Your friend is Jelaluddin of Konya."

There are several versions of their initial meeting. In one, Rumi was teaching by a fountain in a small square in Konya, reading from his fathers *Ma'arif*. Shams cut through the crowd and pushed that book and others off the ledge into the water.

"Who are you, and what are you doing?" Rumi asked.

"You must now live what you've been reading about."

Rumi turned to the volumes on the bottom. "We can retrieve them," said Shams. "They'll be as dry as they were."

Shams lifted one of them out to show him. Dry. "Leave them," said Rumi.

With that relinquishment Rumi's deep life began, and the poetry. He said, "What I had thought of before as God I met today in a human being." His time as a theological scholar ended too. He and Shams spent months together in retreat. Their mystical conversation (*sohbet*) and the mysterious Friendship unfolded.

Some people in the community, though, were jealous. They distrusted Shams and resented his diverting their teacher from his teaching. They forced Shams away to Damascus, but Rumi called him back. Finaly, it seems, some of Rumi's students — probably including one of his sons, Allaedin — killed Shams and hid the body. In his grief Rumi began circling a pole in his garden and speaking the poetry that has come to be regarded as the most intimate record we have of the search for divine companionship. His turning is, of course, the origin of the moving meditation of the Mevlevi dervishes. It is an emblem, simultaneously, of discipline and the abandon of surrender. It is a dance in concert with the galaxies, the molecules, and the spiraling form that is the source and essence of the cosmos. But it is good to remember that Rumi's ecstasy began in grief.

In the meeting of Rumi and Shams, in that vital encounter, healing and the truest life begins. Any form of beauty or wisdom or celebration that puts one back in friendship with the soul is where the opposites find rest. "How can I be separated and yet in union?"

Who is this Shams of Tabriz? The question is often asked if Rumi and Shams were lovers in the sexual sense.

No. Their meeting in the heart is beyond form and touch and time.

The poet Robert Bly and I were flown over to Ankara and Konya by the Turkish government in December 2000 to help celebrate the 727th anniversary of Rumi's death, his *urs,* or wedding night. Robert in 1976 had started me out on this Rumi work by handing me some scholarly translations and saying, "These poems need to be released from their cages." As we came out of the tomb area in Konya, we sat on a stone bench to put our shoes back on. Sort of solemn with the moment, I leaned against him, "Thanks for giving me this." He looked back, "That's like thanking a bird for the wind." That broke the holy and left us laughing. Why do we visit tombs of great souls? Surely there's a resonance that feeds us, a field, a wind the freed birds rest on and ride.

One of the startling prospects that Rumi and Shams bring to the world of mystical awareness, which turns out to be ordinary consciousness as well, is the suggestion that we "fall in love in such a way that it frees us from any connecting." What that means is that we become friendship. "When living itself becomes the Friend, lovers disappear." That is, a human being can become a field of love (compassion, generosity, playfulness), rather than being identified with any particular synapse of lover and beloved. The love-ache widens to a plain of longing at the core of everything: the absence-presence center of awareness. Rumi went in search of the missing Shams. The story is that he was on a street in Damascus when the realization came that he *was* their Friendship. No separation, no union, just he was that at the silent core. I'd have to say that's the *baraka* (a blessing, the particular grace of taking in presence), the mystery of the ecstatic life.

He spoke his poems. They were written down by scribes, and later revisions were made by Rumi on the page, but for the most part his poetry can be considered spontaneous improvisation. All of the poems in his *Divan-i Shams-i Tabrizi* ("The Works of Shams of Tabriz") can be heard as the inner conversation of their Friendship. . . .

The poems in the *Divan* are *ghazals* (often translated "odes" in English), which are composed of a series of independent couplets and sometimes run as short as eight lines, sometimes much longer. The form makes irrational, intuitive leaps from image to image and thought to thought. This agility makes it an appropriate vehicle for Rumi's passionate, longing. Rumi and Shams met in the heart, and their Friendship widens in the poetry beyond all categories of gender and age, beyond romance: beyond any ideas of mentoring and disciple-ship. The poems open to include "sunlight" and "what anyone says." Their Friendship is a universe they inhabit. Instead of being connected by a love, they are the living atmosphere, of love itself. Rumi's poetry breathes that air. The poems feel fresh and new, like something we have not absorbed yet, or understood, here seven hundred years later.

For the last twelve years of his life Rumi wrote one long continuous poem, the *Masnavi*, sixty-four thousand lines of poetry divided into six books. It has no parallel in world literature. It surges like an ocean (his image) around many subjects. It is self-interrupting, visionary, sometimes humorous commentary on the health of the soul and on Qur'anic passages; it is full of folktales, jokes, and remarks to people physically present as the poems were being composed. Rumi dictated this sublime jazz to his scribe, Husam Chelebi, as they walked around Konya, through the nearby vineyards of Meram, during teaching sessions, and in the streets and public baths. Husam was a student of Shams, so this long poem" can be considered an extension of Rumi's conversation with the Friend. The best metaphor for its strange unified diversity is the way Rumi was with the community around him: sometimes he attended to the growth of the group as a whole, sometimes he addressed the needs of individuals. Readers of the *Masnavi* may dive in anywhere and swim around. It is a flow whose refrain is the ecstatic exclamation, "This has no end!" or "This cannot be said. I am drowning in this!"

Rumi died at sunset on December 17, 1273. His tomb in Konya is still visited by thousands each month. It is said that representatives from all major religions attended his funeral. They saw Rumi and his poetry as a way of deepening their own faith. He is often called Mevlana, or Maulana, meaning "master" or "lord." Every year on December 17, the anniversary of his death is celebrated the world over as the night of his union with the divine. It is called his *urs*, or wedding night. Rumi felt this union was something as natural as breathing. He knew it as the core inside each impulse to praise, and he acknowledged it as the presence he calls "beloved" or "Friend." Rather than be exclusively part of an organized religion or cultural system, he claimed to belong to that companion who transpires through and animates the whole universe.

I belong to the beloved, have seen the two
worlds as one and that one call to and know,

first, last, outer, inner, only that
breath breathing human being.

FANA AND *BAQA*: TWO STREAMINGS ACROSS THE DOORSILL OF RUMI'S POETRY

No one can say what the inner life is, but poetry tries to, and no one can say what poetry is, but let's be bold and claim that there are two major *streamings* in consciousness, particularly in the ecstatic life, and in Rumi's poetry: call them *fana* and *baqa*, Arabic words that refer to the play and intersection of human with divine.

Rumi's poetry occurs in that opening, a dervish doorway these energies move through in either direction. A movement out, a movement in. *Fana* is the streaming that moves from the human out into mystery — the annihilation, the orgasmic expansion, the dissolving swoon into the all. The gnat becomes buttermilk; a chickpea disappears into the flavor of the soup; a dead mule decays into salt flat; the infant turns to the breast. These wild and boundaryless absorptions are the images and the kind of poem Rumi is most well known for, a drunken clairvoyant tavern voice that announces, "Whoever brought me here will have to take me home."

"What was in that candle's light that opened and consumed me so quickly!" That is the moth's question after *fana*, after it becomes flame. The king's falcon circles in the empty sky. There is an extravagance in the magnificent disintegration of *fana*. In one wheat grain a thousand sheaf stacks. Which is literally true: a single wheat seed can, after a few years, become thousands of stacks of sheaves. But it's that special praise for the natural abundance of existence that identifies this state. Three hundred billion galaxies might seem a bit gaudy to some, but not to this awareness; in *fana* what is here can never be said extravagantly enough.

Fana is what opens our wings, what makes boredom and hurt disappear. We break to pieces inside it, dancing and perfectly free. We are the dreamer streaming into the loving nowhere of night. Rapt, we are the devouring worm who, through grace, becomes an entire orchard, the wholeness of the trunks, the leaves, the fruit, and the growing. *Fana* is that dissolution just before our commotion and mad night prayers become silence. Rumi often associates surrender with the joy of falling into the freedom of sleep. It's human-becoming-God, the *Ana'I-Haqq* ("I am the truth") of Al-Hallaj Mansour. The arms open outward. This is the ocean with no shore into which the dewdrop falls.

My friend the poet Daniel Abdal-Hayy Moore scolds me for not saying outright that *fana* is *annihilation in*

Allah. I avoid God-words, not altogether, but wherever I can, because they seem to take away the freshness of experience and put it inside a specific system. Rumi's poetry belongs to everyone, and his impulse was toward experience rather than any language or doctrine about it: our lives as text, rather than any book, be it Qur'an, Gospel, *Upanishad*, or sutra.

There is a fierce desolation in *fana*, though, that I may not be communicating. Abdal-Hayy is right. The absence experienced in *fana* is complete. There is no soft focus around anything. It's the hard-edged *jelal* ("majesty") desert sword of Shams. I have much to learn in these matters.

Baqa goes the other way across the doorsill. The Arabic word means "a living within": it is the walk back down Qaf Mountain, where the vision came; life lived with clarity and reason; the turning again toward what somehow always was. The concentration of a night of stars into one needle's eye. A refinement, companionship, two people walking along some *particular* county road. The absorbing work of *this* day. The precise painting of a piece of trim. The arms folding inward across the chest and the bow to one another. Courtesy and craftsmanship. God-becoming-human. The qualities associated with this motion are honesty, sobriety, carefulness, a clarity Rumi sometimes calls "reason," compassion, and work within a community. *Baqa* is also a return from expansion into each's unique individuation work, into pain and effort, confusion and dark comedy: the end of a frayed rope, the deep knowing of absence.

Baqa is where animal and angel meet in an awkward but truly human dance. It's a breathtaking birth, the dying and then being born again that all religions know is the

essence of soul growth. It can be overheard in the poetry
as a conversation between Jelaluddin and the mystery.

Baqa might say:

> *Friend, our closeness is this:*
> *Anywhere you put your foot feel me*
> *in the firmness under you.*

while *fana* asks, in the same quatrain:

> *How is it with this love,*
> *I see your world, but not you?*

Baqa is felt in Rumi's spring-morning poems, very present, green, and alive with the camaraderie of a picnic by
the water.

> *Stay together, friends.*
> *Don't scatter and sleep.*

> *Our friendship is made*
> *of being awake.*

> *The waterwheel accepts water*
> *and turns and gives it away, weeping.*

> *That way it stays in the garden. . . .*
> *Stay here, quivering with each moment*
> *like a drop of mercury.*

You feel a tremulous intensity *within limits.* Bodhisattval service walking to the well. The common joy of ducks riding a flooded river. Kindness and acts of anonymous helping. *Baqa* brings the next stage in the process of prayer: there's the opening into annihilation, then the coming back to tend specific people. A melody, the little German band coming up through Beethoven's *Ninth.* This is the ocean come to court the drops. A fall to the knees, the frustrating satisfaction of the spoken word.

By letting these two conditions, *fana* and *baqa,* flow and exist simultaneously in his poetry, Rumi is saying that they are one thing, the core of a true human being, which he was and out of which these poems are spoken. This is how alive his model of the human psyche is, where the secular and the sacred are always mingling, the mythic and the ordinary, dream vision and street life.

THE QUESTION OF THE PERSONAL

Rumi's poems are not personal in the way we've come to expect in the Western tradition of poetry and poetry readings. We do not learn who Rumi was *as a personality* from his poems. They are not subjective, but rather objective, or iconic. They conduct and transform energies. They do the work of icons: they connect us more deeply with our souls. When we look at an image of Christ or Dionysos, we feel the core of grief and compassion there. When we see the archaic torso of Apollo in the Vatican, we take in some of its graceful balance and power, and we *do* change our lives. The form of

Kali transmits the force of making a clean cut with the past, the edge of focused rage. And try someday to walk into the Kwan Yin room of the Nelson-Atkins Museum in Kansas City. Take in her high humor and grounded acceptance.

Neither of the conditions, *fana* or *baqa*, involves the false self of a personal ego. Rather, they are motions of the essence of a human-divine encounter. Rumi's poetry means to take us beyond the personal into the mystery that is here, the source of dream vision, the spring of longing, into a presence that asks the question, "Who am I?" Ramana Maharshi and. Rumi would agree: the joy of being human is in uncovering the core we already are, the treasure buried in the ruin.

I am told that at the end of a Mevlevi initiation, which consists of various kinds of physical work, *zikr* ("remembering God"), fasting, abstinence, and long retreats, a condition of entrancement called *hulul* is reached.

Rumi's poetry gives a taste of that trance, as well as other stations. All of his poetry continues the work of transformation he experienced with Shams-i Tabriz; it has to, because it comes out of that Friendship.

I have never gone through the Mevlevi initiation, and I do not live in the states of *fana* and *baqa* that Rumi speaks from. No doubt I oversimplify or misrepresent what they are. My own experience of these states; if I can be allowed any claim, comes from remembering my teacher, Bawa Muhaiyaddeen, who told me to do this Rumi work. He lived in both worlds. Also, I get some taste when I move from a wild perception of the vast beauty in and around us to the equally enjoyed attention to my nine-year-old granddaughter's latest written song, which happens to be about the sun.

I feel the source of the power of Rumi's spontaneous poetic derives from his continual balance of surrender and discipline, his visionary radiance held in the level calm of ordinary sight. Splendor and practice, meditation and chore — somewhere in the dynamic of those lies the vitality and validity, the knack of Mevlana.

> *The universe and the light of the stars come through me* (fana).
> *I am the crescent moon put up over the gate to the festival* (baqa).

The "cresent moon" is undoubtedly some plywood device nailed over the fairground entrance. *Baqa* often includes a little joke about the grandeur. . . .

BAQA

Rumi adores this stubborn, horny, mean, radiant, arrogant, hilarious planet we inhabit. He looks at it; he holds up to the light anything human beings do, and uses each action as a lens to examine the growth of the soul.

The most amazing quality of his poetry is that it can also give a sense of the presence our lives occur within. That most elusive mystery that enters every gesture of the hunt — bow, release, the deer's blood, the hunter's eye — each careful stitch of tapestry becomes the ground felt under the poetry.

Rumi caresses the exactness, the distinct shape of the human story, even as he conveys the oceanic intelligence that surges through. This is *baqa*: coming back from annihilation with cleansed enthusiasm for particulars. In the state of *baqa* one reenters the moment fully, doing small quiet work, sewing the robe of absence.

The poet Hayden Carruth survived a suicide attempt and came back from it with a renewed sense of the sheer good luck of being alive. "My happiness was not a state of doing but of being. . . . Is this what St. Theresa felt? I suspect that in its sensational manifestation my happiness is indeed close to religious ecstasy." He wouldn't, but I'd say he was experiencing *baqa*.

Rumi loves animals. Surely one of the oldest joys of human beings is watching them. The cave walls celebrate the animal grace of sentience. Rumi's poetry loves the mixture of animal, human, and spirit, which is the elaborate dance of true human beings.

With dreams, the *baqa* state comes in as one makes some *practical application* of the wisdom given in them. . . .

SPEAKING WITH A GROUP

There's an incident told in Rumi's *Discourses* at the beginning of #10 that I keep returning to for what its trying to show. A government official, the Amir, comes to visit Rumi's father, Bahauddin. Bahauddin tells him he should not have gone to such trouble. "I am subject to various states," he continues. "In one state I can speak and in another I do not speak. In one state I can listen to the stories of other lives and respond to them. In another I withdraw to my room and see no one. In yet another I am utterly distraught, absorbed in God, unable to communicate at all. It's too risky for you to come here on the chance I might be amiable and able to have conversation."

I love the assumption that Bahauddin is not in control of those states. They wash over like weather. In his surrendered life, if the inner weather is right, he can come out and give counsel, attend to questions, and do some good for his friends. Otherwise, it's close the door. He's on retreat with his outrageously imperious soul. This has seemed to me justified behavior in a soul-making artist. Picasso, Georgia O'Keeffe, Coleridge, van Gogh, Beethoven. Don't interrupt their inspired solitudes.

> Beware! beware!
> His flashing eyes, his floating hair!
> Weave a circle round him thrice.
> — Samuel Taylor Coleridge, "Kubla Khan"

And should this not also be true for ordinary mystics? No more scheduled *on* times, no office hours. Let students come if and when and however. The improvisational pianist Keith Jarrett, no ordinary mystic, once, after a few tentative noodlings, stood up from the piano, walked to the front of the stage, and said, "Sometimes these events just don't work out."

Anyone who has taught classes knows that one of the most vital gestures in the universe is how energy (Rumi calls it the *presence*) circulates, palpitates, evaporates, and reconstitutes, moving through a class on a certain day, around the edges of a group, in the memory. There is no describing these prolonged and intricate motions (that's why class evaluations are so absurd), but Rumi finds many images for the dynamic. He calls it an electrical, thunderstorming, conductoring *presence*. He says it looks sometimes like a picture-making quill tip, a candle lighting a face; other times, a flute note, a book opening or being shut, a catch, a blink.

Mutakallim is thought of as one of the names of God. It means "What speaks through us. . . ."

THE INNER MEANING OF RELIGIONS

All acts of praise, contrition, and forgiveness join with the living core at the center of all religions.

His friendship with Shams Tabriz, that ineffable and yet particular connection, consumed the structure of religion for Rumi. The friendship 'became his worship, absorbing Islam, Muhammad, Jesus, and all doctrines in the ocean of its reality, the heart. After his meeting and *sohbet* with Shams, theological discussion was no longer relevant. As he says, Shams's face is what every religion tries to remember ("Your Face").

The *way* that Rumi and Shams clarified for the world of mystical experience is their continuously unfolding friendship. The source of that friendship — sunlight, everything the sun lights, and the mystery of the inner sun — is what he worships. This is a difficulty some traditional believers have with Rumi: he does not stress the *distance* between human beings and Allah, the absolute, but rather a *remembered intimacy*, the original agreement in which friend and friendship become one sea-changing union. He does not stress prayer so much as continuous conversation. If our real consciousness is beyond time and space, the core of worship must be beyond any cultural or religious system.

I don't mean to be dogmatic about this, or even argumentative. There is a Rumi loved by Muslims whose almost every poem is read as a commentary on the Qur'an. This is a true Rumi too, along with my gnostic without-religious-form one. The man is a grace, a *baraka*, a powerful blessing. We can meet and talk and proclaim our takes on his poetry, but all within the embrace of his presence, surely. Kabir Helminski recently published a book of traditional Mevlevi prayers. In it a prayer by the 1910 Mevlevi Sheikh recognizes "Our Mevlana and the Mevlana of the gnostics." I take consolation in that phrase. Evidently there have been others down the line who have also heard Rumi's poems outside of any system, the shared heart, part of no religion and all. . . .

HABITS THAT BLIND THE PSYCHE

Not all of Rumi's poems encourage ecstatic communion. Some are more like practical travel advice. In Bunyan's *Pilgrim's Progress*, the Slough of Despond (the swamp of feeling depressed) must be negotiated and Vanity Fair (the town that encourages talk-show ambitions and conspicuous luxury) passed through. On Rumi's pilgrimage there are dangers and distractions not so openly allegorical as Bunyan's. He warns against conduct that disorients the caravan, self-destructive passion, and whatever blocks kindness and one's connection with a teacher.

Any human action that turns cold can delay the soul's pilgrimage. Everything is about encouraging the deepening of love and compassion. Rumi advises specifically against jealousy, wanting world-power, and toying with fermented drink. His image of the so-called lovers who are cruel to each other is a scene of demented dolls pulling the stuffing out of one another. He also recommends we be slow to blame anyone other than ourselves.

And the corollary to that might be: when you give advice, be sure you can accept it for yourself. A story has come down about Rumi: a woman asks if he would say something to her young boy about his eating too much of a particular kind of white-sugar candy. Rumi tells her to come back in two weeks. She does, and he tells her again to come in two weeks. She does, and he advises the child to cut down on sweets.

"Why did you not say this a month ago?"

"Because I had to see if I could resist having that candy for two weeks. I couldn't. Then I tried again and was successful. Only now can I tell him to try not to have so much. . . ."

MASNAVI

The *Masnavi* is Rumi's heart-breath community voice. This walking-around poem was spoken as Rumi strolled the streets and gardens and orchards of Konya with his scribe Husam Chelebi during the last twelve years of Rumi's life (1261–73). It has that peripatetic feel, a moving vicinity that filters many subjects. I am told that *upanishad* means a sheaf of notes taken by someone at the side of a master. The *Masnavi* is such a collection. Much of it too was spoken in the dervish college Rumi headed, its fluid form reflecting the way a master tends soul growth, sometimes individually, sometimes for the group.

The *Masnavi* is an ocean-openness. As we listen to it, a synchrony rises: They say that sufis don't pray, because they know that *everything* is God. What could they want? Take Rumi's book with you to the mountains. It has a motion that belongs there, a wildness beyond Thoreau or D. H. Lawrence or Nietzsche. This wildness is in the area of Bodhidharma and Niffari, Blake, and Hafez. You feel it in the proliferation and in the fierce shards of its ruin. "All we sell here is *fana* and *baqa*" (VI, 1528).

MUD AND GLORY

There are scandalous episodes in Rumi's *Masnavi*, so much so that one of them at least ("The Importance of Gourdcrafting") has caused a curriculum adoption of *The Essential Rumi* to be cancelled in Berkeley, California! Parents and teachers were offended.

Rumi's stories with their wild moments belong in the tradition of medieval *fabliaux*. They are very like those European and Near Eastern stories, but with a radiant difference. A *fabliau* (Old French, "a little fable") is a raucous peasant tale, often scatological (involving excrement) or lewd. People, mostly men, get themselves in absurd, humiliating postures similar to those assumed in defecation or copulation, but in *fabliaux* the cramped calisthenics take place out in the open for everyone to see. I have vivid memories of such scenes not because I read medieval French, but because in 1959 I took a graduate course at Berkeley with Alain Renoir (son of the movie director Jean, grandson of the painter Pierre Auguste). Alain was a great teacher and a solid medievalist. He retold a few *fabliaux* for us twenty first-semester graduate students in a classroom in Dwinelle Hall. He stomped about putting on shoes filled with imaginary shit, squishing obliviously through swamps and hatfuls of the stuff. He sidled, with his enormous virtual erection, into the chambermaid's pantry.

Perhaps you discovered, dear reader, as I, in your high-school library the naughty minx-wives and daughters of Chaucer's miller and reeve. The musical-bed capers, the snoring and the farts, O country lore of puberty in Nevill Coghill's translation:

That's how the carpenter's young wife was plumbed
For all the tricks his jealousy could try,
And Absalon has kissed her nether eye
And Nicholas is branded on the bum,
And God bring us all to Kingdom Come.

In the *Masnavi* a man is discovered by his wife with his thighs drenched with gism and the vaginal juices of their maid. The husband is pretending to do his daily prayers. "So this is how a man prays, with his balls!" the wife screams (V, 2203).

In another story, Nasuh, a virile young man, works as an attendant in the women's bathhouse. He has acted effeminate to appear harmless in this sensitive job. As the secret of his continuous hard-on is about to be revealed, just at the point of near humiliation, his awareness breaks open and expands beyond the personal.

> *At that moment his spirit grows wings and lifts. His ego falls like a battered wall. He unites with God, alive, but emptied of Nasub.* (V, 2274–76)

Nasuh's breaking into an enlightened state through the threat of sexual embarrassment is perhaps a moment unique in literature. Rumi uses *fabliau* moments, always, to look into soul growth. A glutton has shit in his bed. Muhammad comes to wash the bedclothes. With shame comes an opening.

> *He's quiet and quivering with remorse. Muhammad bends over and holds him and caresses*
>
> *him and opens his inner knowing. The cloud weeps, and then the garden sprouts. The baby*
>
> *cries, and the mother's milk flows. The nurse of creation has said,* Let them cry

a lot, *This rain-weeping and sun-burning twine
together to help us grow. Keep your
intelligence white-hot and your grief glistening, so
your life will stay fresh.* (V, 132–39)

An adulterous judge is hiding in a clothes chest being
carried down the street. He talks to the porter:

*"Tell the court deputy to come and buy this chest
and take it, unopened, to the judge's house."*

"Is this the voice of God or a genii talking to me?"
(VI, 4493–95)

Like scenes from a Marx Brothers film or a Charlie
Chaplin skit, or perhaps more accurately, from the raw,
priapic interludes of Greek drama or, later, the Italian
Commedia del Arte, such shenanigans we have with us
always. Rumi uses them to look at, and love, our insistent,
stubborn, insatiable desire-bodies, the hypocrisy of hiding them, and the wisdom of not identifying with them.

Bill Clinton, ole buddy, helped us feel something of
this human crux more recently. The foolishness of those
months in 1998 seems almost wistful now. Larry Flynt's
roll call of matching Republican sleaze, the beautiful
black clergy standing quietly in the Rose Garden. Wonder
what the poor pasty, sexless slug Ken Starr is examining
now, whose spattered dress?

Rumi lets the judge speak from within his box.

*A lover of world-things has put himself in just such
a box.
Though he appears to be free,*

he can see nothing but the inside of his chosen chest.
(VI, 4496–97)

How do these ridiculous and sometimes horrifying incidents (a woman is killed having sex with a donkey [V, 1333–1405]) fit in this poet's wider vision? Beautifully, I would say, with an openness about experience that is still difficult for us to accept.

T. S. Eliot says of William Blake's poetry, "It is an honesty, against which the whole world conspires, because it is so unpleasant." The same is true of Rumi's details of embodiment. He uses grungy specifics to say truths about transcendence. Consider "Two Ways of Running," (V, 2163–2204), in which the agile energy with which a husband runs after his desire, the young maid, and the way the wife runs, who is trying to catch him at his lust, are contrasted; the former motion is like that of the lover of God and the latter like the heavy tread of the literalist or the rule enforcer. Rumi honors the direct, more necessary enthusiasm of the husband rather than the mean-spirited, "gotcha" mentality of the wife.

As the humbling, and healing, truth finds voice, the outrageous boxes of personae pretense (false egos) fall open, and the impulse is to laugh and weep at once. So Rumi's ecstatic vision includes this kind of *shadow work*, if it can be called that, attention to the *nafs* ("the wantings"), to the shame attached, and to its uncovering. He is a surgeon lancing infection, unbandaging armored crust, or at the least waving away the flies, his image for our self-protecting excuses.

> *Put your vileness tip to a mirror and weep. That's*
> *when the real art, the real*
>
> *making, begins. A tailor must have a torn shirt to*
> *practice his expertise.* (I, 3205–9)

The empty mirror is Rumi's metaphor for what the heart becomes within quietness and meditation. There is a necessary grief at the inception of ecstatic art. I want a howling hurt! ("Not Here," chap. 22). We Americans are familiar with this because Emily Dickinson is one of our national poets; she specializes in ecstatic grief.

As Rumi takes away the self-protecting excuses, the making of soul comes in.

> *Don't believe you're healing yourself!*
>
> *Prayer is an egg. Hatch out the helplessness.*
> (III, 2175)
>
> *Your defects are the ways that glory gets manifested.*
> (I, 3210)

He celebrates the clearing and refreshment that pours through when we acknowledge the animal energies, the *nafs*, and the shadow side of personality. Singing those out loud, we wake each other up. We empty out a libation of tears. Rumi reminds us to bring what is taboo or repellent in ourselves to awareness because that difficult attention opens the heart and keeps us intensely in the moment where the clearer passion lives.

These spectacular, in some ways comic, instances of soul-making happen in the theater of shame. Also there's some evolutionary revisioning going on, along with the sheer delight of creation in this land of fuddle and cruelty. Some mysterious opening of essence builds as we turn the refuse of mistakes over in the sun, like garbage being composted on a Damascus street ("*Mashallah*," chap. 11). Rumi hears mistakes as a music we ride, the chant of *mashallah*, the divine presence inside desire. "Kiss the snake that guards the treasure" ("Cleansing Conflict," chap. 11). "Good and bad are mixed. If you don't have both, you don't belong with us."`

In a startling image he contends that love is a courtroom *where we must bring in harsh evidence* ("Cleansing Conflict"). Rumi says that he is in love with God's mercy and forgiveness and that he is also in love with God's wrath and destruction. I do not claim to live in that space, though I can say this: working with rage and jealousy and other fears, such as the fear of abandonment, impotence, or embarrassment, leads to the breakthroughs necessary for depth in relationship, which can open the soul to possible enlightenment.

Living in such dynamic mutability, we must constantly admit we don't know how the outcomes will go by saying, *Inshallah*, "If God wills." Rumi hears this as the acknowledging of an original human agreement with the divine. That agreement is most clearly felt as we understand how knowing with the linear mind is different from the way of the heart. Rational linear proof is what the mind demands. The heart's way begins when one lays ones head on a person's chest and drifts into the answer. Such knowing grows with being in harmony with the mystery of another human being, which includes remembering, listening, and the ecstatic sense of a sacred universe. As more identifications with body and personality drop away, the center of the self grows more vital.

Someone might say that center is Rumi's *companion*, Shams, the inner core, Friend, or beloved. Someone might name what walks along with, and within, him. I can't, though I hear it playing in the high-trickster humor. I hear it in the conversation Solomon has in his morning refuge, and in the "double music of existence" (Book IV, p. 319).

Rumi's bawdy stories are about opening and reading the body's letter to the creator of the universe. He says this reading is our most courageous work (Book IV, p. 318). Majnun slides down from the high camel that has been carrying him in his sleep, on its own low errands away from the direction of his longing for Layla (Book IV, p. 316). But what shall we ever say of longing and what the longing's for?

The clear bead at the center changes everything.
There are no edges to my loving now.
— ("The clear bead. . . .," chap. 5)

The shocking, off-color segments have to do with the

periphery of that center, with being in a body, the fury and mire of human veins (Yeats), with love as it washes through the senses. Erect penis, wet vagina, sneeze, snore, fart, eyes-shut come cry, piss-relief sigh. Rumi puts every body noise, especially the grunting and humping, the nibbling and groans of erotic trance, in the foreground. He listens to learn what that section of human experience says of soul growth. In the *fabliau* pieces of the *Masnavi* Rumi takes us down the spine to the lower chakras. In those stories we feel the force of their pulling; then he helps us know something. The escapades always make a point about the quality of the cruder energies and their potential for transformation.

> *The Caliph was sexually impotent, but his, manli-ness was most powerful. The kernel of*

> *true manhood is, the ability to abandon sensual indulgences. The intensity of the captain's*

> *libido is less than a husk compared to the Caliph's nobility in ending the cycle*

> *of sowing lust and reaping secrecy and vengefulness.*

Like the captain and the caliph, we each have a different, specific work to do. The stories of the *Masnavi* help us discover what that is. Rumi explores one metaphor for this in Book IV, the world as a bathhouse (p. 274). There are furnace stokers and there are those who bathe. The fire-building energies and the emptying-out longings for purification cooperate to let the bathhouse flourish. There's a competitive atmosphere among the ones who, heat up, the fierce furnace workers, and a relaxation, a peace, in the ones who lean back and lave. But it's the action of both that lets the full range of human awareness thrive. And sometimes, members of the groups change places! The intensity-lovers and the meditators work the same shift. A "stoker" in a public bath was socially looked down on, but in Rumi's bathhouse that snobbery dissolves; stoker and bather do one work, and there are beauty and symmetry to the energy exchange. Maybe the fury that feeds intensity takes the purification deeper, or maybe the bathhouse has hidden purposes only the lover inside all love knows, the ultimate creative, morphogenetic field, deepest companion. At any rate, Rumi's bathhouse world, in the many modes and messages of the *Masnavi*, is trying to say some whole, elusive truth of human life — how lotus grows from mud, how bawdy and sublime are near of kin, and how Majnun must slide down off the camel and break his leg on the way to Layla. We leave him lying in the road. The point may be a simple one: that the life energies in passion and compassion, in lust and in the expanded state of vision, have one source. But the implications for soul growth are profound and difficult for me to say. The mystery of this "marriage of heaven and hell" we live is that *without contraries is no progression.* Soul growth moves with *both* sides of the bathhouse, reason and energy, in meditation and in the flames of our wanting.

THE FORM OF THE WHOLE

I was asked once whether I thought Rumi's *Masnavi* was finished. It's a good question. The *Masnavi* doesn't have a satisfying beginning, middle, or end; it seems composed of strands and fragments, but I contend it is whole, complete as a day is, or a human life. There's no beginning or end to, the flowing of heart energy.

T. S. Eliot on the long poem: "You cannot create a very large poem without introducing a more impersonal point of view, or splitting it up into various personalities." Rumi's extra large long poem (six books, sixty-four thousand verses) is a community, an ocean with layers of different temperatures that support the various life-forms of a dervish college.

For me, the best image for the form of the *Masnavi* is how an enlightened master is, and talks, with those around him or her, those held in the *nazar*, the realm of the master's *glance*. The *Masnavi* is complete, because it comes from the whole. I can't prove this, of course, or say anything more. Experiment with it. Enter the poem anywhere and swim around; listen for resonance; experience the motions. Let its filaments connect with your life. Synchronicity, I propose, is the matrix. Or say that any great artwork is a field, that the *Masnavi*, like the *Divan* of Hafez, spreads out a spontaneously exploratory, tending region of consciousness. The concept of *morphic resonance* applies. Works of literature are agents in the continuous revisioning of the language of who we are and are becoming. A rosebush lineage of old masters meets with us there in the work and prompts new energies, new grief, new ways of creating. Or it may be some other unprovable invisible reality, like love.

I had a dream recently that might be trying to show something of how these fields perform. I am walking around composing poems *about* walking around streets and gardens. I am reading the poems to a moving audience who has before them, in some form, although not pages, the growing text that I am composing. I come to a stopping place. I don't have the words. A friend in the audience gives me his text, which has my additions, though in somewhat different lineation and phrasing. I say that I'm going to use his changes. So it goes, communal, generous, and very friendly, the *making* and the stroll.

The concept of the *qutb* is that there is an infinitely complex divine field presiding over all at every moment. Maybe Rumi's *Masnavi* is a product of the working of such a field.

In the ocean there are many bright strands
and many dark strands like, veins that are

seen when a wing is lifted up: Your hidden
self is blood in those, those veins that are

lute strings that make ocean :music, not the
sad edge of surf, but the sound of no shore.

Or say the *Masnavi* is the magnificent, symphonic mess we are: the gallery of scamps I have lifted my yardstick to could have included many more: Faraj, the servant who is fooled on his wedding night by the substitution of a boy for his aristocratic bride, but keeps on with his unstoppable fumbling. And the military captain of *el grand libido* who leaps from lovemaking to kill a lion roaming the camp and immediately returns, with no diminishment of tumescence, to his much-relished game, barely missing a beat. The animal energy of the strong and salad young, and not so young, is celebrated, not in D. H. Lawrence's dark-god sense, but as flutes for the divine flow streaming through.

Surely we have felt such music moving in us. The God-self flows in all mediums, but God, that's hard to know at the time! The animals embodying the animal energy in humans are prominent notations for that music in Rum's poetry. It's a menagerie, an ark with everything from dugong to ant to parrot and porcupine, with Noah there supervising, and that's the point: we're connected *through energy* to the animals. Rumi strongly senses the human-animal bond, as did the cave-drawing masters." The natural energies flow directly to our opening hearts and the clearing vision of the witness. They give the process juice and joy. They propel a widening of perception.

A lotus flower must grow out of mud: compassion and enlightened seeing flow through Rumi's stories from the moments of getting caught red-handed, *with our dangly bits in the air*, to wisdom. Sometimes he calls those animal strands the "rooster of lust," the "duck of urgency," the "peacock of wanting to be famous," and the "crow of acquiring stuff." For soul growth, one doesn't kill the animals, but *incorporates* them. You can learn much from the dog of desire, Bawa kept telling me, but don't let it drag you all over town from one piece of dung to the next thrown-out fish head to whatever piss signals others have strewn along the street. Keep your dog tied up, take it for walks at your own pace, and give it scraps from time to time. If you don't, you may find yourself on stage, where it will become more publicly obvious how you must recognize and transform the animals into the great love vision and way that Rumi's poetry, and every enlightened master from every and no tradition, draws us out onto the high plain of Caravan fires in the middle distance. We'll be in their company by dark.

Rumi's parables of ridiculous embarrassment make fine additions to those of Jesus (we've been wanting them), the hadith ("traditional sayings") of Muhammad, the Zen sutras, Mayan stories, and contemporary poems, the camp-circle words that help us live with and within unconditional love and widen the concentric knowing that is our poignant mystery.

BEING GOD'S SPIES

It is rare that an enlightened being is also a great poet. Why is this? Putting aside the enormous difficulty of agreeing on what either "enlightenment" or "great art" is, it may be that someone who surrenders to living the unsayable truth most often has little interest in tending to the details, the craft of language.

My theory about why the combination of great art and enlightenment is so unusual involves the dance with the shadow and with the animal soul that I've been trying to discuss. That work helps the enlightened being grow as an artist. Shakespeare's treatment of the breakthroughs made in jealousy and ambition and aging petulance leads to this enlightened kindness passage at the end of *King Lear*.

> *Come, let's away to prison:*
> *We two alone will sing like birds i' th' cage:*
> *When thou dost ask me blessing, I'll kneel down*
> *And ask of thee forgiveness: so we'll live,*
> *And pray, and sing, and tell old tales, and laugh*
> *At gilded butterflies, and hear poor rogues*
> *Talk of court news; and we'll talk with them too,*
> *Who loses and who wins, who's in, who's out;*
> *And take upon's the mystery, of things,*
> *As though we were God's spies. . . .*
>
> (V, iii, 8–17)

An enlightened artist takes on the mystery of *things*, and the beauty and power of the art has to do with the lively specificity of embodied energies, the song in prison. "Pray you undo this button," says Lear. Or the *fabliau* close-up: Juhi's (Nasruddin's) hand moving up the woman's thigh, so he can determine the length of her pubic hair, which is the *theological* point he's occupied with (V, 3325–50). It's true that Rumi caresses the world, as a great artist must, even as he hears the great wind of leaving it rising. Galway Kinnell says that the core of soul art is a *tenderness toward existence*. Rumi's poetry loves full sun *along with* the willow's silky shadow moving on the ground. . . .

In the early 1990s — it was December — I was sitting in meditation under the green dome that houses Rumi's tomb in Konya. Someone came up and gave me a green shawl. As you might imagine, I treasure it still and use it in my meditation. I love the wrapped, rapt feeling.

Going in, feeling the limpid contentment in being oneself and the endless discovery there: the green shawl is that, reminiscent of a child's tent-making delight, the rainy-day times when you spread a sheet over a card table and a chair, anchored it with safety pins, and crept under the shelter where imagination could flower. How we forget this *tent making* for such long spans is a mystery in itself.

Rumi tells of Solomon's practice of building each dawn a place made of intention and compassion and *sohbet* (mystical conversation). He calls it the "far mosque." Solomon goes there to listen to the plants, the new ones that come up each morning. They tell him of their medicinal qualities, their potential for health, and also the dangers of poisoning.

I suggest we all get green shawls. "Remember, the entrance door to the sanctuary is *inside* you" ("Entrance Door"). Mary's hiding place and the real warehouse ("What Was Told, *That*") arc other images of the listening tent, where conversation thrives and love deepens.

Rumi often hears it as the birdlike song-talk that begins at dawn under the dome of meditation. Build a far mosque where you can read your soulbook and listen to the dreams that grew in the night. Attar says,

Let love lead your soul.

Make it a place to retire to,
a kind of cave, a retreat
for the deep core of being.

ENTRANCE DOOR

How lover and beloved touch is
familiar and courteous, but there

is a strange impulse in that to
create a form that will dissolve

all other shapes. Remember, the
entrance door to the sanctuary is

inside you. We watch a sunlight
dust dance, and we try to be that

lively, but nobody knows what music
those particles hear. Each of us

has a secret companion musician to
dance to. Unique rhythmic play, a

motion in the street we alone know
and hear. Shams is a king of kings
like Mahmud, but there's not another
pearl-crushing dervish Ayaz like me.

LAO TZU

c. 550 B.C.

Nothing is known of the life of Lao Tzu, the legendary founder of Chinese Taoism (Daoism). The oldest biography (c. 100 B.C.) claims he held official rank. He was first mentioned by Zhuangzi. Taoist tradition attributes their classic text, the Daodejing (Tao Te Ching) *to Laozi, but it was written in the third century B.C. By the second century A.D Taoists claimed he had lived more than once and had travelled to India, where he became the Buddha. (Later he was claimed to have founded Manichaeism.) The Tang emperors (618–906) claimed descent from him.*

PREFACE
by Alan Watts

IN THE LITERARY TRADITION of Taoism, the legendary Chinese philosopher Lao Tzu is often referred to as a contemporary of Confucius. According to some accounts, Lao Tzu was supposed to have been a court librarian who wearied of the insincerity and intrigue of court life and decided to leave the city and go off and live in the mountains. But before he left, the guardian of the gate is said to have stopped him and said,

"Sir, I cannot let you go until you write down something of your wisdom."

And it is said that he sat down in the guardhouse and recorded the book known as the *Tao Te Ching*, the book of *Tao* and *Te*, of the Way and its power.

The core of Lao Tzu's written philosophy deals with the art of getting out of one's own way, learning how to act without forcing conclusions, and living in skillful harmony with the processes of nature instead of trying to push them around. Lao Tzu didn't actually say very much about the meaning of Tao; instead, he simply offered his advice.

It is now believed that although this work was probably rendered in a single hand during the time of Confucius, or shortly thereafter, the author incorporated the wisdom of a much older folk tradition. One school believes that Taoist literature was inspired by the oral teaching of shamanic hermits in ancient times. Another holds that the *Tao Te Ching* was an attempt to bring the practical, conventional wisdom of the Chinese people to the ruling class in order to help them to rule with greater wisdom and compassion. Both schools are probably partially correct, and in either case Taoist thought remains among the most accessible of the world's great religious philosophies, and is perhaps the only one to retain a sense of humor.

My favorite picture of Lao Tzu is by the master Sengai, and it shows him in the sort of disheveled and informal style that is so characteristic of Taoist humor, and was later assimilated in Zen Buddhism. This playfulness is one of the most delightful characteristics of the whole of Taoist philosophy and, as a result, I know of no other philosophical works besides those of Lao Tzu and his successor Chuang-tse that are so eminently readable. Of all the great sages of the world, they alone have a sense of the enjoyment of life just as it comes.

Lao Tzu literally means "the old fellow," since Lao means "old" and tzu means "fellow," or sometimes "boy." So Lao Tzu is the old boy, and he is sometimes shown as a white-bearded youth, which is of course symbolic of his great wisdom at an early age.

Long before Buddhism came to China in about 60 A.D., Lao Tzu's philosophy had revealed to the Chinese that you cannot characterize reality, or life itself, as either being or nonbeing, as either form or emptiness, or by any pair of opposites that you might think of. As he said, "When all the world knows goodness to be good, there is already evil."

We do not know what any of these things are except by contrast with their opposite. For example, it is difficult to see a figure unless there is a contrasting background. Were there no background to the figure, the figure would vanish, which is the principle of camouflage. Because of the inseparability of opposites, therefore, you realize that they always go together, and this hints at some kind of unity that underlies them.

In Lao Tzu's philosophy this unity is called Tao. Although it is written t-a-o, in Chinese it is pronounced almost as if it were spelled d-o-w. It has the sense of a rhythmic motion, of going on and stopping, and also a sense of intelligence, and so you get an idea of a sort of rhythmic intelligence that ebbs and flows like the tides.

The word has two general meanings. One is perhaps best rendered into English as "the way," "the way of things," or "the way of nature." The other sense of the word means "to speak," so when the opening words of Lao Tzu's book say,

The Tao that can be spoken is not the eternal Tao,

it makes a pun in Chinese. It says literally, "The Tao that can be Tao is not Tao," or if you read it like a telegram, "Tao can Tao no Tao." The first meaning of Tao is "the way," and the second meaning of it is "to speak," or in other words,

The way that can be expressed is not the eternal way.

I prefer not to translate the word Tao at all because to us Tao is a sort of nonsense syllable, indicating the mystery that we can never understand — the unity that underlies the opposites. In our deepest intuition we know that there is some sort of unity underlying these various opposites because we find that we can't separate one from the other. We know that a whole universe exists, but we can't really say what it is. So Tao is thus a reality that we apprehend deeply without being able to define it.

A Chinese poet put it this way:

Plucking chrysanthemums along the eastern fence,
gazing in silence at the southern hills,
the birds fly home in pairs,
through the soft mountain air of dusk.
In all these things there is a deep meaning,
but when we're about to express it,
we suddenly forget the words.

Lao Tzu also said, "Those who speak, do not know; those who know, do not speak." And another Chinese poet satirized him by saying, "Those who speak, do not know;

those who know, do not speak; thus we have heard from Lao Tzu, and yet how does it come that he himself wrote a book of five hundred characters?" The point, then, is that his whole book does not in any way define what the Tao means. He speaks not so much about it, but rather speaks with it, using it, as it were, as the power by which to express himself.

So what is the reason that Tao is inexpressible and yet at the same time the basis for a philosophy? The reason is that we cannot have any system of thought — whether it be philosophical, or logical, or mathematical, or physical — which defines its own basis. This is an extremely important principle to understand. In other words, I can pick up a paint brush with my right hand, but I can't pick up my right hand. My right hand picks itself up. If I try to pick up my hand, what would I pick it up with? There always has to be something, as it were, that isn't picked up, that picks itself up, that works itself and is not worked upon.

In the same way, you will find that if you look up "to be" in a dictionary, it is defined as "to exist." Then when you look up "to exist," you will find it defined as "to be." And are you any the wiser? A dictionary cannot really completely define itself; ultimately it can only put words together that correspond to other words.

In this sense, to try to say anything about the Tao is like trying to eat your own mouth, and of course you cannot get outside of it to eat it. Or to put it the other way, anything you can chew is not your mouth. Anything that is expressed about the Tao is not the Tao.

LAO TZU

by Max Kaltenmark

C HINESE PHILOSOPHICAL thinking emerged and developed during a long period of warfare that wrought profound changes in China's political and social structure. In the fifth century B.C., China was still divided into a large number of feudal states; in 221 B.C., the state of Ch'in won supremacy over its rivals, and its leader became the first emperor of a united China, assuming the title Ch'in Shih Huang Ti. The historians' name for these three centuries (the fifth to the third centuries B.C.) is the "Period of the Warring States"; "Period of the Philosophers" would be equally appropriate, for never was speculative thinking so widely and so freely practiced as in those troubled times. Philosophers gradually turned away from traditional religious and moral thinking, and elaborated a metaphysics that was to remain virtually unmodified for centuries, except for a limited borrowing of ideas from Buddhism.

Early in the fifth century B.C., K'ung Ch'iu (Confucius) founded the first school of wisdom in the small state of Lu, in modern Shantung. This event was of unusual importance, for Confucius's doctrine, as developed by his disciples, was destined to leave a deep impression on the Chinese mind, providing the almost immutable bases of moral and political philosophy for more than two thousand years.

Confucius's life (551–479 B.C.) falls at the end of the period preceding the Period of the Warring States, a time when signs of decadence had already become apparent in the social structure and when both the traditional order and the ideals that justified it were in danger. Confucius considered it his mission to save that order and those ideals. His conception of history and society was Utopian: an orderly society, as he saw it, was a society organized on feudal lines, with tradition and religion keeping some sort of balance between the rival barons. Feudalism in this sense refers to more than just economic or juridical relationships; it refers to a system of relationships pervading society as a whole, in its spiritual as well as its material existence. Moreover, ancient Chinese conceptions of nature and the universe were often little more than projections of social values: the world was seen as a hierarchical system modeled on human society. To be sure, human society necessarily conformed to the celestial order; but since the celestial and earthly orders were interdependent and closely linked by "correspondences" and magico-religious "participations," human behavior in its turn had an influence on nature, and the least disorder in society put the whole universe in jeopardy. We can easily understand the anguish of the "intellectuals" who held these views, the custodians of an ancient tradition, when that tradition began to break up before their eyes. They were incapable of imagining any culture but their own, which they believed had existed since the dawn of civilization. Civilization itself was a harmonious corpus of perfect, immutable institutions laid down by the so-called sage-kings of antiquity, the great founders of dynasties, and in particular the kings of the reigning Chou dynasty.

The Chou dynasty succeeded the dynasty of the Shang (also called Yin) in the eleventh century B.C. The Shang capital was not far from modern Anyang, in northern Honan; archaeologists working on the site where it stood until 1111 B.C. have unearthed various building foundations, tombs, and miscellaneous objects, including the earliest written documents of China.

Despite these discoveries, we still have very little information about the Shang dynasty and the early Chou monarchs. The Chou domain seems never to have been very large, and by the eighth century B.C. the Chou rulers' power had been greatly reduced. The king, who bore the title Son of Heaven, still had religious prestige, and his traditional role as the barons' suzerain and arbiter was still respected. But little by little, as the great feudal lords grew more ruthless in the pursuit of their ambitions, the old rules of conduct lost their authority. Contact with the barbarians forced the peripheral Chinese states to adopt new principles of organization and to change their forms of government, agriculture, and warfare. Population increases and the invention of iron and the plow also contributed to the overthrow of the established order. Confucius attempted to save the edifice of traditional civilization by providing it with deeper moral foundations. Though his attempt failed, his many disciples spread his teachings throughout China; and they did their job so well that Confucianism gradually came to be recognized as the authentic repository of civilization. Unfortunately, not all the Master's disciples were faithful to his thinking. Whereas he had preached an ethics based on the perfecting of the individual mind, a thorough going self-cultivation that he saw as the prime requisite for good government, his successors too often opted for a formalized ritualism. If we except the obligation to study the Confucian Classics (*ching*), the main duties of every respectable member of Confucian society were to observe the rites and to respect the hierarchies.

Though Confucius's school was the first to be founded, it was quick to acquire rivals, which soon became so numerous that the Chinese now call them the "Hundred Schools." One was the school founded by Mo Ti in the second half of the fifth century B.C.: violently anti-Confucianist, Mo Ti condemned both music (which was highly valued by Confucius) and the rites, and preached a doctrine of universal love, heroism, and justice. Unfortunately, his teachings are marred by a simplistic utilitarianism and a mean-spirited aestheticism. Another, typical of the period, was the Legalist school. Resolutely realistic and bent on innovation, the Legalists sought to ensure effective government by the promulgation of universally valid penal laws, and by a rational (and brutal) organization of the state's economy and military power. Still other schools were the Sophists, the Politicians, the Diplomats, and the Strategists. Most important of all, there was the school of philosophers called Taoists, whose patron is said to be Lao Tzu.

This wealth of philosophical schools did not survive political unification. From the Han dynasty on, the only ones to remain active were Confucianism and Taoism. The first became the official doctrine of the monarchy, combined with elements borrowed from other currents of thought, in particular from Legalism. But if official morality and public life were stamped with the die of Confucianism, the influence of Taoism remained alive, and often predominant, in the spiritual life of individuals.

Together with Confucius, Lao Tzu is probably the most eminent personage in Chinese antiquity, and one of those whose names are most familiar in the West. The book that bears his name, which is also known under the title *Tao Te Ching*, has been translated far more often than any other work of Oriental literature. Although the text is difficult and the translations are often little more than fanciful interpretations, Lao Tzu's popularity has never diminished. For all that, we know next to nothing about him. We know so little that specialists, whether Chinese, Japanese, or Westerners, do not even agree on his historicity, some maintaining that he is a purely legendary figure, others conceding that he really lived but holding divergent views on when he lived and on certain episodes in his biography.

In the last analysis, these discussions have only limited significance for our purposes. Those concerning the *Tao Te Ching* are more important. But even these we cannot go into here, where we must limit our discussion to the main questions raised by the author and the book.

Around 100 B.C. Ssu-ma Ch'ien was working at the first history of China, the *Shih Chi* (Historical Memoirs). This major work, one of our main sources of information about ancient China, contains a biography of Lao Tzu. Unfortunately, it is abundantly clear that even at this early date Ssu-ma Ch'ien had only uncertain and contradictory information about his subject. He frankly admits that he is puzzled, and simply presents the hodgepodge of opinions he has managed to collect with an avowal that, all things considered, no one can be sure what they add up to.

The account of Lao Tzu's origins with which Ssu-ma Ch'ien opens his biography is itself subject to caution. "Lao Tzu was a man from the village of Chu Jen, district of Lai, county of Hu, in the kingdom of Ch'u. His surname was Li, his given name Erh, and his public name Tan." Ssu-ma Ch'ien's indication of Lao Tzu's birthplace corresponds to the modern town of Luyi (City of the Deer) in the province of Honan, about forty li from the town of Pohsien (formerly Pochow) in Anhwei. There was a sanctuary here as early as the Han period, and a temple, the T'aich'ing Kung (the Palace of the Great Purity), still stands on the spot traditionally held to be the philosopher's birthplace; an imposing statue of Lao Tzu, almost twelve feet high, stands there also. Nearby, it is possible to visit what are said to be the tombs of Lao Tzu and his mother. This may seem surprising, seeing that the Taoists considered both to be exceptional beings who could never have died like ordinary mortals. For another thing, none of the sources states that Lao Tzu died or was buried at his birthplace. These two tombs, if they are tombs, are definitely not authentic. Furthermore, the Memoirs declare that Lao Tzu disappeared after heading toward the west, into the land of Ch'in, and that some people claim he died there. Local tradition places his tomb at Hwaili (the Village of Pagoda Trees) in Shensi, a few miles west of Sian.

Lao Tzu's names pose problems that are almost unsolvable. According to the cited passage in the *Shih Chi*, Lao Tzu's real name was Li Erh (surname and given name) or Li Tan (surname and public name). The earlier texts never call the philosopher by either of these forms; he is always Lao Tzu (Master Lao) or Lao Tan. If Ssu-ma Ch'ien calls him Li, it is probably because a Shantung family of that name claimed to be the descendants of Lao Tzu; their genealogy appears at the end of Ssu-ma Ch'ien's biography, though their claim is historically worthless. The surname stuck, however, with one important consequence: it led the emperors of the Tang dynasty (A.D. 618–907) to consider him their ancestor.

But what, then, was his real surname? We don't know, though Lao seems improbable. This word, meaning old or venerable, seems to have been a name often given to more or less legendary sages. Old age was considered to be the sign of great vitality and wisdom. And Lao Tzu was, almost by definition, a very old man: Ssu-ma Ch'ien records opinions that he reached the age of 160 60 or even 20 or more. Lao's other two names, Erh (ears) and Tan (long ears), are also connected with the idea of long life and wisdom, sages often being portrayed with long ears.

The historian's account of Lao Tzu's career contains three assertions that would be of great interest if they could be considered authentic: (I) Lao Tan was the court archivist of the kings of Chou; (2) he was visited by Confucius; (3) he finally went off toward the west, dictating his book during the journey, and then disappeared without a trace.

The meeting between Lao Tzu and Confucius is famous; if true, it would allow us to assign an approximate date to Lao Tzu's activities. Here is Ssu-ma Ch'ien's account of it:

> When Confucius went to Chou, he asked Lao Tzu to instruct him in the rites. Lao Tzu replied, "Even the bones of those you mention have fallen into dust; their only remains are their words. Furthermore, when a gentleman lives in favorable times, he hastens to court in a carriage; but when he lives in unfavorable times, he drifts with the wind. I have heard it said that a good merchant hides his wealth and gives the appearance of want; if endowed with a rich supply of inward virtue, the superior man has the outward appearance of a fool. Get rid of that arrogance of yours, all those desires, that self-sufficient air, that overweening zeal; all that is of no use to your true person. That is all I can say to you." Confucius withdrew and told his

disciples, "I know a bird can fly; I know a fish can swim; I know animals can run. Creatures that run can be caught in nets; those that swim can be caught in wicker traps; those that fly can be hit by arrows. But the dragon is beyond my knowledge; it ascends into heaven on the clouds and the wind. Today I have seen Lao Tzu, and he is like the dragon!"

The meeting is related again in another chapter of the *Shih Chi*, but Lao Tzu's discourse is different:

When he took his leave, Lao Tzu saw him off, saying, "I've heard it said that the man of wealth and power makes parting gifts of money, and that the good man makes parting gifts of words. I could never be a man of wealth and power; but I sometimes dare to think myself a good man. So I will show you out with a few words, which are as follows: The man who is intelligent and clear-sighted will soon die, for his criticisms of others are just; the man who is learned and discerning risks his life, for he exposes others' faults. The man who is a son no longer belongs to himself; the man who is a subject no longer belongs to himself."

As Edouard Chavannes, the translator of the *Historical Memoirs*, points out, this speech is a condemnation of the intelligence, filial piety, and loyalism that are the essential principles of Confucius's teachings.

This scene was so popular in Han times that sculptings of it can be seen on several Shantung tombstones dating from the second century B.C. We continually come across accounts of it in both Taoist and Confucianist writings; unfortunately, the accounts give differing versions of the place, the date, the number of meetings that occurred, and what Lao Tzu said or did not say, with the result that it is hard to believe that the two great philosophers ever met at all.

For a while, then, Lao Tzu took up residence at court, but in time, perceiving the decadence of the House of Chou, he left, heading west toward the state of Chin. The way led through the Han-ku Pass, whose keeper, Yin Hsi or Kuan Yin, begged Lao Tzu to compose a book for him. To comply with this request, the philosopher wrote "a book divided into two sections and containing more than five thousand characters, in which he set forth his ideas concerning the Tao and Te; then he departed and nobody knows what became of him." The Keeper of the Pass (Kuan-ling) Yin Hsi, has become an important Taoist personage; he has even been credited with the authorship of a book, the *Kuan Yin Tzu*; however, he is most probably purely legendary.

Ssu-ma Ch'ien later mentions two well-known figures whom some people identified with Lao Tzu: Lao Lai Tzu, a contemporary of Confucius, and the great astrologer and archivist Tan, who lived much later and who made an obscure prediction in 376 B.C. concerning the destiny of the Chou and their elimination by the state of Ch'in. The historian then concludes: "No one in the world can say whether all this is true or not. Lao Tzu was a hidden sage."

Thus Ssu-ma Ch'ien frankly admits to uncertainty: all

the material he has managed to gather about Lao Tzu is so vague and contradictory that he cannot draw a single definite conclusion from it. He explains this dearth of information by describing Lao Tzu as a "hidden sage" and summing up his teachings as follows: "Lao Tzu cultivated the Tao and the Te; according to his teachings, men must strive to live in an obscure and anonymous manner." The description of the philosopher as a "hidden sage" suggests that after leaving his post at the royal court Lao Tzu lived in obscurity. Throughout China's history there have been men who, though members of the intellectual class, have chosen to remain aloof from public life, shunning the cares and rewards of the world, which in all candor they considered a morass.

Confucius, who had occasion to meet some of these people, found their ideas distinctly Taoist in character. One of them was Lao Lai Tzu (the same Lao Lai who was sometimes identified with Lao Tan). According to Chuang Tzu, Lao Lai Tzu harshly reproached Confucius for his narrow-mindedness and pride — faults that were frequent enough, no doubt, in certain teachers of moral philosophy, and that the Taoists were fond of attributing to Confucius himself. Another "hidden sage," the Madman of Ch'u, sang at Confucius's door: "O Phoenix, Phoenix, how your virtue has degenerated! Your past I cannot set to rights, but for the future there is still time to save you. Desist! Desist! In these days men who serve the government are in danger!" (*Analects*, XVIII, 5).

People of this persuasion often adopted the peasantry's rustic way of life, or, in the regions of rivers and lakes in the state of Ch'u, the ways of simple fishermen. Others, more radically inclined, took refuge in the mountains, beyond reach of civilization and princely influence. The very existence of these extremists, especially the more radical, challenged everything a prince stood for and was, in effect, a permanent condemnation of his reign. But authority had no hold over them: their superior holiness made them inviolable. There was only one way for a prince to get rid of a troublesome sage: to offer him the throne in the hope that this insult would make him jump into the river holding a rock — as several sages actually did, according to Chuang Tzu.

These hermit sages have played an important role in the history of Taoism: indeed, most of the ancient Taoist philosophers lived in just this way, refusing to take part in public life. Among them were Chuang Chou, the author of the *Chuang Tzu*, Lieh Yü-k'ou, the supposed author of the *Lieh Tzu*, and doubtless many others who are unknown to us. Ssu-ma Ch'ien was therefore reasonably correct in putting Lao Tan in this category.

It would be wrong to imagine, however, that all the hermits were Taoists. Indeed, the Taoists took some hermits severely to task for their fanaticism and puritanic zeal, which marks them out as embittered Confucianists rather than as disciples of Lao Tzu. When the Taoists opted for a life of obscurity, they did so on principle and not out of resentment. Sages like Lao Tzu and Chuang Tzu differed from all other hermits in still another way: they had schools of followers. These schools probably existed as small, tightly exclusive groups, in which over many years an essentially oral teaching was transmitted from masters to disciples, the latter sometimes taking notes. This was, in fact, how most of the ancient books were written; only much later on, it seems, did the masters begin directly composing their own works. What, then, were the circumstances surrounding the composition of the *Tao Te Ching*? In the end that is the question that concerns us, for Lao Tzu the man remains shrouded in impenetrable obscurity.

THE *TAO TE CHING*

The book attributed to Lao Tzu was originally given the title *Lao Tzu*, in keeping with the practice followed for almost all the ancient philosophers. Thus Meng K'o's (Mencius's) work is called the *Meng Tzu*, Hsün Ch'ing's is called the *Hsün Tzu*, and Chuang Chou's is called the *Chuang Tzu*. The title of *Tao Te Ching* (Sacred Book of the Tao and the Te) was accorded the *Lao Tzu* under the Han; the effect was to give it the same status as the Confucian Classics, which had long since been called *ching*. The character *ching*, whose basic meaning is "warp of cloth," here means "moral canon." The *ching* comprise teachings of outstanding moral value; they are sacred texts revealed by Holy Men or gods. The Buddhists later borrowed the term *ching* to translate "sutra."

The *Tao Te Ching* is also frequently referred to as the *Book of Five Thousand Characters*. In fact, the existing text has more, and the number varies from version to version.

GOD'S LIGHT

The book is split up into eighty-one short chapters divided into two parts, the first part ending with Chapter 37. The division into two parts, upper and lower, is of ancient date, but the division into chapters varies in the early versions. The number eighty-one was chosen because of the mystical value of nine and three. The upper part is sometimes referred to as *Tao Ching* (Book of the Tao), and the lower part as *Te Ching* (Book of the Te), but in the existing version the only justification for this distinction is that Chapter 1 deals with the Tao and Chapter 38 with Te.

If Lao Tan, a contemporary of Confucius, is the author, as tradition says he is, the work dates from the sixth century B.C. However, most scholars believe that the *Lao Tzu* cannot have been written at so early a date, and various other dates have been proposed. Western scholars generally plump for the end of the fourth century B.C. or the beginning of the third century, but their arguments are rather vague. Recent work in China and Japan (the Japanese analyses are particularly thorough) has proved the following points beyond all doubt: (1) that the existing text cannot have been written by Lao Tan, the contemporary of Confucius; (2) that a text similar to the one we possess existed at the end of the Warring States period; (3) that many aphorisms found in the *Tao Te Ching* were well known in Chinese philosophical circles from an early date and were not always attributed to Lao Tan.

Scholars have observed, moreover, that neither the style nor the thought of the book is internally consistent. Some passages are in rhyme and others not; in the rhymed passages there are several very different meters.

An examination of the rhymes reveals anomalies that can be accounted for only by assuming that they occur in passages written down in different periods or different regions. As for the content, a considerable number of passages are closer to the tenets of such schools as the Legalists, the Politicians, and the Strategists than to Lao Tan's thought as the ancients understood it, which is the dominant strain of the book.

These passages are not clumsy interpolations, however, but a result of the way the *Lao Tzu* was compiled.

We should not think of the philosophical schools of ancient China as exclusive sects. Even the two schools that appear to be the most distinctive — those of Confucius and Mo Ti — were far from being closed groups. Above all, no Taoist school as such existed before the Han. It was the Han historians and bibliographers who drew up a classification of the ancient philosophers by schools, one of which they called the school of the Tao (*tao chia*). During the philosophers' own era they were not as a rule classified into distinct movements, and it is accordingly not always easy to label them. Given these circumstances, it is conceivable that different currents of thought may have derived from common sources and authorities, and that philosophers of various schools took pleasure in ascribing apothegms to such universally revered sages as Lao Tan of the Long Ears or the Yellow Emperor, Huang Ti. The Taoists considered Huang Ti, a purely mythical figure, as much their founder as Lao Tan; many works were ascribed to him, and during the Han dynasty Taoism was known as the "Huang-Lao" doctrine.

Early quotations from the writings of Huang Ti have survived; some of them are very similar in style to the *Tao Te Ching*, and in one case (Chapter 6) the text is identical.

All things considered, the *Lao Tzu* appears to be an anthology of apothegms borrowed partly from the common stock of wisdom, partly from various proto-Taoist schools. The anthology was built up gradually and did not take on a more or less definitive form until the third century B.C. Before then many different versions must have been in circulation, which explains the extremely numerous variants found in the various recensions of the existing text as well as in the ancient citations. Indeed, it is possible that as far back as the sixth century B.C., a stock of aphorisms in verse served as a basis for oral instruction in the close-knit groups of "Taoists." These groups differed from the other philosophical schools by virtue of their quietist and mystic ideal. It was in them that true philosophical thinking first began to develop. Thus, surprisingly enough, Taoism came to influence Legalism, whose spirit is the opposite of quietism, partly because it alone offered the ontology that Legalist theory needed.

It is certain that the *Tao Te Ching* cannot have been written by Lao Tan in the sixth century B.C., and the attribution to the great astrologer Tan of the fourth century B.C. is without serious foundation. We must face the fact that we simply do not know by whom, where, and when the work as it has come down to us was compiled; we must also realize that it is, to a significant extent, composite. Clearly, however, its ideas are carefully worked out and form a coherent whole. We must, then, posit the existence of a philosopher who, if he did not write the book himself, was the master under whose influence it took shape. There is no reason why we should not go on calling this philosopher Lao Tan or Lao Tzu, and that is what we shall do, if only for the sake of convenience, in our discussion of the *Tao Te Ching*. We should bear in mind, however, that Lao Tzu may in fact be several thinkers, and that the personality of the last man to have had a hand in the text, probably in the first half of the third century B.C., may have played a central role in determining the version that has come down to us. . . .

All life is governed by the same permanent law: the return to the origin. To know this law is to possess a superior intelligence that Lao Tzu calls Light (*ming*). But the Holy Man is not content with merely knowing this law intellectually; he realizes it within himself by returning to the Tao in person. The import of this returning is spiritual: it is a matter of identifying oneself with the Tao through an inward realization of its unity, simplicity, and emptiness.

Knowledge of the Tao is no ordinary knowledge. The Taoists condemn mere learning as dangerous, for it is a source of dissipation: its multiplicity destroys the unity of being. In order to maintain or restore unity, and to struggle against the temptations of discursive knowledge, the intellect has to be purified. The first step in this purification is a disciplining of the organs of the senses and passions, for "The five colors blind man's eyes. The five notes deafen his ears. The five tastes deaden his palate. Riding and hunting madden his mind. Hard-to-get goods impede his labors" (*Tao Te Ching*, Chapter 12).

So the Taoist is required to practice a measure of asceticism: the senses are not condemned altogether, but moderation must be observed in their normal use. In Chinese physiology, the sense organs are also "openings," through which vital fluid will escape unless a close watch is kept. The passions cause a gradual loss of life that is, at the same time, a loss of soul. For as Ho Shang Kung points out in his commentary on the above passage, we then lose both our spiritual light and our faculty for hearing the voices of silence, and we can no longer taste the "savor of the Tao."

Contrary to the Confucianists, who make study a basis of their system of morals, Lao Tzu condemns all learning, particularly the pseudoscience of the values taught by the moralists and realists. These philosophers treat values that are as relative as the notions "long" and "short" as if they were absolute. Furthermore, every affirmation of this kind gives rise to the opposite affirmation:

In this world, everyone recognizes the beautiful as being beautiful, and that is why ugliness exists; and everyone recognizes the good as being good, and that is why bad exists. "There is" and "there is not" produce each other; "easy" and "difficult" give rise to each other; "long" and "short" exist only comparatively with each other; "high" and "low" are interdependent; there are no notes without harmony; there is no "before" without an "after" to follow it.

Therefore the Holy Man ensconces himself in inaction [wu-wei], *and practices a teaching without words.*

(Chapter 2)

This relativist attitude is not skepticism, and we shall see that the *wu-wei* is not purely negative. The Taoists considered all social values to be prejudices, and as such, wrong, because they cloud reality and land us in the vicious circle of contradictions. The point is to get out of this circle by transcending it. To do this, we need only look at things from the standpoint of the Tao, for in the Tao all contradictions are reconciled and cancel out. As Lao Tzu says, the Principle is the common refuge of all things and all notions: "The Tao is the mysterious granary of the Ten Thousand Creatures. It is the sacred treasure of the good man, the refuge of the bad" (Chapter 62).

All creatures issue from the Tao and return to the Tao; hence it is their common repository or "granary." Here the text has the word *ao*, which meant the southwest corner of the house, a dark place for storing grain and also the place where the mistress of the house slept. Closely linked with the life and fecundity of the family, it was particularly holy in peasant homes. What the *ao* was to the common people, the treasury (*pao*) was to the nobility: every noble family had a treasury of sacred objects with a protective value, veritable talismans ensuring the happiness and continuity of the family. The Tao, then, is all this: a source of life, of happiness, and of salvation, even for the wicked. The Tao (and the Taoists) reject no one, for in Taoist thinking no one is really good or really wicked: "The Holy Man is a good savior of men and rejects no man; he is a good savior of creatures and rejects no creature" (Chapter 27).

For the evildoer, Virtue is a pole of attraction and a refuge; it converts him to better ways without his knowing it. This is far from being the attitude of the other philosophers, who dogmatically reject everything that contradicts their beliefs. Hence the virtues preached by the Confucianists, for example, are utter degradations of the Tao:

> *When the great Tao falls into disuse, the virtues of humanheartedness and righteousness arise.*
>
> *When intellect emerges, the great artifices begin.*
>
> *When discord is rife in families, dutiful sons appear. When the State falls into anarchy, loyal subjects appear.*
>
> (Chapter 18)

> *Banish wisdom, discard knowledge, and the people will benefit a hundredfold.*
>
> *Banish humanheartedness, discard righteousness, and the people will return to the true familial virtues.*
>
> *Banish ingenuity, discard profit, and there will be no more thieves and brigands.*
>
> *Something is missing from this threefold advice, so I shall propose this addition: Be without false adornments; preserve inborn simplicity; lessen selfishness and desire; banish knowledge in order to live a carefree life.*
>
> (Chapter 19)

Humanheartedness (*jen*) and righteousness (*i*) are the supreme virtues of Confucianism. In Mencius they became the foundations of the ethical code of the nobility — the conservative nobility, at any rate. Active beneficence, righteousness (i.e., respect for convention, law, and duty), intelligence (where the moral and ritual laws are concerned), filial piety (including the duties inherent in ancestor worship), loyalty (to the ruler) — all these attitudes and notions would be pointless if men knew how to make their behavior conform to the natural order. Every step away from the Tao leads them further and further down the slope toward moral and political anarchy:

> *The man of superior virtue is not virtuous, and that is why he has virtue.*
>
> *The man of inferior virtue never strays from virtue, and that is why he has no virtue.*
>
> *The man of superior virtue never acts, and yet there is nothing he leaves undone.*
>
> *The man of inferior virtue wants to act, but he is apt to leave things undone.*
>
> *The man of superior humanheartedness wants to act, but finds no particular occasion for acting.*
>
> *The man of superior righteousness wants to act, and finds reasons for acting.*
>
> *The man of the rites wants to act, but meeting with no response, rolls up his sleeves and resorts to persuasion by force.*
>
> *When people abandon the Tao, they resort to Te; when they abandon Te, they resort to humanheartedness; when they abandon humanheartedness, they resort to righteousness; when they abandon justice, they resort to the rites. The rites are a mere husk of loyalty and faith and the beginning of*

anarchy. Fore-knowledge is merely the glitter of the
Tao, and the beginning of folly. Hence a man worthy
of this name chooses the solid and not the flimsy, the
gem and not the glitter.

(Chapter 38)

Lao Tzu is here playing on two different values of the word Te: superior Te is in fact hard to distinguish from the Tao, whose efficacious virtue it is. So the Holy Man has no virtue other than superior Te; he has no virtue, hence merit, particular to himself. On the contrary, the man of "inferior virtue," as Wang Pi explains, takes pride in the virtues, those Confucian virtues that the vulgar people take for goodness. But we know that the notion of goodness implies and gives rise to that of badness: by "never failing in virtue" a man thus moves away from the Tao. Now, if the Tao is absolute perfection, primordial nondifferentiation, even superior Te is already slightly less perfect than it, for it is the start of a descent into the virtues, i.e., into multiplicity. The highest of these virtues, *jen*, or humanheartedness, which in its superior quality is close to inferior Te, is already an activity, but it is still a directionless activity with no reason to manifest itself, i.e., it is not directed at particular objects. But when *jen* becomes a conscious activity limited to particular objects, it is degraded in its turn: a still more inferior virtue crops up, deliberate generosity, righteousness, and lower still, ritual-mindedness, when acts are prompted merely by a desire to make a handsome gesture, by decorum and etiquette. The rites are indeed the opposite of the Taoist ideal; they were instituted to mark distinctions, divisions, and

332

classes. In the relationships that humans have among themselves and with the world, the rites concretize the artificially hierarchized values that official doctrine presents as holy and intangible.

This is why the prime requisite is to repudiate all false wisdom and the pseudosciences, which are nothing more than knowledge of others — and hence pretensions of dominating them; rather, true holiness consists of knowing oneself (Chapter 33). The Taoist can then "know the whole world without crossing the doorstep; see the Heavenly Tao without looking out the window. The further you go, the less you know. Therefore the Holy Man knows without stirring, identifies without seeing, accomplishes without acting" (Chapter 47).

Since the Taoist repudiates pseudoscience for himself, he is naturally against its being taught to others. In Chapter 3, Lao Tzu affirms that the Holy Man rules by "emptying their hearts [their minds] and filling their bellies, weakening their will and toughening their bones, striving to keep the people ignorant and desireless." The formula is undeniably rather harsh, but this is due to the quietists' aversion to the proliferation of all kinds of doctrines that divided the people's minds and led to strife. The "people," in this context, can hardly mean the peasantry; it more likely means the nobility and the philosophers, for they, and not the commoners, are responsible for the proliferation of ideas and ambitions. "Filling their bellies . . . toughening their bones" is to be understood, not as a social economy program, but as an allusion to practices for prolonging life. The expression "filling their bellies" is in no way pejorative in Chinese. Being richly fed was a mark of the aristocracy, and the Chinese have always looked upon stoutness with respect. As for the bones, ancient beliefs held them to be the repositories of the subtlest and most precious life principles. Thus Ho Shang Kung reminds us that chastity results in our having plenty of marrow within solid bones.

Chapter 3, then, does nothing more than proclaim the necessity of renouncing the dangerous temptations of overpolite society in order to return to healthy original simplicity: the heart, the centrifugal seat of the intelligence, the will, and the desires, is opposed to the belly, the centripetal receptacle of the organs of nutrition and the life principles.

WU-WEI

We come across the expression *wu-wei*: "without doing," "absence of action." Wu is not the same as nothingness, and *wu-wei* is not an ideal of absolute inaction; on the contrary, it is a particularly efficacious attitude since it makes all doing possible. "The man who applies himself to study, each day increases [his efforts and ambitions]. The man who applies himself to the Tao, each day diminishes [his activity and desires]. From diminution to diminution, he manages to stop acting altogether; once he has stopped acting, there is nothing he does not do" (Chapter 48). In "ensconcing himself in

wu-wei," the Taoist merely imitates the Tao, whose effi-
cacy is universal for the very reason that it is "inactive."
"The Tao never acts, yet there is nothing it does not do"
(Chapter 37).

There is nothing the Tao does not do because the Tao
is the same thing as universal spontaneity. Everything in
nature comes about of itself, without any particular kind
of intervention, such as might be the act of a divinity or
of providence. Similarly, the Holy Man takes good care
not to intervene: he lets all creatures develop according
to their own nature, and thus obtains the best practical
results. It is important that the ruler act the part of a
Taoist; it is he, in fact, that Lao Tzu has in mind as his
reader. The majority of the aphorisms in the *Tao Te
Ching* are formulas for good government. Chapter 37
continues:

> *If lords and kings could be like the Tao and persist
> in this attitude of nonintervention, the Ten
> Thousand Creatures would soon follow its example
> of their own accord; and if they should then show
> any passion, I would tame them with the simplicity
> of the nameless, and then they would be passionless.
> Being passionless, they would be still, and peace
> would follow naturally.*

So the ruler must pass unnoticed:

> *The best [of all rulers] is he whose existence is
> unknown; next best is he who is loved and praised;*

next, he who is feared; next still, he who is despised.

Whoever claims the right to rule over the people must submit to the people in his words; whoever claims the right to guide them must follow them.

Thus the Holy Man dominates without making the people bend beneath his weight; he guides without making the people suffer any harm.

(Chapter 17)

Wu-wei is the only means to true success: sooner or later, deliberate intervention always results in failure. "I foresee the defeat of those who would presume to gain power by action" (Chapter 29). And Lao Tzu speaks a warning to men of ambition: the empire that they would conquer is like a precious vessel, easily broken by handling; and "ruling a large kingdom is like cooking small fish," the less stirring up the better (Chapter 60). Not surprisingly, Lao Tzu points out that it is the law that makes the thief (Chapter 57).

The Holy Man's policy of nonintervention is nothing more than congruity with natural law, the "Heavenly Tao that conquers without striving" (Chapter 73). For Lao Tzu wants to persuade the ruler that *wu-wei* and nonviolence are the most effective means of getting power and holding on to it. Since all action gives rise to reaction, the normal counterpart of a seemingly right action will be wrong. The only action that does not entail this consequence is the natural action of the Heavenly Tao:

The Tao of Heaven takes away from what has too

much, and adds to what has not enough. The Tao of the ordinary man is something else; this Tao takes away from what has not enough and gives it to what has too much already. Who is capable of offering the world what he has in excess? Only he who possesses the Tao.

(Chapter 77)

So *wu-wei* is not pure passivity; indeed, the above passage — which expresses an ideal of social justice quite exceptional in ancient Chinese thinking — goes on to say: "Therefore the Holy Man, when acting, expects no reward for his actions; once the good deed has been done, he does not bask in his merit; he does not show off his talents."

Nothing is more dangerous than vanity, which is so dangerous that the best means of causing somebody's downfall is to lift him up with pride (Chapter 36). . . .

INSIPIDITY OF THE TAO

Lao Tzu's calm, reflective mysticism makes no call upon the violent emotions. Nothing in the *Tao Te Ching* suggests that ecstatic dancing or other inducements to trance were resorted to. Nor is there any borrowing from the language of love to describe actual experiences. The only path to ecstasy seems to be a long cathartic meditation. Lao Tzu is fully aware of the initial unattractiveness of his doctrine:

Music and fine food make the passerby pause.

How different is that which the mouth utters about the Tao! How tasteless, how lacking in savor!

For if you look at it, you can see nothing; if you listen to it, you find nothing to hear; if you use it, you can never use it up.

(Chapter 35)

When the superior man has heard of the Tao, he hastens to follow it.

When the average man has heard of the Tao, he sometimes thinks about it, sometimes forgets it.

When the inferior man hears of the Tao, he bursts out laughing: if he did not laugh, it would not really be the Tao. Hence the proverb has it:

The illumined Tao seems obscure;

The Tao that goes forward seems to go backward; The Tao that is smooth seems rough. The superior Te seems hollow like a valley.

The purest whiteness seems sullied.

The most abundant Te seems scanty;

The sturdiest Te seems fragile;

The most solid truth seems specious.

The greatest square has no corners,

The greatest vessel takes the longest to finish,

The greatest music cannot be heard.

The greatest image cannot be seen.

The Tao is hidden and nameless.

The Tao alone excels in beginning and finishing.

(Chapter 41)

> *My words are very easy to understand and to put into practice, yet no one in the world is capable of understanding them and putting them into practice. . . . This is why the Holy Man dresses in homespun and hides a jade within his bosom.*
>
> (Chapter 70)

If the Tao is insipid, the Taoist who, as it were, embodies it, is no less so, for the light that he bears within stays hidden; to be authentic, it must not be apparent to the vulgar. Not only must his holiness go unrecognized, but the true Taoist must, in his perfect simplicity, give the appearance of a fool:

> *While the crowd is feasting at a great sacrifice or going up to the terraces for the springtime festivities, I remain alone in impassive immobility, like an infant who has not yet learned how to smile.*
>
> *I am like a homeless wretch. While the others have more than enough, I alone seem to have lost everything.*
>
> *How stupid I look! How boorish!*
>
> *How brilliant people are! I alone am dull.*
>
> *How self-assured they are! I alone am vacillating.*
>
> *They all have some particular talent, and I alone am as ignorant as a churl.*
>
> *Different from the others, I alone prefer to suck my mother's breast.*
>
> (Chapter 20)

Taoism as a whole is a complex and often disconcerting phenomenon: side by side, we find profound insight and puerile suppositions, lofty mysticism and superstitious magic, exhortations to absolute purity and the most primitive obscenity. It must be said at once that these contradictions are often only apparent: Taoist minds and Western minds (perhaps we should say modern minds) categorize their thoughts quite differently. Yet the synthetic, "organicist" thinking of the ancient Chinese is proving worthier of interest as our knowledge of it increases. This is as true for the history of science as for the history of ideas: the very mysticism of the fathers of Taoism contained some elements that could have favored the rise of a scientific movement. Other factors prevented this from happening, but the Taoist spirit contributed largely to the growth of the graphic arts and many crafts.

The fact remains that, because of the anarchical way it developed, Taoism is very heteroclite. From the very earliest days, the philosophers were exposed to all kinds of influences: literati, hermits, artisans, magicians, and priests and priestesses of the popular religion. Even in later periods, religious Taoism was never brought under the discipline of a central spiritual authority; the doctrine was never organized into a system or expressed in a dogma. This accounts for the proliferation of sects, some esoteric, others open to all. The Taoists replied to the challenge of Buddhism by borrowing some of its ideas (retribution and reincarnation) and institutions (monasticism). But, like everything else in Taoism, the Buddhist-inspired Taoist hell is unmistakably Chinese.

One of the most interesting aspects of Taoism is *nei*

tan. Whereas the Confucians hold that a man's whole life depends on Destiny (*ming*: decree of Heaven), the Taoist adepts of *nei tan* believe that our destiny depends on ourselves and not on Heaven. True, these introverts seem to limit the application of this precept to their own internal hygiene, but we should remember that increasing one's vital potency (Te) is a prerequisite, if not for acting, at least for influencing others. As we have seen, the *nei tan* exercises go together with the elimination from consciousness of everything extraneous to pure self, which means expelling the social self in favor of a cosmic self — a unified, global, and potent consciousness instead of a plethora of lesser states of awareness. Even the most bizarre *nei tan* techniques aim at achieving this higher state of consciousness, which is held to confer, not immortality, in which few educated people still believe, but prolonged youth.

It seems that Taoism can no longer be practiced openly in continental China, but in Taiwan it still has a remarkable following. Its close links with popular religion have led some observers to confuse the two. In fact, very large numbers of Taoist temples exist on the island, some of them old, very many others brand new. The *tao-shih*, who belong to the Heavenly Masters Sect, still observe the same age-old liturgy. This continuity is remarkable, when we think that the tradition was established by the first Heavenly Masters nearly two thousand years ago. The funeral ritual is very impressive. The *tao-shih* also officiate for village or urban communities on the occasion of important periodic festivals. It is these occasions that have given rise to the confusion mentioned above: the strictly Taoist ceremony takes place inside the temple while the popular celebrations go on simultaneously outside, a kind of carnival entailing ostentatious display and squandering of the community's wealth. But let there be no mistake about this: for Taoists, the serious business happens inside, where the gods come to dwell within the main officiant, who convokes them by his prayers and contemplates them with his "inner gaze."

In addition to this Taoism with popular affinities, a more official Taoism is gaining ground on the island, thanks to the initiative of Chang En-p'u, the latest in the line of Heavenly Masters, who has claimed sanctuary at Taipei. Chang En-p'u is said to be the sixty-third member of the same Chang family to hold the rank of Heavenly Master in the succession that began with Chang Tao-ling. The Heavenly Masters lead the Cheng-i sect, which, together with the Ch'üan-chen sect, is the most representative of all the modern Taoist sects since the Sung dynasty. The Cheng-i specializes in magical practices. Chang En-p'u still prepares talismans, confers diplomas on priests, and conducts ceremonies at festivals or upon private request. Besides this, he has set up two associations, the Adepts of Taoism (about a hundred members in 1958) and the Taiwan Taoist Association (four thousand members in 1958).

The Ch'üan-chen sect, more recent than the Cheng-i, is also known as the Internal Alchemy Sect, Tan-ting. The famous White Clouds Monastery (Po Yün Kuan) in Peking was one of its dependencies. Whereas Cheng-i priests are married, Ch'üan-chen monks practice celibacy; there seems to be no Ch'üan-chen monastery on

Taiwan, but there are 2,800 Taoist temples. The lay adepts of Ch'üan-chen have no form of collective observance, but perform daily meditation and charitable works.

If we ask what future there can be for Taoism, the answer, at first flush, must be rather pessimistic. On the continent, the Communists are particularly hostile toward Taoism because it is suspected of housing subversive secret societies. Even in Taiwan, Taoism has a poor reputation among officials and intellectuals. Some of them realize, however, that this religion, which has counted for so much in traditional Chinese culture, merits respect: it is, after all, the only truly national religion; for Confucianism is not, strictly speaking, a religion, and Buddhism came in from abroad. On the other hand, Taoism's connection with popular beliefs and practices, some of which are wrongly held to be superstitions, does it much harm. And then, Chinese scholars who readily parse the thought and language of the *Lao Tzu* or the *Chuang Tzu* generally know little about popular customs, village Taoism included, even though the aboriginal inhabitants of the island, like the mountain peoples of South China before them, have been the object of thorough ethnological surveys. This state of affairs is unfortunate, for there is every reason to believe that religious Taoism is destined to disappear, in its present form at least, if only to adapt itself to modern conditions.

Philosophical Taoism still arouses considerable interest throughout the world, as can be seen from the innumerable translations of the *Tao Te Ching* published in the West and the many studies of it published in China and Japan. One reason for the extraordinary appeal of this short text is certainly the cryptic nature of the apothegms themselves; another, perhaps, is that our frantic world is fond of hearing about the virtues of *wu-wei* and absolute tranquility. In a sense, the doctrine of nonintervention accords perfectly with our conception of the true scientific spirit, which, first and foremost, means respect for natural laws. But by way of antithesis, the real interest of Taoism for us today lies in the psychological value of some aspects of it (very close to yoga) and, above all, in its spiritual content.

CONTRIBUTORS

KAREN ARMSTRONG is one of the world's foremost scholars on religious affairs. She is the author of several bestselling books, including *The Battle for God, Jerusalem, The History of God*, and *Through the Narrow Gate*, a memoir of her seven years as a nun. She lives in London.

COLEMAN BARKS has become the primary conduit for bringing Jelaluddin Rumi's mystical consciousness into English, translating and publishing fifteen collections of Rumi's poems, most recently *The Illuminated Rumi* (1997) and *The Essential Rumi* (1995). Barks recently retired from the University of Georgia, Athens, where he taught for thirty years and was named Professor Emeritus of English.

THICH NHAT HANH is a Vietnamese Buddhist monk. His lifelong efforts to generate peace prompted Martin Luther King, Jr. to nominate him for the Nobel Peace Prize in 1967.

He lives in exile in France where he works to help refugees worldwide. He is the author of numerous books including *Anger: Wisdom for Cooling the Flames* and *Living Buddha, Living Christ.*

ZORA NEALE HURSTON ranks among the most influential writers of the twentieth century, not simply for her influence on subsequent African-American writers but also for the passionate voice she gave to black culture in this country. She was a folklorist and the author of the seminal 1937 novel *Their Eyes Were Watching God.*

MAX KALTENMARK was Director of Studies at École Pratique des Hautes Études (Institute for Advanced Research) in Paris, 1957–78. He is the Author of *Lao Tzu and Taoism.*

JACK KORNFIELD is a teacher, author, and psychotherapist. His books include *A Path with Heart; Seeking the Heart of Wisdom* (with Joseph Goldstein); and *Stories of the Spirit, Stories of the Heart* (with Christina Feldman). He currently lives with his family in California.

STEPHEN MITCHELL is an author and revered translator. His many books include *The Book of Job, Tao Te Ching, Parables and Portraits, The Gospel According to Jesus, A Book of Psalms, Ahead of All Parting: The Selected Poetry and Prose of Rainer Maria Rilke,* and *Genesis.*

SEYYED HOSSEIN NASR was born in Tehran, Iran. He received his advanced education at M.I.T. and Harvard and returned to teach at Tehran University from 1958 to 1979. He is the author of *Islam: Religion, History, and Civilization* and *The Heart of Islam: Enduring Values for Humanity*. He is currently professor of Islamic studies at The George Washington University in Washington, D.C.

REYNOLDS PRICE is a novelist, poet, and essayist. He was born in 1933 in North Carolina and is the author of more than thirty critically acclaimed books, including *Roxanna Slade, Great Circle,* and *Three Gospels*. He lives in North Carolina and is James B. Duke Professor of English at Duke University.

HUSTON SMITH is the author of over seventy articles in professional and popular journals, and his book *The World's Religions* (formerly *The Religions of Man*) has sold several million copies and has been the most widely used textbook for courses in world religions for many years. Currently he is Visiting Professor of Religious Studies at the University of California, Berkeley.

MOTHER TERESA, whose original name was Agnes Gonxha Bojaxhiu, was born on August 27, 1910 in what is now Skopje, Macedonia. She devoted her life's work to helping the poorest of the poor around the world and set up her order in the heart of indigent Calcutta, India. She received the Nobel Peace Prize in 1979.

DEVI VANAMALI, a contemporary Hindu contemplative and teacher, lives in a small ashram in Rishikesh, an ancient place of pilgrimage in the foothills of India's holy Himalayas. She is the author of *The Play of God: Visions of the Life of Krishna*.

ALAN WATTS was a philosopher, writer, and speaker. He wrote over twenty books and numerous articles on subjects such as personal identity, the true nature of reality, and the pursuit of happiness. He become widely recognized for his Zen writings and for *The Book: On the Taboo Against Knowing Who You Are*. He died in 1973 at his home in California.

ELIE WIESEL's is one of the strongest voices against the horrors of the Holocaust. A survivor of Auschwitz, where he lost nearly his entire family, he received the Nobel Prize for peace in 1986. He is the author of more than forty books of fiction and non-fiction, including *Night*, *A Beggar in Jerusalem*, *The Testament*, and *The Fifth Son*. He lives with his family in New York.

PHILIP ZALESKI is senior editor of *Parabola*, editor of *The Best Spiritual Writing* series, and the author or editor of a number of books including *The Book of Heaven* and *The Recollected Heart*.

ACKNOWLEDGMENTS

Excerpt from *Teachings of the Buddha*, edited by Jack Kornfield. Copyright © 1993, 1996 by Jack Kornfield. Reprinted by arrangement with Shambhala Publications, Inc., Boston, www.shambhala.com.

Excerpt from *The Heart of the Buddha's Teaching* (1998) by Thich Nhat Hanh. Reprinted with permission of Parallax Press, Berkeley, California, www.parallax.org. Paperback edition, 1999, Broadway Books, New York.

Excerpt from *No Greater Love* by Mother Teresa. Reprinted courtesy of New World Library.

Excerpts from *Three Gospels* by Reynolds Price. Copyright © 1996 by Reynolds Price. Reprinted with the permission of Scribner, an imprint of Simon & Schuster Adult Publishing Group.

Acknowledgments

Excerpt (Foreword) from *The Illustrated Rumi: A Treasury of Wisdom from the Poet of the Soul*, translated by Phillip Dunn and Manuela Mascetti Dunn & R.A. Nicholson. Copyright © 2000 by The Book Laboratory, Inc. Foreword by Huston Smith. Reprinted by permission of Harper-Collins Publishers, Inc.

Excerpts from *The Soul of Rumi: A New Collection of Ecstatic Poems*, translated by Coleman Barks. Copyright © 2001 by Coleman Barks. Reprinted by permission of HarperCollins Publishers, Inc.

Excerpt from *What is Tao?* by Alan Watts. Reprinted courtesy of New World Library.

Excerpts from *Lao Tzu and Taoism* by Max Kaltenmark, translated from French by Roger Greaves. Copyright © 1965, 1969 by Max Kaltenmark. Originally published by Editions du Seuil in 1965. Reprinted by permission of Stanford University Press.